THE GREAT SIOUX UPRISING

C. M. OEHLER

The
Great
Sioux
Uprising

New York Oxford
University Press 1959

Printed in the United States of America

FOR *POLLY*

PREFACE

Caravans of prairie schooners, some loaded with land seekers and others with hunters for gold, crawled across America's western plains long before white control of the land had been achieved.

The Plains Indians, occupants of the prairie, raided caravans once in a while or killed settlers here and there, but offered no massive resistance to the newcomers; they were more often a nuisance than a menace.

Then, in August 1862, the easternmost Sioux killed hundreds of Minnesota settlers; took scores of women and children captive; sent thousands of homesteaders fleeing eastward in panic; and launched a frightful week of arson, looting, rape, and murder.

It was the bloodiest Indian massacre the West ever knew, ten times as deadly as the Fetterman disaster, and with four times the fatalities of Custer's tragedy. Most of its victims were unarmed civilians. Shameless retaliation at Sand Creek and Wounded Knee did not even the score, killing only one-third as many Cheyenne women and children and one-fourth as many Sioux.

Dwarfed by even grimmer events of the Civil War's second year, the Minnesota outbreak got little attention. Not until two years later, when the War on the White Race erupted in the Cheyenne and Teton Sioux country, was there time to notice what was happening on the western frontier.

From the 1862 outbreak sprang tales which are now part of the lore of thousands of families. From it came stories told and retold at hundreds of Indian campfires and councils, sometimes to encourage the guardians of the plains to think that the invaders could be repulsed with ease. The uprising delayed by three decades the time when the West would be safe for the whites, and set a dreadful example for the ultimate conquest.

The outbreak started as a sneak attack and not with a declaration of war. It caused far more civilian suffering than military damage. Its losers were not treated as military prisoners; they were punished as civilian criminals. Other conflicts following this pattern have been regarded as wars, and that is what the Sioux outbreak was called.

Some would say its causes were real-estate quarrels or racial, cultural, religious, or ideological differences. As in most wars, though, the issues were less simple than they seemed to be. Not one was resolved, then or thereafter.

Much real estate changed occupants during the three decades following the uprising. Paleface supremacy came to the Great Plains. A more sanitary, less pagan, and less brutal way of life was imposed on the Sioux and Cheyennes. The self-righteous would comfort themselves with the thought that the Plains Indians were the ultimate winners. Sentimentalists would deplore the perpetual loss of an indigenous culture. Others, peering a century later at the world beyond the plains, would seek a sign that some issue had been truly resolved, but would look in vain.

C. M. O.

Wilmette, Illinois
October 1958

CONTENTS

ACKNOWLEDGEMENTS

Anyone who investigates events long forgotten must be grateful to many not listed in bibliographies. He owes gratitude to everyone who aids his quest for information, supplies him with facts, suggests where he may turn, answers his questions, hears his half-developed ideas, points to flaws in his interpretations, or criticizes the form of his expression.

Except for 'Polly,' to whom this volume is dedicated, no one person did all of these things, but many did some of them.

Some whose aid is gratefully recalled may not have known they were being helpful at the time, may think they only acted in line of duty, or may since have forgotten the help they gave. They include Russell Fridley, Lucille Kane, Gene Becker, and Lois Fawcett of the Minnesota Historical Society; Miss Elizabeth R. Baughman of the Chicago Historical Society; Mrs. Roberta B. Sutton of the Chicago Public Library; Dr. Ruth L. Butler of the Ayer Collection, Newberry Library, Chicago; Mrs. Eva Roberts, secretary of the Murray County Historical Society; Ole Lervaag and Arthur Mitty of the Lake Shetek vicinity; Mr. and Mrs. L. A. Kaercher, Kermit Small, Elmer Sleight, Van Allen Bradley, William Hurst, Dale Fisher, John Devaney, Phil Kobbe, Bobb Chaney, Mr. and Mrs. Richard Nowinson, Richard S. Barnes, W. R. Gillen, and Thomas M. Beers.

Pictures of events at Birch Coulee, Sacred Heart Creek, South Bend, and New Ulm are from re-discovered panorama paintings recently acquired by the Minnesota Historical Society.

Little Crow's portrait is from an 1860 painting. Those of other Lower Sioux Chiefs are from group photographs taken in 1858. The Society's permission to use this material and to reproduce the Fort Ridgely map from W. W. Folwell's *History of Minnesota* is appreciatively acknowledged.

Three drawings (page 61 and subsequent pages) are from the 1863 edition of Isaac V. D. Heard's *History of the Sioux War.*

LIST OF ILLUSTRATIONS

LINE ENGRAVINGS

HALFTONE PLATES
between pages 144 and 145

TIMETABLE

AUGUST 17, 1862 *Sunday*	Four young Sioux from the encampment of Red Middle Voice murdered five settlers in Meeker County, Minnesota, during morning. At midnight Red Middle Voice and his nephew, Young Shakopee, conferred at the latter's village.
AUGUST 18, *Monday*	Before dawn most of the Lower Agency tribes attended council at Little Crow's house. Houses and stores of Lower Agency attacked at dawn. Traders, physicians, interpreters, teamsters, and others killed; women and children taken captive. Captain John Marsh and troops from Fort Ridgely ambushed at Redwood Ferry. More than half of command killed. Settlers' cabins along Minnesota and Cottonwood rivers, and in Renville County along Beaver, Sacred Heart, and La Croix creeks, raided during day and night. Over 400 civilians killed here and at Lower Agency. Private William Sturgis rode to carry word of outbreak to Fort Snelling, one hundred and sixty-five miles away. At midnight looting of Yellow Medicine (Upper) Agency stores begun.

AUGUST 19
Tuesday

Whites, led by John Otherday, departed from Yellow Medicine at dawn.

Indian council met on prairie west of Fort Ridgely.

Troops led by Lieutenant Timothy Sheehan arrived at fort after overnight march from Glencoe, forty-two miles distant.

Forty thousand settlers began flight from all parts of the valley.

Missionaries, led by the Reverend Stephen Riggs, started from Hazelwood.

Private Sturgis arrived at Fort Snelling in afternoon, eighteen hours after leaving Ridgely.

Henry Hastings Sibley assigned to quell uprising.

Four companies of soldiers supplied.

Minor attack on New Ulm, led by soldiers' lodge.

AUGUST 20
Wednesday

First attack on Fort Ridgely.

Lake Shetek settlers surrounded in 'Slaughter Slough.'

AUGUST 21
Thursday

Attacks at Big Stone Lake, Eagle Lake, and other more distant localities.

AUGUST 22
Friday

Refugee population of Ridgely swelled to three hundred.

Major attack on Fort Ridgely.

Sibley arrived at St. Peter from Fort Snelling, ignored New Ulm request for aid.

Riggs party reached Fort Ridgely, but continued down-river.

AUGUST 23
Saturday

All-day attack on New Ulm repulsed, but one-third of town destroyed.

AUGUST 25
Monday

New Ulm evacuated. Sibley remained at St. Peter, awaiting more troops and calling for more supplies.

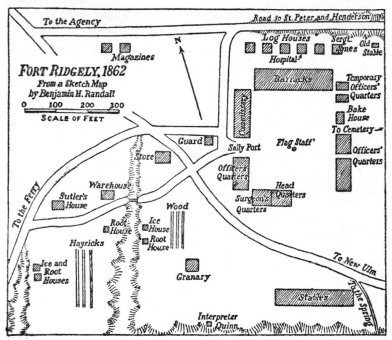

AUGUST 26 *Tuesday*	Lower Agency Indians started moving up-river to Yellow Medicine area.
AUGUST 27 *Wednesday*	Citizen horsemen arrived at Fort Ridgely to announce Sibley's troops were nearing fort.
AUGUST 28 *Thursday*	Sibley and fifteen hundred troops reached Fort Ridgely.
SEPTEMBER 2 *Tuesday*	Two companies surrounded in dawn attack at Birch Coulee, thirteen miles from the fort.
SEPTEMBER 3 *Wednesday*	Relief party from Fort Ridgely reached Birch Coulee thirty-one hours after start of attack. Twenty-three in coulee dead or mortally wounded. Hutchinson, Forest City, and herds grazing near Fort Abercrombie are raided.

SEPTEMBER 18   Sibley's troops, now numbering sixteen hun-
Thursday   dred, started toward Yellow Medicine after
                 waiting at Fort Ridgely for more munitions and
                 supplies. Indians have debated killing or sur-
                 rendering captives, with surrender advocates
                 sending messengers urging Sibley to hurry.

SEPTEMBER 22   Having advanced thirty-six miles, column en-
Monday   camped for night near Wood Lake, four miles
                 from Yellow Medicine.

SEPTEMBER 23   Morning effort to ambush column failed. One-
Tuesday   third of Sibley's troops see action.

SEPTEMBER 24   Little Crow and hundreds of other leaders of
Wednesday   outbreak departed for Canada, Devils Lake,
                 or western plains.

SEPTEMBER 26   White and half-breed captives freed at Camp
Friday   Release, forty days after start of uprising.

SEPT. 28—NOV. 5 Nearly four hundred Indians and half-breeds
                 tried by 'military tribunal.' Three hundred and
                 six sentenced to be hung.

DECEMBER 1   President Abraham Lincoln estimated white
                 casualties at 'not less than 800.'

DECEMBER 6   Lincoln listed those to be hung.

DECEMBER 26   In mass execution at Mankato, thirty-eight In-
Friday   dians and half-breeds were hung.

JULY 3, 1863   Little Crow, on raid to obtain horses, shot by
Friday   settler's son near Hutchinson, Minnesota.

THE GREAT SIOUX UPRISING

I YOU ARE AFRAID OF THE WHITE MAN

Before white men cut the trees, a great forest, mostly of oak and maple, covered much of the eastern half of Minnesota. It was called the Big Woods. In the forest were deer, beaver, otter, occasional bears, and smaller game of many kinds. Elk and even buffalo grazed in its clearings. To Indians on the plains west and south of it a century ago, the Big Woods was the best hunting ground east of the Missouri. Only distant buffalo herds ranging the prairies farther west could offer the hunter as much.

A rough wilderness road, the Pembina-Henderson Trail, ran along part of the western edge of the woods. A few other trails, including one from St. Paul to Glencoe and another between Fort Snelling and St. Peter, cut through the southern part of the timbered wilderness.

Early one Sunday in August, 1862, four Indians who had been hunting during the previous five days in the Big Woods emerged at its western margin and turned south on the Pembina-Henderson Trail, heading toward home. They were from the Rice Creek encampment on the Minnesota River, nearly forty miles south. All four were under thirty years of age. They were Wahpetons, married to Medewakanton women. Rice Creek was a Medewakanton village. Both tribes were 'annuity' Dakotas. All four of the young Wahpetons were related to each other: brothers, half-brothers, or cousins.

Two were dressed in trousers and shirts, as white men, and two in blankets, as Indians. One wore two eagle feathers;

another wore one. A feather in his head-dress signified its wearer had killed an enemy, touched him with a coup-stick, taken a scalp, or otherwise demonstrated valor in battle.

In English the names of the four were Brown Wing, Killing Ghost, Runs Against When Crawling, and Breaking Up.[1] Their hunt had not been successful; nobody was carrying game. The dried meat they had brought from Rice Creek was gone, and all were somewhat hungry. When they emerged from the shade of the forest they began to be thirsty as well.

Turning east when the trail veered, they sighted the cabin of Robinson Jones, a casual acquaintance, and knew they were in Meeker County, where numbers of new settlers had taken up claims.

Between the road and Robinson Jones's split-rail fence was a hen's nest containing a handful of eggs. One of the young Indians paused and scooped up the eggs.

'Don't take them!' snapped a companion. 'They belong to a white man and we may all get into trouble.'

The boy who had picked up the eggs threw them to the ground in sudden anger, and turned to face his critic. 'You are a coward,' he sneered. 'You are afraid of the white man. You are afraid to take even an egg from him, though you are half starved. Yes, you are a coward, and I will tell everybody so.'

One of the eggs, landing on the grass, had failed to break. The boy who had been called a coward reached out a foot and smashed the egg. 'I am not a coward. I am not afraid of the white man,' he said hotly. 'To show you that I am not, I will go to the house and shoot him. Are you brave enough to go with me?'

'Yes,' hooted the other boy. 'I will go with you and we will see who is the braver.'

All four were now opposite the home of Robinson Jones and turned in. It was what was known as a 'public house' because Jones kept for sale a small stock of merchandise and because his wife sometimes prepared sandwiches or even meals for wayfarers. The Acton post office, opened the previous year, was located in the house.

In addition to his other wares, Jones displayed a barrel of low-priced whisky which could be bought by the drink. He seldom sold whisky to Indians [2] and the Rice Creekers did not ask for it. They did not ask for food, either, after learning Mrs. Jones was not at home. She had gone for a Sunday morning visit at the home of Howard Baker, her son by a previous marriage. Baker, with his wife and two children, lived on a homestead east of the Jones claim. His cabin was across the road, within sight of Jones's house.

Present when the Rice Creekers entered, in addition to Robinson Jones, were two children of a deceased relative. One was a fifteen-year-old girl named Clara Wilson. The other, asleep in an adjoining room, was Clara's half-brother, eighteen months of age.

When they entered the Indians were talking loudly and engaging in a bombastic quarrel. They were so rowdy that Jones decided they did not want to buy anything, but not so boisterous that he had any qualms about leaving the children with them. He motioned to Clara. 'I told Howard I'd be over, too,' he said, and left for the Baker home. As most frontiersmen did, he carried his gun.

Shortly after Robinson Jones left his house the four Rice Creekers followed. They were no longer quarreling loudly, but the young egg taker could not resist taunting his critic about the failure to shoot the white man. They arrived at the Baker home nearly as soon as Jones.

At the Baker place were Mr. and Mrs. Viranus Webster, new arrivals in the neighborhood. They were using their covered wagon, left in Baker's yard, as a temporary home while scouting for land on which to file a claim.

Everyone sprawled on the doorstep or on nearby stumps. The Wahpetons knew a few English words and Jones spoke

a little Dakota. Baker and Webster listened attentively, trying to memorize Sioux words they had not heard before, and
interrupting with occasional questions.

Someone proposed target practice. Baker summoned his
wife, and Mrs. Jones, and put a block of wood on a stump to
serve as a target. Everyone fired at the mark in turn. After
each shot, the Indians reloaded their guns. This was customary, but the whites were not as careful to follow custom.

Of the marksmen, Jones was the most successful. One of
the Wahpetons wryly suggested Jones had a superior gun.
The men were 'bantering for a gun trade' as Mrs. Baker turned
to follow Mrs. Jones into the house.[3]

'The next thing I knew, I heard the report of a gun and saw
Mr. Webster fall,' Mrs. Baker told a coroner's jury the next
day. 'Another Indian aimed his gun at my husband, fired,
but did not kill him. He then shot the other barrel and my
husband fell dead. My mother-in-law, Mrs. Jones, came to the
door and another Indian shot her. She turned to run and fell;
they shot her twice as she fell.'

One of the Indians leveled his gun at Robinson Jones, who
stood, astounded and uncertain, in the dooryard. Jones jumped
to one side and fell near Webster's wagon, mortally wounded.
When the coroner's helpers found his body 'It was seen that
in his death agonies he had torn up handfuls of grass and turf
and dug cavities in the ground, while his features were horribly distorted.'

No shots were fired at Mrs. Baker, Mrs. Webster, or the
two Baker children. The four young Indians left hastily. Mrs.
Baker and Mrs. Webster, screaming hysterically, huddled together in the yard, too shocked and terrified to do anything else.

A mentally defective resident of the neighborhood named
Cox, riding a prancing horse along the trail, added a macabre
touch. Mrs. Baker and Mrs. Webster shouted for his attention.
He danced his horse into the dooryard. The excited and sobbing women told him what had happened and implored help.

Cox laughed heartily, shook his head, and called them liars. In incoherent anguish, the women pointed at the bodies of their husbands. The horse shied sharply and whirled around. Cox laughed again. 'They are just drunk. They have the nose-bleed, and it will do them good,' he chuckled. Kicking his horse lightly, he turned back to the road, shrugging and snickering, and rode away.

Later, with Mrs. Baker clutching the hands of her children, the survivors reached the home of Nels Olson, a neighbor. The oldest Olson boy leaped on a horse and raced excitedly to Forest City.

Trembling with terror and now realizing fully what they had done, the four Rice Creekers turned toward the west when they left the Baker cabin and started to run. As they ran past the Robinson Jones house they saw Clara Wilson, the fifteen-year-old foster daughter, standing in the doorway. She had heard the sounds of shooting, assumed it was target practice, but now saw the four Indians racing along the road. One of the Rice Creekers stopped, raised his gun, sighted on Clara, and pulled the trigger. Clara toppled backward into the room, dead.

Her half-brother remained asleep. When the coroner's men who galloped out from Forest City found him he smiled, tried to tell them Clara had been hurt, and indicated that he was hungry.

Clara had not been molested and her body was not mutilated. The whisky barrel was undisturbed; there was no indication the Rice Creekers had helped themselves to liquor either before or after the killings. There was no evidence the murders had been premeditated.

At first nobody knew what to make of the Acton crimes and found it nearly impossible to believe the reports about them.

J. H. Adams, a settler living fifteen miles away, first heard about the affair from a neighbor. 'Some of those to whom he told the story did not believe it,' said Adams, 'and some did.

Some believed the murders were done by a few drunken Indians, and some believed it was a general massacre. Those who did not believe the report stayed at home. Others of us got together and watched the remainder of the night.' [4]

Those who remained at home were, temporarily, as safe as those who watched through the night. The four from Rice Creek had left the Acton neighborhood. After they shot Clara Wilson they turned south, running across country and thinking regretfully of the two good teams, Baker's and Webster's, they had left behind. It was now nearly noon. Even with fresh horses, it would be impossible to get home before nightfall.

They ran to the cabin of Peter Wicklund, where Wicklund's daughter and son-in-law were Sunday dinner guests. The horses of the son-in-law were tied to a hitching post. Two Rice Creekers jumped on each horse, and they rode off in search of additional mounts. Then, their horses covered with lather, they careened wildly over short-cuts toward the river.

The score at Acton was five dead and five survivors. No buildings were burned. Nothing was stolen. No captives were taken. Nobody was raped. The corpses were not mutilated.

Sunday's happenings would recede into the background and seem almost inconsequential after the events to follow on Monday and Tuesday.

Brown Wing, Killing Ghost, Runs Against When Crawling, and Breaking Up reached Rice Creek village after dark but before most of the fires were out. Shouting above the pounding of their horses, they had decided exactly what they would do when they arrived. As their exhausted mounts staggered into the encampment they leaped to the ground. 'Get your guns!' they shouted. 'There's war with the whites, and we have begun it!' [5]

Cries of surprise and exultation sounded through Red Middle Voice's camp. Within moments a drum throbbed a steady, vibrant undertone for the whooping of a swarm of young braves surrounding the four. The sound of the war drums carried across the river to settlements on Beaver and Sacred Heart Creeks.

At the Earle homestead the three older sons, for Sunday evening amusement, had been 'making tolerable music' with violins and a melodeon. Radner, aged fifteen, closed the door at bedtime. He remarked to his brothers, Chalon and Ezmon, how distinctly the Indian drums could be heard.

'The sound was unusual,' said Ezmon, 'but we were not disturbed.'[6]

II PLANT A GOOD DEAL OF GROUND

In 1862 the West ended in Ohio, Lower Michigan, Indiana, and Illinois. Civil War volunteers joining the ranks in Kentucky were regarded as coming from the West. Morgan's Raiders operated in the West when they invaded Tennessee in behalf of the Confederacy.

Wisconsin, Iowa, and Minnesota were the Far West. Beyond them, in Dakota or Nebraska Territory and farther away, were red-skinned savages, wild animals, a few avoiders of mankind who had settled in Oregon, and a few Argonauts burning with gold fever who had gone to California.

Among the residents of New England, New York, Pennsylvania, and other eastern states and in Germany, Ireland, Scandinavia, and elsewhere overseas, intense excitement prevailed. For a filing fee of one dollar, or at most for a dollar and twenty-five cents an acre, anyone could have a quarter section of land in the Far West. Almost for the asking he could have a farm, deep with black soil, soon to be worth at least fifteen thousand dollars. Free land in the Far West afforded a less hazardous and far more certain road to fortune than chasing rainbows in California.

'Nothing but a parcel of old fogies will be found in Vermont five years hence,' predicted the *State Banner* of Bennington, Vermont, in 1856.

'Probably not less than a quarter of a million people will emigrate this year to our frontier states and territories,' observed the New York *Independent.* 'Never was there such excitement before. . . . The most talented in all quarters are taking possession of the soil as a surer foundation for permanent prosperity than can be found in any other vocation.'

The more remote and least-settled parts of the frontier became focal points of the excitement. Minnesota was one of these. Not attaining statehood until 1858, it had the advantage of novelty and the appeal of the unknown. Yet it could be reached by prairie schooner over rough roads through Wisconsin or Iowa or by boat on the Mississippi. Railroads would reach it very soon. The frenzied way people from all over were swarming into the new state was sensational.

In 1850 Minnesota, one year old as a territory, had a population of six thousand whites and more than twice as many Indians. Six years later, two years before its admission as a state, the territory's representatives in Washington proclaimed the white population had been multiplied by thirty-three and was now two hundred thousand.[1]

St. Paul, the new Utopia's capital, had grown from a population of ten white inhabitants in 1846 to more than ten thousand within a decade. St. Anthony, a sawmill town ten miles farther up the Mississippi, had a single cabin before 1848, but now was a city of five thousand. Across the river a new village named Minneapolis had grown from nothing to a town of several hundred.

From their new reservation along the upper Minnesota River, six thousand Dakotas watched the tide of white settlement with misgivings. The eagerness and the air of finality with which whites were pouring into lands just vacated by the Dakota Sioux were disquieting. Could it be the Indians had sold out too cheaply? Had the chiefs made a dreadful mistake in surrendering the tribal lands? With whites swarming in by the thousands, spoiling the hunting, would the Indians ever again have enough to eat? Would the piddling annuities for which they had sold out (about nine dollars cash a year for each person) make up for the loss of twenty-eight million acres of hunting land?

A series of treaties begun in 1851 between the Indians and the United States made possible the influx of whites.

Before 1851 much of Minnesota and parts of Wisconsin comprised the homeland of the easternmost branch of the enormous Siouan linguistic[2] family. The Sioux, who were abidingly suspicious of newcomers,[3] included the Yanktons, the Tetons with their sub-bands, the Brule's, Ogalallas, Hunkpapas, Sans Arcs, and other western tribes. For centuries, warlike and aloof, they dominated much of the area north of the Platte River between the Great Lakes and the Rocky Mountains.

Under an 1851 agreement the eastern Sioux ceded their tribal homeland to the Americans. In exchange, they were to receive three million dollars in annuities, payable over the next fifty years. They were assigned to a reservation on the upper Minnesota River, one hundred and fifty miles long, running from the head of the river to a point within seventy miles of the settlement of Mankato, extending roughly between present-day Ortonville and a point ten miles up-river from New Ulm, Minnesota. The reservation was twenty miles wide, extending ten miles on each side of the river. When they moved to their new home in 1853, the chiefs of the bands were supposed to get $475,000 in cash to defray moving costs.

Five years after they had occupied the reservation the Dakotas were induced to cede the northern half of it, at thirty cents an acre,[4] for an additional $266,880.

At the time of the 1851 and 1858 treaties there was little outcry against them.[5] Missionaries who were trying to Christianize the Sioux, Indian agents who sought to make farmers out of them, and all others who wanted the Indians to become civilized, maintained that concentration of the Dakotas in a smaller area would speed the process of transformation.

In the year 1700, Pierre Le Sueur, ascending the Minnesota for futile investigation of a reported copper out-cropping, had advised the Dakotas to 'plant a good deal of ground.'[6] Ever since then whites had campaigned to induce the Indians to become farmers. At last the crusade seemed to have a chance to succeed.

Certainly the million acres of land remaining to the Dakotas on the south side of the river was ample for a farm population of six thousand. Surely nobody could say the Indians had been relegated to barren waste land and told to scratch a living from it. Their valley, carved in ice-age times by a great glacial river, was rimmed by handsome wooded bluffs and contained rich, well-watered bottom lands as wide as five miles across. Few more fertile and beautiful tracts could have been found in which to transform wild Indians into civilized farmers.

Probably there was nothing inherently evil or unfair about the treaties of 1851 and 1858, if one accepted the inevitability that North America some day would be occupied in the main by Europeans and their descendants. But the manner in which the terms of the treaties were fulfilled was an altogether different matter. It was this that caused Indian indignation and gave the whites no reason for pride.

Whenever annuities or any other funds were to be paid, a yelling swarm of traders, fur company representatives, half-breeds, lobbyists, advisers, ex-agents, and petty opportunists appeared, demanding part or all of the money. 'You owe me nine dollars for sugar,' 'Eighteen for pork,' 'Ten for lard,' they would shout, and nobody, least of all the Indians, could produce any records to prove otherwise.

Some Indians may sometimes have owed some money for goods bought on credit. Some, though, always settled ahead of time, paying furs, and never owed anyone anything. It did not matter; the Indians were always told they owed money, and received, at most, only part of the funds due them and their families.

'I saw a poor fellow one day swallow his money,' reported an observer. 'I wondered he did not choke to death. He said, "They will not have mine, for I do not owe them." I was surprised they would allow such cheating.'[7]

Money picked up at the time of annuity payments was only small change; truly massive claims were filed and allowed when major sums were at stake.

Against the $475,000 to be paid when the Dakotas moved to their new reservation, Henry Hastings Sibley filed a claim for $145,000 in behalf of the American Fur Company; Hugh Tyler, a lawyer-lobbyist representing traders and half-breeds, demanded a fee of $55,000; Bailly and Dousman, a trading firm, asked $43,000; and more modest sums were sought by others. Some of the larger claims were reduced when the total of the demands was found to exceed the amount due the Indians, but in the end Alexander Ramsey, ex-officio Indian agent, paid more than two-thirds of the $475,000 to Hugh Tyler for distribution to the traders, fur companies, and half-breeds. Many Dakotas complained they received nothing.

Of the $266,880 the tribes were to get for the north half of their reservation, more than $12,000 went to Henry Hastings Sibley and $155,000 to thirty-four other 'certified' claimants. Almost $90,000 was allowed on the claims of three groups of traders, the Myricks, the Roberts, and the Browns.[8] The 'Upper' Indians (eighteen villages of Sissetons and Wahpetons) were able to divide about $100,000, but the 'Lower' tribes (ten villages of Medewakantons and one of Wahpekutes) received nothing.

Consideration of claims was supposed to take place at an open council where Indians would have a chance to acknowledge or deny the validity of alleged debts. No such council was held to consider claims against the $266,880. Instead, there was a closed meeting, attended by Little Crow, most prominent of the Medewakanton chiefs, who emerged from the meeting with the promise of a new wagon.

When Little Crow got his new wagon tribesmen who had received nothing from the $266,880 fund tended to suspect he had been bribed to concede the validity of some of the claims.

Two federal investigations probed the handling of Indian funds. Alexander Ramsey, former territorial governor and ex-officio Indian agent, was 'exculpated from any censure,' but many Dakotas, having received little or nothing from sale of half the remaining real estate, felt they somehow had been treated unfairly.

Use of some of the tribal funds to give special assistance to farmer Indians did not appease the nine-tenths of the Dakotas who rejected the suggestion that all Indians should take to agriculture. The policy of aiding farmer Indians from the general fund caused jealousy and indignation.

Out of tribal funds due from the settlement of 1851 Indian agents furnished seed corn and oats, enough cattle to start small dairy herds, fencing, plows, houses, and sheds. They even were willing to pay farmer Indians as much as two dollars an acre for plowing the land, and after the sod was broken and the harvesting done the farmer was welcome to keep the crop. It was a glorified form of subsidized farming.

Sawmills were built to cut lumber from the trees on the bluffs. Carpenters were hired to build houses, chapels, and schools. Teachers were employed to instruct Indian children. Physicians were induced to live on the reservation.

Two villages, called Lower or Redwood Agency and Upper or Yellow Medicine Agency, were built on the new reservation. In or near them lived sawmill operators, carpenters, teachers, clergymen, physicians, interpreters, traders and their clerks, half-breeds,[9] and Indian officials.

Major[10] Thomas Galbraith, who had replaced Major Joseph Brown as Dakota agent in 1861, lived with his family at Yellow Medicine Agency.[11]

Any family head who wanted to become a farmer Indian could have eighty acres of choice bottomland assigned to himself. Then the government would set him up, with a minimum of effort and at almost no expense on his part, as a self-sustaining farmer.

It seemed an ideal situation for the transformation of wild savages into civilized Christians, but it had not worked very well. More than eight years after the Dakotas moved to their beautiful new reservation only one family head in ten had become a farmer Indian, donned trousers and shirt, and had his hair cut.

Nine out of ten continued to wear blankets; hooted at the farmer Indians as 'Cut-Hairs,' 'Dutchmen,' and 'Pantaloons'; scorned to accept the eighty acres offered; mourned the twenty-eight million acres the Dakotas had surrendered during the previous decade; and tried to make a living hunting, fishing, and trapping in a land rapidly being overrun by whites.

Whenever hunting was unrewarding, or the small cash annuities were delayed, the blanket Indians converged on the farmer Indians and helped them dispose of any surplus crops they happened to have.

It was a divisive and confusing situation, and did not make either the farmer or the blanket Indians very happy. The agents and missionaries found consolation in the belief that drastic readjustments took patience and time. Eventually all of the Indians would be farmers, the annuities would become unimportant, and all would be harmonious and prosperous along the upper river. From the beginning of time, hunting and fighting had been the Dakota way of life. A Sioux boy became a man when he brought down a buffalo or killed an enemy. Now the buffalo herds were moving away and killing enemies was outlawed. As yet the young men had not accepted farming as a substitute for either, but in time they would.

III THE GREATEST AMONG THE CHIEFS

Because the four young Indians who spent a Sunday morning killing whites at Acton were Wahpetons, they were 'Upper Sioux' by birth. But since they had married Medewakanton women and lived in Red Middle Voice's village on Rice Creek, they were 'Lower Sioux' by marriage and residence.

The two designations, first coming into use when the Dakotas moved to their new reservation, derived from the fact that Medewakanton and Wahpekute villages were clustered in the vicinity of Redwood or Lower Agency, while most of the Wahpeton and Sisseton villages were nearer Yellow Medicine or Upper Agency.

Best known among the heads of the eleven Lower Sioux bands was a Medewakanton[1] chief named Little Crow. His band and their near neighbors later would become known as the Santee Sioux.[2]

Little Crow[3] had been born in 1820 at Kaposia on the Mississippi. His native village, not far from the mouth of the Minnesota, was on land presently to be occupied by the frontier hamlet of Pig's Eye, present-day site of the city of St. Paul.

As a youth, the oldest son and thus in line to inherit chieftainship of the village, he was in 'ill-favor with his father's band, a Lothario in morals, a debauchee in habits, and of a haughty and overbearing disposition.'[4] Obliged to leave Kaposia 'because of threats against him by certain husbands he had wronged,' the young chief lived with the Wahpekutes

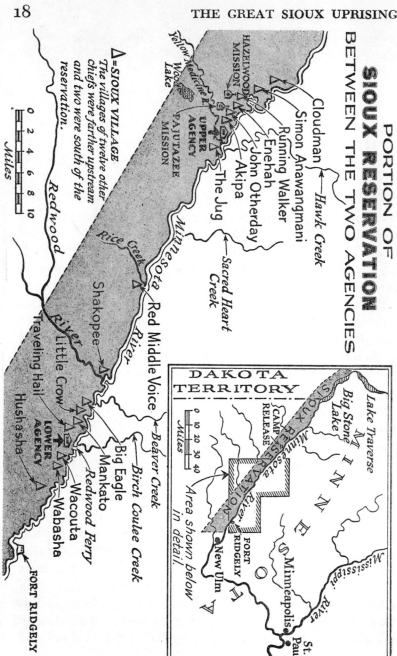

PORTION OF
SIOUX RESERVATION
BETWEEN THE TWO AGENCIES

Cloudman → Hawk Creek
Simon Anawangmani
Running Walker
Enehah
John Otherday
Akipa
The Jug → Sacred Heart Creek

HAZELWOOD MISSION
Yellow Medicine R.
Wood Lake
UPPER AGENCY
PAJUTAZEE MISSION

△=SIOUX VILLAGE
The villages of twelve other
chiefs were farther upstream
and two were south of the
reservation.

0 2 4 6 8 10
Miles

Redwood

Rice Creek
Minnesota
Red Middle Voice River
Shakopee

Traveling Hail
Little Crow

Hushasha
Big Eagle
Mankato
Redwood Ferry
Wacouta
Wabasha

Beaver Creek
Birch Coulee Creek

LOWER AGENCY

FORT RIDGELY

DAKOTA TERRITORY

0 10 20 30 40
Miles

Area shown below
in detail.

Big Stone Lake
Lake Traverse
CAMP RELEASE
MINNESOTA RIVER
SIOUX RESERVATION
FORT RIDGELY
New Ulm
Minneapolis
St. Paul
Mississippi River

M I N N E S O T A

long enough to marry and discard two wives, and then among the Wahpetons, where he acquired four permanent mates, all sisters.[5]

His father once said of Little Crow that he 'had very little good sense.' But after his second wave of matrimony the youthful Medewakanton became a sober and stable citizen, much admired for his 'smooth speech and agreeable manners.' He was no longer a debauchee; the worst that could be said about him was that he seemed lazy, disliked hunting, and rarely joined war parties against the Chippewas.[6]

When Little Crow was twenty-five years old his father died. The heir apparent returned to Kaposia. Two half-brothers, aided by some of the wronged husbands, disputed his claim to the chieftainship. But part of the band, having heard the late chief bequeath the scepter to Little Crow—'because this is now the best I can do'—upheld the claimant.

During the resistance, bullets shattered the heir's wrists. A tribal medicine man extracted bone splinters, and bound the wounds in ointments of roots and herbs. Little Crow emerged with disfigured arms and the sympathetic support of the Kaposia band.

As if to show he had more good sense than his father had credited him with, the new chief set out 'to stop whisky drinking, to encourage members of his band to become industrious and thrifty, and to promote morality among them.' For wronged husbands who recalled incidents of the chief's youth, Little Crow had an answer: 'I was only a brave then; I am a chief now.'[7]

Although he avoided any such tribal heresy as calling himself a Christian, a year after becoming chief, Little Crow invited Dr. Thomas Williamson to establish a mission at Kaposia. Years later, on the Sunday morning four Lower Sioux killed settlers at Acton, the chief and a Winnebago guest, Little Priest, attended Episcopal services at the Reverend Mr. Hinman's Lower Agency chapel.

A white acquaintance called Little Crow 'the greatest man among the chiefs of the Dakotas.' The same admirer described his oratory as 'bold, impassioned, and persuasive, and his arguments are nearly always forcible and logical.'[8]

No Sioux leader was more ideally amenable and tractable in negotiations with the Americans. Little Crow helped push through the 1851 treaty over the remonstrances of Wabasha, Traveling Hail, and other more cautious chiefs. In 1858 he and a score of other leaders adorned in tall plug hats were escorted to Washington to sell the north half of the reservation.

'He was a man of greater parts than any Indian in the tribe,' said Charles Flandrau, once Sioux agent, of Little Crow. 'I had used him on many trying occasions, as the captain of my bodyguard, and my ambassador to negotiate with other tribes, and always found him equal to any emergency.'[9]

Most whites who met the chief commented on his natural dignity, but few called him handsome. Excepting for thick lips, his features were sharp and angular. His hazel eyes, generally described as piercing, were set rather closely together.

On state occasions he often wore a black frock coat with a velvet collar. His head-dress for tribal ceremonies was made of weasel tails, two polished buffalo horns, ribbons, and 'strings of buckskin tied in knots and colored gaily.'[10] Little Crow's supporters asserted he was a military strategist of unusual ability and a fighter of uncommon courage. Skeptics cited lack of eagle feathers in his head-dress as evidence that the chief's bravery had never been tested. Little Crow himself declared that he had killed dozens of Chippewas and dangled an impressive array of scalps from his lodge pole. At least once, a contemporary artist painted his portrait with two feathers.[11]

When the Dakotas transferred to the upper valley, Little Crow announced he would become a farmer. He had his hair cut shoulder length. Then he moved, with his wives and seven

of his ten children,[12] into a two-story frame house on the bluffs
two miles above Lower Agency, across the river from the site
of the present town of Morton, Minnesota. The house, constructed of upright boards plastered on the inside, consisted
of a large room with an attached cooking shed on the ground
floor, and two smaller rooms on the second.[13] Several tepees
pitched near it provided additional sleeping capacity. Agent
Galbraith, wanting to encourage the most prominent farmer
Indian, proclaimed a brick house would be built for Little
Crow before 1862 ended.

Some of the young blanket wearers among the Lower
Sioux, dismayed by the spectacle of the chief becoming a
complaisant farmer, derided him as a 'Dutchman,'[14] and 'Cut-
Hair.' They had muttered about the new wagon, and now
suggested the new brick house to be built with tribal funds
could be considered an additional bribe. Little Crow, according to some of the braves, had forsaken his people, selling
out to the corrupt, swindling whites.

Their suspicions received tangible expression early in August, two weeks before the Acton murders, when the Medewakantons met in council to elect their head speaker. Candi-
dates for the honor were Little Crow, Traveling Hail, and
Big Eagle. Traveling Hail, candidate of the 'Progressive
Whiteman's Party,' was personally popular, but represented
a cause in which he did not really believe. Soft-spoken Big
Eagle was a warrior of renown and wore six eagle feathers in
his head-dress, but had been a chief only a few years.[15] Little
Crow expected an easy victory.

Dignified deliberation was not a notable characteristic of a
Sioux election council; instead, extravagant praise and violent
malediction were standard procedure. One orator after another would arise, gesticulate, shout, plead, threaten, screech.
Dazzling tributes would be paid each candidate by his supporters. Each candidate would be denounced and accused by
friends of his opponents.

Little Crow heard himself extolled as a leader of exceptional vision, ability, and courage. Patient and unperturbed, he heard himself condemned as a scheming, trouser-bedecked scoundrel who had betrayed his people for a wagon and a brick house.

Then the incredible happened: Traveling Hail won the speakership.[16] It was a severe shock to Little Crow. His chief-tainship of his village was not affected, but his pride had been harshly jolted. He remained the greatest man among the Lower Sioux, but his prestige had lost some of its splendor.

How could it have happened? Did most of the Medewakan-tons believe in the policies of the Progressive Whiteman's Party and support Traveling Hail for that reason? No, that could not be the explanation. Traveling Hail had opposed the treaties, had signed them under protest, and questioned the wisdom of Indians' being induced to become farmers over-night. If the Lower Sioux had favored the doctrines espoused by the Progressive Whiteman's Party they would have sup-ported Little Crow, who had advocated the treaties, per-suaded others to sign them, and become a farmer. The support of Traveling Hail, all things considered, was bewildering and confusing.

Wabasha, by heredity, was a more important chief than Little Crow. Wabasha, along with Wacouta and other con-servative leaders, had joined Traveling Hail in opposing the treaties, and now had supported Traveling Hail for the speakership.

So also, and surely for altogether different reasons, had young Shakopee and his uncle, Red Middle Voice, not really a chief, but head man of the Rice Creek village.

Young Shakopee, also known as Little Six or Little Shako-pee, had his village eight miles upstream at the Redwood River's mouth, near the present town of North Redwood. His was the largest of the Medewakanton villages, and this had meant a lot of votes for Traveling Hail. Old Shakopee, aloofly friendly to Americans, had died earlier in the year. His son bitterly detested the whites. The conservative chiefs considered Young Shakopee a depraved wastrel; his morals were similar to the early morals of Little Crow.

Not far upstream from Shakopee's village were the tepees of Hochokaduta[17] or Red Middle Voice. Shakopee's uncle, long-time rival of Old Shakopee, had led a group of malcontents away from his brother's village to form a separate encampment on Rice Creek.[18] Among the traditionalist chiefs, Red Middle Voice was regarded as little better than an outlaw.

At the speakership election, orators from Shakopee's village and Rice Creek had sneered contemptuously at Little Crow's farming pretentions. They had derided him as a bribed minion of the whites. Ignoring the fact that Traveling Hail represented the Progressive Whiteman's Party, they had advocated his election.

Disunity was not confined to the lower bands. There was nearly as much dissension and confusion among the Wahpetons. Christianity was a Wahpeton cause of contention. Little Paul, head speaker, and four Wahpeton chiefs, John Otherday, Simon Anawangmani, Akipa, and Cloudman, heads of villages near Yellow Medicine Agency, had declared themselves Christians, to the joy of Dr. Thomas Williamson and the Reverend Stephen Riggs, whose missions were near their villages. Almost alone among upper band leaders, the Christian chieftains encouraged their tribesmen to become farmers.

Two-thirds of the Wahpeton chiefs, including Spirit Walker, Extended Tail Feathers, and Sleepy Eyes, thought the religious pretentions of the Christian chiefs were absurd.

Red Iron, principal Wahpeton chief, had established his village twenty miles upstream from Yellow Medicine in the Lac qui Parle region. Based on his observations of Christianity among the whites, Red Iron regarded the white man's religion with skepticism. As for farming, he considered it an occupation wholly unworthy of Indians. His village was distant enough from white settlements so that hunting, at least thus far, was not entirely futile.[19]

Differences of opinion about religion and agriculture did not plague the Sissetons. More than the other bands they enjoyed a measure of unity. It resulted from a common suspicion of the whites and, excepting for tillers of a few patches of corn near Big Stone Lake, a universal abhorrence of farming.

Most important of the Sisseton leaders was Standing Buffalo. Convinced by experience with traders and agents that all Americans were liars and swindlers, Standing Buffalo had resolved to stay as far away from them as possible. He had located his village between Big Stone Lake and Lake Traverse. From here, at the extreme northwestern end of the reservation, his tribesmen hunted buffalo in Dakota Territory and obtained all the game they needed. Unless they traded for ammunition or went to obtain such annuity funds and provisions as they were offered, Standing Buffalo's band did not need to have much contact with the whites.

White Lodge and Lean Bear, also Sisseton chiefs, moved by the same considerations, had located their villages on lakes sixty miles south of the reservation.

A special cause of annoyance irritated the Dakotas during the summer of 1862. The first of July had come and gone, but no annuities, either in the form of cash or provisions, had been paid.[20] Vast quantities of flour, lard, pork, and sugar were known to have been unloaded at Yellow Medicine warehouses, but no messenger had arrived to announce a distribution date. Thousands of Upper Indians, expecting to be summoned to Yellow Medicine any day, remained home from a customary July buffalo hunt.

When no messenger came all month, four thousand Upper Indians, by now hungry as well as puzzled, gathered at Yellow Medicine. The funds, explained Major Galbraith, had not arrived. No distribution would be made until the money as well as the provisions were at hand. The new agent could give no reason for the delay, but a conviction grew that the Civil War had bankrupted the government and that no funds would come.

To the hungry horde it seemed unreasonable to hold the provisions in storage. On August 4 one of the warehouses was broken open. Reluctantly, Galbraith distributed part of the supplies and sent the Upper Indians home to await word of the main annuity payment.

More rankling to the Indians than a delay in payment were several constant sources of irritation: the persistence with which traders defrauded the Indians, collusion between agents and crooked traders,[21] evident indifference or helplessness of Sioux chiefs in protecting the interests of their people, and the fact that agents rather than the chiefs handled distribution of tribal funds.[22]

In the summer of 1862, after nine years of seething over these irritations, young men of the Lower Sioux determined to do something about them. To give substance to their protest, they formed a special soldiers' lodge.[23]

Soldiers' lodges, ordinarily an outgrowth of seasonal hunts, have no present-day social or governmental counterpart. During the hunts they operated as self-directing units of military police, and between hunts were continued in each village as a convenience for hunters and warriors.

Ordinarily soldiers' lodges existed independently of chiefs. Customarily their membership was confined to young braves from a single village. Generally their activities related only to hunting and warfare. Characteristically, soldiers' lodges did not concern themselves with internal affairs of their bands. But the 1862 organization was not cut to any ordinary pattern. It came into being at Rice Creek, reportedly at the instigation of Red Middle Voice and his nephew. It recruited members from most of the Lower Sioux villages and promptly achieved a membership of one hundred and fifty. From the start it announced an intention to take a hand in matters normally the concern of chiefs. At the outset it expressed strong dissatisfaction with treaties signed by the chiefs and subsequent execution of treaty provisions.

'As far as I was able to learn through spies and informers, its purpose was to prevent traders from going to the pay tables,' reported Agent Galbraith.[24]

In common with soldiers' lodges, Indian chiefs functioned in what has been described as 'a society without a government.' The influence of chiefs rarely extended beyond their own villages, and even there they did not have absolute power. They were not monarchs in the Asiatic or European sense.[25] They were arbitrators, advisers, and spokesmen, but could not punish the unruly or disobedient. They achieved discipline by persuasion, example, or ridicule, but not by compulsion. Such authority as they possessed was based on prestige; as such, it was subject to variation.

On rare occasions, if a chief's prestige collapsed entirely, he might be deposed, or even killed. Then, by common consent, his functions might be delegated temporarily, until his successor was determined, to the soldiers' lodge of his village.

At first, at least, the Rice Creek soldiers' lodge intended to operate within the framework of such law as existed on the reservation. Soon after its formation its members trudged to Fort Ridgely, down-river from Lower Agency. There the braves asked Captain John Marsh, commander of the post, whether his soldiers proposed to help the traders collect claims if and when annuities were paid.

Although he had not been long in the Indian country, the captain had been there long enough to have formed a clear opinion of proceedings at the annuity payments. 'My boys are soldiers; they are not collection agents for the traders,' he assured his callers.[26]

Word of Marsh's attitude promptly got back to the traders at Redwood and Yellow Medicine Agencies. They quickly called a meeting at which they agreed no credit would be extended to Indians under any circumstances until the annuity funds had been received and claims had been paid.

'They will starve if the money doesn't come soon,' observed an interpreter present at the meeting.

'So far as I am concerned, if they are hungry let them eat grass!' snapped Andrew Myrick, a Lower Agency trader.[27]

The next day signs appeared in all the stores: NO CREDIT FOR INDIANS.

'Let them eat grass!' became a rallying cry, repeated hundreds of times during the next few weeks. It won the Rice Creek soldiers' lodge hundreds of sympathetic supporters and made Andrew Myrick the focus of bitter hatred.

Sunday afternoon, August 17, a council of the soldiers' lodge convened at Rice Creek. It listened to routine complaints about lost hunting grounds, the delayed annuity funds, Trader Myrick's insult, and the failure of chiefs to cope with fraudulent claims, but adjourned without having decided on any new course of action.

Those attending did not know four Rice Creekers, including two members of the lodge, had committed murder at Acton earlier in the day and soon would gallop into camp with thrilling news of war on the whites.

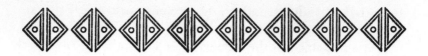

IV LITTLE CROW WILL LEAD THEM ALL

Four Indians under thirty years of age could not, by themselves, launch much of a war against the Americans. It did not matter how enthusiastic the support of their soldiers' lodge might be, or how great their fear of punishment for their Acton crimes.

Red Middle Voice, Rice Creek chieftain, was immediately sympathetic. He listened, eager and fascinated, to detailed accounts of how the victims had died. He asked dozens of questions about the dead and others about the survivors. Soon he became nearly as excited as the four who had galloped into the village.

A war decreed by a few Rice Creekers without consent of the tribal leaders and support of other bands would not last, he knew, beyond noon of the first day. Then the Rice Creek warriors would be declared renegades and banished from the tribe. Thereafter the Lower Sioux would make vigorous efforts to turn the four murderers over to the soldiers.

Red Middle Voice, not even considered a chief by some, could rally little support among most of the Medewakanton bands, and he knew it. He decided a meeting with Shakopee was desirable.

With eager soldiers' lodge members trailing close behind, Red Middle Voice and the four killers went down-river to Little Shakopee's village. The news got there a moment ahead of them. Some of Shakopee's braves were gathered near the center of the village, making a show of checking their guns.

Roars of welcome and jubilant war whoops greeted the Rice Creekers.

Everyone else remained outside when Red Middle Voice and the murderers entered Shakopee's tepee. Shakopee sat on the floor pulling at his pipe. He had known from the roars and whoops when the visitors reached camp.[1]

There was not even a momentary doubt that Shakopee sided with the Rice Creekers and approved their deeds. But, like his uncle, he could not promise tribal backing for a general war. He was much the youngest and most untried chief. Considering his was the largest of the lower bands, it was humiliating to know how seldom the great men of the tribe sought or accepted his advice. He remembered the consultations in which his father's advice had been asked, and how often momentous decisions were discussed with him in advance.

Shakopee stared upward at Red Middle Voice, held by the excitement shining from his uncle's face. Both men knew soldiers would come for the killers in a day or two. If anything was to be done it needed to be done at once.

Red Middle Voice's lips twitched. Shakopee had never seen his uncle look more agitated. The older man returned Shakopee's steady stare. Uncle and nephew both knew what was needed, and each recognized his own and the other's helplessness to supply the need. One by one they discussed the leaders of the lower bands.

There was Wabasha. He had the authority and prestige to lead the Sioux against the whites, but both men knew Wabasha would never do it.

There was Traveling Hail, the newly elected speaker. Traveling Hail, it was necessary to admit, had the heart of a white man. Probably, like Wabasha, he would oppose any general attack on the white men.

Possibly Big Eagle or Mankato could be persuaded to lead a war. Both were warriors of renown. Neither could be said to love the whites. But they were young. Their prestige and authority did not carry very far beyond their own bands.

That left Little Crow. More than anyone else, he had the prestige and stature that was needed.

It was true Little Crow had advocated farming. True, he had taken the side of the whites in more than one important matter. But Little Crow had lost the speakership election, and his face had been black at the defeat. Maybe he was beginning to know he had been a fool.

'Let us go down and see Little Crow!' cried Shakopee, jumping to his feet.[2] The older Indian's black eyes glowed as they might before a battle with Chippewas.

Shakopee threw back the tepee flap and shouted at the younger men. He asked them to notify Wabasha, Big Eagle, Mankato, Traveling Hail, and all the others that a big council would meet at once in Little Crow's house.

The young men sped into the darkness.

By the time the group starting from Shakopee's tepee reached Little Crow's house it had swelled to a whooping multitude of over one hundred warriors, most of them painted and carrying guns. Only two hours remained before dawn.

Little Crow slept in the big room on the ground floor. His bed was two strips of carpeting covered by blankets. Little Priest, the Winnebago guest, emerged with a few of his warriors from a tepee near the house. They joined the throng.

Young braves from the villages of Wabasha, Wacouta, Mankato, Big Eagle, and other nearby encampments flowed from the night and merged with the crowd. Their chiefs and head soldiers came with them or appeared a moment later.

Little Crow's room was large, but not nearly large enough. Shakopee stood in the door and held back those who were not to enter. He shoved Red Middle Voice and the four killers into the room, and admitted chiefs and head soldiers as they arrived. Mankato, Wabasha, Wacouta, Big Eagle, and their head soldiers entered. Shakopee saw Little Priest and motioned him through the door. Then he forced his own way into the room, leaving the door open for any others who could get in. Nearly two hundred remained out of doors, excitedly discussing the reasons for the council.

At the far side of the room, legs crossed, Little Crow sat on his bed. He tugged a blanket over his bare shoulders and listened intently while Red Middle Voice and Shakopee related the happenings at Acton. As he listened great beads of sweat formed on his forehead. His glance moved slowly around the room.

'Why do you come to me for advice?' he growled. 'Go to the man you elected speaker and let him tell you what to do.' [3]

'Little Crow is the greatest among the chiefs,' said Red Middle Voice softly. 'Where he leads all others will follow.'

From the blackness outside the door came the sound of the mob. At first it had been a tumultuous medley of loud talk, shouts, and whoops. Now it had ceased to be a roar and became a steady howl with a shrill undertone, unlike anything anyone in the room had ever heard.

'What do you want?' rasped Little Crow.

'They want to kill all whites,' said Red Middle Voice. 'They would drive the Americans from the valley and get back our country.'

'Red Middle Voice is a fool,' snapped Little Crow.

Wabasha, Wacouta, and young Big Eagle nodded agreement. Mankato, Shakopee, Little Priest, and others scowled in silence. Nobody in the room said anything for a moment.

Then Shakopee moved forward a step. 'Our people must pay the traders more for pork and sugar than the white man pays in New Ulm,' he said. 'Then the traders put up signs saying they will sell nothing to Dakotas on credit. They say if the Dakotas are hungry they can eat grass. The money for the land goes to Hugh Tyler, and no Dakota knows who Hugh

Tyler is. The annuity does not come. Some say it will never come again. If it does, the white man will say it is his and take it away.'

It was quite a speech for Shakopee. Several of his listeners nodded agreement as he made each point.

Medicine Bottle, who was not a chief, pushed through the crowd to stand by Little Crow's bed.

'When Inkpaduta killed whites at Okoboji, the agent said the Dakotas must kill Inkpaduta or bring him in. Inkpaduta was not a Dakota and has not been since the Wahpekutes drove him out twenty years ago, but the white man said if the Dakotas did not bring him in the annuity would stop.' [4]

Even Little Crow nodded in agreement when Medicine Bottle finished his recital. This was what Medicine Bottle had wanted; Little Crow had been the only Dakota to take the threat seriously enough to pursue Inkpaduta, but he had sneered a little at the white man's inability to protect his own settlers.

'All the white soldiers are in the South fighting other white soldiers,' said Red Middle Voice. 'The Americans are so hard pressed the agent must take halfbreeds and traders' clerks from the reservation to help them.[5] Before a better time comes for the Dakotas to take their country back, the land will be full of Dutchmen.'

'The Dakotas will not stand alone,' predicted Medicine Bottle. 'The Yanktons and Yanktonais do not love the Americans. If the Dakotas start driving them out, others will help, and Little Crow will lead them all. The Winnebago reservation is near. The Chippewas hate Dakotas but they hate Americans more, and maybe even they will help.' [6]

Little Priest nodded when the Winnebago tribe was named. Reference to the Chippewas provoked low snorts of derision even from some who wanted war.

Emboldened by acceptance of his first talk, Shakopee moved forward again. 'Little Crow has said the rulers of British America, after the war in 1812, told his father's father they would help if the Dakotas ever needed help.'

'That was long ago,' muttered Little Crow. 'Now the English are ruled by a woman. She will know two white women were killed.'

'We have no choice. Our hands are already bloody,' intoned Red Middle Voice. It was intended to be a clinching argument.

Traveling Hail had come in. He stood with Wabasha, Wacouta, and Big Eagle. Wabasha, who had not yet spoken, stepped forward and faced Red Middle Voice. 'Those are the words of a child,' he said clearly. 'Red Middle Voice well knows blood will not wash off blood.'

'Does Red Middle Voice want hundreds of Dakotas to die so four will be saved?' demanded Wacouta.

'Dakotas who were not killed would be driven from such land as they have,' said Big Eagle gently. 'When the messenger came with word of the council and the reason for it, thirty-two of my warriors painted themselves and asked if I would lead them. I said, "Yes, and you will have all the war you want. We will almost surely be defeated at last, but we are brave Dakotas and will do the best we can." My braves are outside, painted and carrying guns. They want war, and I have promised to lead them, but I think war would be the act of a foolish child, and am opposed to it.'

'We should not talk about war with the Americans,' said Traveling Hail. 'Dakotas are brave and proud; they are not fools. Red Middle Voice and Shakopee talk, but what comes from their mouths is the babble of children, as empty as the wind. We have no cannon and little ammunition. There are few Dakotas and many Americans. The Americans are as many as the leaves on the trees in the Big Woods. Count your fingers all day long and white men with guns will come faster than you can count.' [7]

For the first time the council seemed to be turning against the Rice Creekers. Red Middle Voice decided it was time to use one of his final arguments. 'It is not Red Middle Voice who wants to kill the whites and drive the intruders from the land of the Dakotas,' he said softly. 'Listen to the voice of the young men.'

Through the door came the howl, even louder than before and with an undertone more strident.

'They want to kill,' said Red Middle Voice slowly. 'If the chiefs stand in the way, they will be the first to die.' Red Middle Voice's gaze flickered from face to face. No chief's face showed fear, but on several was helpless rage.

Little Crow cleared his throat and moved to sit more erectly on his strips of carpeting. 'Dakota chiefs do not fear to die,' he said calmly. 'They will do what is best for their people, and not what will please children and fools. What Red Middle Voice proposes is madness.'

Now the hot excitement faded from Red Middle Voice's face and was replaced by cold cunning. He had expected the council to be difficult, but not like this. Quickly he stepped forward and towered over Little Crow's bed. His voice rang loudly enough for all in the room to hear. 'Little Crow,' he said, 'is afraid of the white man. Little Crow is a coward.'

Almost before the words were out Little Crow had leaped to his feet, snatched the eagle feathers from Red Middle Voice's head, thrown them to the floor and ground them under his foot.

'Little Crow,' he screamed, 'is not a coward, but he is not a fool. When did Little Crow run from his enemies? Is he without scalps? Look at his war feathers! Behold the scalp-locks of his enemies hanging there on his lodge poles! [8] Braves, you know not what you are doing. You are like dogs in the hot moon, when they run mad and snap at their own shadows. The white men are like locusts when they fly so thick the whole sky is a snowstorm. Kill one, two, or ten, and ten times ten will come to kill you.' [9]

It was Little Crow at his most eloquent. Nobody had seen

the chief so enraged before, or could remember such fiery oratory. Red Middle Voice drew back a step or two. His heart sank, but he dared not interrupt.

'Yes,' shouted Little Crow, 'the whites fight among themselves. Do you hear the thunder of their big guns? No! It would take you two moons to run down to where they are fighting. All the way you would be among white soldiers as thick as tamaracks in the swamps of the Chippewas. Yes, they fight among themselves, but if you strike one of them, they will all turn upon you and devour you.'

This last seemed to be proving Red Middle Voice's contention Little Crow was afraid of the white man. A sardonic smile spread over the Rice Creek chieftain's face. Wabasha, Wacouta, and Big Eagle, spokesmen for peace, heard Little Crow's words with grins of relief. But Little Crow had more to say, and what he said filled their faces with sudden horror.

'Fools!' he cried. 'You will die like rabbits when the hungry wolves hunt them. Little Crow is no coward. He will die with you!'

Were Little Crow's final words intended as part of the argument that he was no coward? Or had he glimpsed the sardonic grins of the war advocates and suddenly, in a fit of fury, changed his mind about war? Or had he remembered the temptation: 'Little Crow will lead them all'?

Nobody waited to learn. Those who wanted peace had no time to ask questions. Even those who wanted war wondered for a moment if their ears had betrayed them. Only the four who had been at Acton were instantly sure they had been granted a reprieve. They burst from the house with whoops of triumph, and the meeting exploded in a mighty shout.

Runners were not sent at once to the upper bands. Nobody issued instructions to the swarm around the house. It was neither possible nor necessary for anyone to do so.

'Kill the whites and kill all these Cut-Hairs who will not join us'[10] became a general order, and nobody knew where it came from. Nobody had seen Little Crow nod approval or heard him give orders, but everyone was certain he had, and considered him, temporarily at least, commander in chief. Little Crow did not claim he had been misunderstood or deny responsibility for the outcome of the pre-dawn council. Even the peace spokesmen concluded that he had agreed to war.

'Little Crow gave orders to attack the agency and to kill all the traders,' was the way Big Eagle recalled the council's outcome. The impression of Big Eagle, who did not want war, was shared by two hundred who did. Long before noon it would be too late for disclaimers of any kind.

Flames lighted by the council, and soon thereafter by the Sand Creek massacre in Colorado,[11] blazed into war between the Plains Indians and the United States, the longest war in the nation's history.

Before it ended in 1890 the war had involved most of the Cheyennes, some of the Arapahoes, and all the Teton Sioux. From time to time and place to place its leaders would be Little Wolf, Dull Knife, Crazy Horse, Sitting Bull, Red Cloud, and dozens of others.

Some would debate whether Little Crow actually meant to start a war, but none would doubt that he succeeded.

V LET MYRICK EAT GRASS

All was calm when the first light showed east of Redwood Agency in the early hours on Monday. Most of the tumult in Little Crow's village, absorbed by trees, did not travel far from the buildings and tepees on the bluffs two miles away. Only a gentle lapping and murmuring came from the stream passing the north side of the agency. The river was resolute but not turbulent. There was no frenzy and little exclaiming in its sweep toward the Mississippi.

A few birds, aroused by dawn, began to twitter in oaks and maples on the ridge to the south and in willows lining the river. Somewhere a worried cow began to bawl for a calf separated from her during the night. From the down-river meadows came the tinkling melody of a bell worn by a young steer given to straying.

Having gone down with the sun, a thin breeze began to revive with the first light. It could be heard on only the nearest trees.

The sole sound of any consequence before full daylight was the uneasy barking of two dogs. They were responding to provocative noises from the bluff, not audible to humans.

It was daylight when the throng from Little Crow's house flowed downhill to the agency. As it drew near, the mob divided into small groups of four or five. Each group, as it broke away, surrounded a separate store, shop, mill, or dwelling.[1]

The third building in the upper part of town was the store of Nathan and Andrew Myrick, most hated of the traders. It was the first place surrounded.

Nathan Myrick was away, but Andrew was at home. Like most of the traders and their employees, Andrew lived on the premises. He occupied a room on the second floor of the building.

Another room was occupied by James W. Lynd, thirty-two years of age, a clerk in the Myrick store. Lynd was the father of two daughters by Mary Napashue and of an unborn child by another Indian girl. He was unmarried, spoke Dakota fluently, and had written a book, as yet unpublished, concerning Sioux customs, history, traditions, and the language.

It was now about six o'clock. Both Andrew Myrick and James Lynd were awake. Lynd was the first downstairs. He stood in the doorway watching the Indians approach, surprised to see them. Plenty of Hail, young brave of Little Crow's band, shot him dead. It was the first killing of the day.

Another clerk, G. W. Divoll, was inside the Myrick store. He heard the shot that killed Lynd, and was murdered an instant later as he walked to the door to find out what was happening.

Andrew Myrick remained upstairs. He heard the commotion and shooting and knew, from an attacker's snarl of denunciation, what was going on.

His first impulse was to hide under a packing case, but the Indians knew he was upstairs. One of them shouted they would set the place on fire. Myrick swung out of a window and slid down a lightning rod to a lean-to shed. From its roof he leaped to the ground. He ran toward a clump of willows. Just before he reached the thicket a bullet brought him down.

When Andrew's bloated and decomposed body was found two weeks later by his brother, Nathan, it bore, in addition to bullet holes, numerous arrows and a hay scythe. A large tuft of dried grass, caked with blood, protruded from Myrick's mouth. A safe inside the store had been broken open before the building was plundered and burned. Gold from the safe had been stuffed into the mouths of Lynd and Divoll, and pieces of gold were scattered near Andrew's corpse.[2]

The stores of William Forbes, Louis Robert, and François La Bathe, the other traders with posts at the Lower Agency, were attacked at nearly the same time.

At Forbes's store Joe Belland and Antoine Young were shot dead and George Spencer was wounded. Spencer, shot on the stairway of the store, was the beneficiary of one of the rare humane acts of the day. A witness later testified the Forbes attack was led by Medicine Bottle and Little Crow.

'Not expecting to live a great while,' Spencer said, 'I threw myself upon a bed, and while lying there could hear them opening cases of goods and carrying them out, and threatening to burn the building. I did not relish the idea of being burned to death very well. . . . I had been upstairs probably an hour when I heard the voice of an Indian inquiring for me.'[3] The Indian was Wakinyatawa, until that moment head soldier for Little Crow, but clearly unsuitable to continue.

'If you had killed him before I saw him,' Wakinyatawa said to the others when he found Spencer, 'it would have been all right, but we have been friends and comrades for years, and now that I have seen him I will protect him or die with him.' Spencer was taken to Wakinyatawa's tepee and his wounds were dressed with roots.[4]

No other white man at the agency, except those who fled when the shooting first started, lived through the day.

At Louis Robert's store the Indians killed the head clerk, Patrick McClennan, and another, Henry Belland.

They killed Trader François La Bathe and a clerk at La Bathe's trading house.

John Lamb, a government teamster, was shot dead; so was A. H. Wagner, white superintendent of farms at the Redwood Agency.

William Taylor, corpulent and jolly colored barber, escaped across the ferry but was shot two miles beyond. Taylor had given Little Crow a daguerrotype of himself dressed as an Indian a few days before. After he was dead it was said that had Little Crow been present he would not have permitted this killing.

Philander Prescott, nearly seventy years of age, had lived among various Santee tribes as interpreter for forty-five years. He had married a Sioux woman and fathered a family of half-breeds. When the shooting started, his wife persuaded him she was in no danger and induced him to run to the ferry. As he fled toward Fort Ridgely a party of Indians overtook and killed him. Medicine Bottle testified later that he 'and one other Indian shot at him.' [5]

Among the earliest risers at Redwood Agency were J. C. Dickinson, operator of the government boarding house, and the girls who worked in his kitchen and dining room. The first boarders reported an unusual stir among the Indians. The next arrivals reported hearing shots in the upper part of the agency. Dickinson, his family, and a wagonload of girls, were among those who crossed the river in time. They were the first survivors to reach Fort Ridgely with a report of events at the agency.

The Reverend Samuel D. Hinman, Episcopal missionary, to whose sermon Little Crow had listened the previous day, got across the river with his children. His wife was away on a visit.

Dr. Philander Humphrey, Lower Agency physician, crossed with his sick wife and three children. They started for the fort. At the abandoned home of a settler Humphrey sent one of his sons to a spring for water. 'While the child was gone the Indians killed his father and burned his mother and the other two children in the house.' [6] The boy hid, watching helplessly, while other Indians came and chopped off the head of his father, whose throat had already been slashed.

John Nairn, government carpenter, remained south of the river. With his wife and four children he fled through the woods and over the prairie. The fugitives did not cross the river until afternoon, when they were nearly opposite Fort Ridgely.

Nairn's assistant, Alexander Hunter, who had taken a half-breed bride a month before, was less fortunate. The Hunters started out with the Nairns. Hunter's toes had been frozen off a few winters before. Lameness forced him to drop behind. He and his bride hid in the woods all night. Early in the morning they encountered Hinkanshoonkoyangmane, who killed Hunter and made a captive of his wife.

Unlike the Nairns and Hunters, most of the fugitives fled to the north side of the river, using the Redwood ferry as long as it remained in operation.

Presently 'the agency buildings and the traders' stores were in flames and hundreds of shouting savages were surging about the government warehouse, shrieking and brandishing their weapons.' Now no doubt remained in anyone's mind that it was necessary to flee, but the ferry by that time had 'a dense crowd surrounding it.' [7]

Hero of the morning was the operator of the ferry, Hubert Millier,[8] generally known as Old Mauley. He kept the ferry running until the 'dense crowd' was temporarily safe on the north side. There is no record anyone was killed at the south approach. But the Indians presently found out what was taking place. They eliminated the ferry as an escape route by murdering and disemboweling Old Mauley, who might have lived had he fled after one of his first trips across.

Looting the stores and warehouses was even more exciting than killing whites, and the material rewards were greater. More than anything else, this diversion gave some residents time to flee. With the exception of Spencer, white men who did not escape were killed. Some, like Dr. Humphrey, Prescott, and Hunter, were murdered while they fled, but others succeeded in reaching the fort. Women and many children who did not get away were made captives. The entire operation did not take very long. Before noon most of the buildings were destroyed and all former residents of the agency were fugitives, had been killed, or were in captivity.

Mrs. Joseph DeCamp, wife of the government sawmill operator, was alone Monday with her three young sons. Her husband had gone to St. Paul on business the previous day. The DeCamp house was far enough from the traders' stores and the warehouse, and behind enough trees, so that Jannette DeCamp did not learn of the attack until ten o'clock. She was fortunate enough to meet, at the start, opponents of the war.

First she encountered Wacouta's mother, who urged her to flee, grabbed the four-year-old DeCamp son, and led the family toward Wabasha's village. On the way they met a crowd of warriors, 'sullen and scowling,' who closed in, 'raising their tomahawks as if ready to strike.' Wabasha, however, was with them, and 'called them cowards and squaws for wanting to kill women and children.' He explained to Mrs. DeCamp that it was 'the upper Indians who were doing all the mischief,' assured her he would see the family was not killed, and then rode away. Mrs. DeCamp did not see him again until two weeks later.

Almost immediately, though, she saw Wacouta, who led the DeCamps to an empty house in his village, where they hid, hungry, frightened, uncomfortable, but safe, until the Lower Agency villages were vacated.

Here Mrs. DeCamp later saw some young warriors who had often come to her 'to learn English words.' Overhearing them discuss the attacks, she asked 'what had instigated them to do the deeds they had done.'

The Indians laughed. 'It is fun to kill white men,' they told her. 'They are such cowards. They all run away and leave their squaws to be killed. One Indian can kill ten white men without trying.' [9]

During the morning scores of latecomers from the villages of Shakopee, Red Middle Voice, Little Crow, and even from the bands of chiefs who had advocated peace, continued to swarm into the Lower Agency. There they viewed the smoking ruins, enviously saw the stacks of plunder obtained from the stores and warehouse, and hastily planned to look for excitement and loot elsewhere.

At the Redwood River, within a mile of Shakopee's village, lived the family of Joseph Reynolds. Both Reynolds and his wife, Valencia, were instructors in a government school at the edge of Shakopee's village. Their home, on the road between the two agencies, was a 'public house' to the extent that meals were served to passers-by. Their household included two hired girls named Mary Anderson and Mary Schwandt, and a niece, Mattie Williams of Ohio.

A Yellow Medicine trader, Francis Patoile, stopped for breakfast Monday morning. During breakfast word of the Lower Agency attack arrived. Everyone decided to flee at once.

Joseph Reynolds got out his one-horse buggy. Patoile, having a wagon, offered to take the three girls. Reynolds and his wife climbed into the buggy. All agreed on New Ulm as a destination.

They started on the road toward the Lower Agency, Reynolds intending to drive his buggy on the bluff later to avoid the agency. Patoile considered it safer to head for the prairie as soon as his wagon was across the Redwood River. A short distance from home the two instructors encountered Shakopee and two other Indians.

'What is the matter, Little Shakopee?' called Reynolds.

'I do not know,' answered young Shakopee, uncomfortably, troubled at seeing the only two whites he had almost considered friends.

'He kept motioning us with his hand,' reported Valencia, 'to go out upon the prairie.' [10]

Thinking the buggy would make better time on the road, Reynolds did not drive out on the bluffs to the right until the agency buildings were nearly in sight. He drove behind a low ridge which would permit the buggy to pass the agency without being seen.

'We crawled up to the crest of the ridge on our hands and knees,' said Mrs. Reynolds. 'The doors of the stores were open and Indians were all about.'

Nobody sighted the buggy, and the teachers continued their flight. Below the agency, though, they saw sixty Indians half a mile away and encountered, much nearer, 'a naked savage on foot.' The naked savage, armed with a double-barreled gun, 'raised the gun to his face and snapped both caps, but they failed to ignite the powder.'

Mr. and Mrs. Reynolds hastily substituted Fort Ridgely as their destination. It was across the river and much nearer than New Ulm.

At the fort Joseph Reynolds was handed a gun and became a citizen soldier. Valencia helped make cartridges, assisted the post surgeon's wife in caring for the sick and wounded, and soon became exceedingly busy.

Patoile and the three girls who started in his wagon did not fare as well. Like the teachers in the buggy, they passed the agency without being seen. From a down-river point, said Mary Schwandt, 'we could see the smoke of burning buildings, as we supposed them to be, if the Indians were indeed killing the whites, of which we were not yet entirely certain.' [11]

When they were within ten miles of New Ulm, Patoile [12] and the girls had the misfortune to meet fifty Indians, 'very noisy and perfectly naked,' returning from an afternoon of murdering and looting at Milford and Leavenworth, where they and other Lower Agency raiders had killed over two score, mostly Germans. The towns were hamlets along the

Cottonwood and the Minnesota. The fifty included Tazoo, Hapan, Mazabomdoo, and Wyatahtowa, recognized despite their nakedness, and Godfrey, who later claimed to have been an unwilling participant.

Patoile was shot at once, 'four balls entering his body, and he fell out of the wagon, dead.' Next Mary Anderson was 'shot through the lower part of the body, the ball entering at the hip and coming out through the abdomen.' She did not die until four days later.

Mattie Williams and Mary Schwandt, together with the wounded Mary Anderson, were hauled away as captives, and were housed in the building in Wacouta's village in which Mrs. DeCamp and her children were concealed.

'After a while,' reported Mary Schwandt, a number of Indians came to the house and, 'after annoying me with their loathsome attentions for a long time, one of them laid his hands forcibly upon me. When I screamed one of the fiends struck me on the mouth with his hand, causing the blood to flow very freely. Then they took me out to an unoccupied tepee near the house and perpetrated the most horrible and nameless outrages upon my person.'

Mary Schwandt was fourteen years of age. Mary Anderson, shot through the hip, the bullet 'coming out through the abdomen,' was treated similarly. Four days later, when the lower villages were abandoned and the Indians moved temporarily to a new location near Rice Creek, Mrs. DeCamp and her children were hauled in the wagon occupied by Mary Anderson. When the wagon reached Little Crow's village, said Mrs. DeCamp, 'the Indian who claimed the dying Mary came up and said she must get out there. I told him she was dying and to let her go on with me so I could be with her till the last,' but the Indian told Jannette DeCamp to 'get along out!' Mary Anderson 'lived about an hour after' and was 'buried there with an old tablecloth wrapping her.' [13]

On Saturday George Gleason, government storekeeper at

the Lower Agency warehouse, had escorted Agent Galbraith's family to Yellow Medicine. There, when the first unconfirmed rumors of the Sunday killings at Acton began to be circulated Monday noon, Dr. J. L. Wakefield, Upper Agency physician, implored Gleason to take Mrs. Wakefield and their children to Fort Ridgely. It was a reasonable enough request, since Gleason planned to return to the Lower Agency anyway, and the fort was only thirteen miles beyond. Gleason, driving the wagon in which he had made the up-river trip, called for his passengers at two in the afternoon.

Mrs. Wakefield, who weighed two hundred and three pounds, ordinarily was cheerful and jovial. She had made numerous friends among the Upper Indians since she, her husband, and the children, Nellie and James, had lived at Yellow Medicine. Physical violence terrified her, and the faintest whisper of 'trouble with the Indians' caused her to shiver violently and started her teeth chattering.[14]

Almost as soon as the wagon started for the fort, she began trying to persuade Gleason to turn back. Gleason, anxious to get home, scoffed at the notion that the Lower Sioux might be a source of difficulty. He offered to 'send four or five hundred lower Indians to protect the Yellow Medicine whites' in case the Upper Indians made trouble.

Halfway to Redwood the wagon party saw a column of smoke. Mrs. Wakefield, sure the agency was being destroyed, began to cry and attempted to leap from the wagon. Gleason, trying to reassure her, 'became more lively than I ever knew him, laughing, singing, shouting, and saying he'd never take us anywhere again.'

As the wagon neared the Joseph Reynolds' house Gleason called Mrs. Wakefield's attention to the fact the house stood intact and predicted safe arrival at Fort Ridgely by eight o'clock.

At this moment two young Indians appeared on the road ahead.

'Mr. Gleason,' whispered Mrs. Wakefield, 'take out your pistol.'

'Be quiet!' retorted Gleason. 'They are only boys going hunting.'

Gleason pulled the reins and slowed the horses. He sat on the front seat. Directly behind him, on a second seat, rode Mrs. Wakefield, Nellie on her lap and James at her right.

As the wagon passed the Indians, one of them wheeled and fired. Gleason, struck in his right shoulder, slumped wordlessly backward. The Indian fired again. This shot also hit Gleason. It knocked him out of the wagon. The startled horses lunged forward. The Indian who had done no shooting jumped ahead of the wagon and clutched the bridles of the frightened team.

'Are you the doctor's wife?' asked the Indian who had stopped the horses.[15]

'Yes,' quavered Mrs. Wakefield in a tiny voice, shaking with terror.

'Good. If you were the agent's wife, he would cut you to pieces.'

The Indian drew near and spoke in a low voice to Mrs. Wakefield. 'Don't talk much. He has had too much whisky.'

Gleason writhed on the ground, groaning. Mrs. Wakefield saw the Indian who had shot her escort reloading his gun. He approached the wagon.

'Spare me!' begged Mrs. Wakefield. 'Spare me for the sake of my children. I'll sew, wash, cut wood, or cook for you, but spare me.' Her chattering teeth and quaking voice made her plea almost incoherent.

Both Indians scowled at her. The one who had cautioned her against talking shook his head furiously. Hapa, the one who had fired the first two shots at Gleason, fired at him again, and the writhing figure lay still.

Both Indians then climbed into the wagon. Chaska, who had done no shooting, warned Mrs. Wakefield against looking back toward Gleason's body as they drove away.

'Hapa is very cross,' he whispered, 'and will kill you if you turn around.'

'Those children!' said Hapa, holding his gun on James and Nellie. 'They will be trouble when we go to the Red River, I will kill them.'

'No,' protested Chaska, promptly. 'You will have to kill me first. I will take care of them.'

Mrs. Wakefield had heard of Chaska, but had not previously seen him. He was a member of Shakopee's band. Dr. Wakefield had been summoned to attend him and other wounded Dakotas after a battle with the Chippewas, and had been credited with having saved Sioux lives. Chaska had gone to the school taught by Reynolds, could speak, read, and write a little English, had dressed as a white man for several years, and was a farmer. His wife had died a few months before. Hapa was 'a wild Rice Creek Indian' whose wife was Chaska's sister.

Chaska took Mrs. Wakefield and the children to his tepee,[16] where they met his mother, and then to a bark house where another captive, a German woman who spoke little English, was held. The German captive's husband, father, sister, and brother had all been killed and her household possessions looted or destroyed, 'but she was mourning only for her feather beds, moaning and sobbing.'

When the captives alighted from the wagon at Chaska's tepee, 'the squaws cried and spread carpets for us to sit on.' In the bark house the captives found 'a good fire, candles, and as good a bed as could be expected.'

'Sleep!' ordered Chaska before he left for his mother's tepee. 'We leave for Red River in the morning. When you wake up, go to the tepee and get a different dress from my mother. You will be safer dressed as a squaw.'

Chaska erred in predicting early departure for the Red River. In the morning the braves who left camp went in the opposite direction, saying they planned to attack Fort Ridgely.

VI THE FUN OF KILLING THE WHITES

While flames were still leaping in the agency wreck-
age, scores of Dakotas called at cabins of settlers on the road
toward the fort, in the Milford and Leavenworth areas, and
across the river on land sold to the government four years
before. Often the callers greeted their hosts as old friends,
shook hands warmly with everyone, and kissed some as a
token of special esteem.

Then the visitors split the hosts' skulls, clubbed children to
death, raped daughters, hacked heads from the dead, slashed
breasts from the corpses of women and genitals from the
bodies of men, took what food and furnishings they could
carry, cut, chopped, or smashed the rest, and set fire to the
ruins before leaving for the next cabin.

Hundreds of palefaces perished, but not one Indian was
killed or seriously hurt by a settler that day.[1] Cowardice contributed to the uneven score, but deception, surprise, and
incredulity were even more important.

Few of the newcomers were seasoned frontiersmen, and few
had guns. They had come to farm rather than hunt. They were
on prairie land and not in deer country, and such guns as they
had were shot-guns instead of rifles. Especially in the recently
opened areas, many immigrants would not have known how
to shoot a weapon if they had owned one.[2] Firearms, in the
long-established world from which they had come, had never
been a part of their lives.

Some men carrying clubs or rocks dropped them and ran when their families were surrounded, leaving wives and children to cope with the incredible new menace.

Many who heard early reports of happenings at the agency thought the rumors were absurd. Some who watched Indians galloping over the prairie shrugged off the sight. 'Just another raid on the Chippewas,' they supposed, and returned to whatever they had been doing. The worst that could happen, they believed, was that some of their own horses might be driven off. Panicky gossip and warnings to flee seemed ridiculous.

At Leavenworth on the Cottonwood, and in the Milford area³ west of New Ulm, bands from the Lower Agency suddenly appeared, shook hands all around, were greeted as friends not seen for a while. Then they slaughtered the families of Elijah Whiton, Bastian Mey, George Raeser, Anton Mesmer, and dozens of others. It was not necessary that the adults be at home; when they were not, the attackers murdered children. At Milford they killed two daughters and a son of Anton Hanley, confident that when the parents came home they would take warning and leave the area.

On the road between Redwood Ferry and Fort Ridgely lived the Edward Magner family. When the first escapees from the agency came screaming past, the family fled, not entirely convinced flight was necessary. Magner had not finished watering his livestock. Feeling a trifle sheepish, he turned back to complete the job before entering the fort, met Indians with axes near his pump, and was chopped to death.

Ole Sampson lived with his wife and three children near the Magners. Their cabin was shielded from the road by trees and they missed seeing the earliest survivors. Sampson was shot dead by the first party of Indians to get that far from the agency. His wife, carrying the children, pleaded frantically with drivers of overloaded ox carts for help in getting to the fort. Finally the family hid in a canvas-covered wagon near their cabin. The Indians found the hiding place, grabbed Mrs. Sampson's baby, threw it into the grass, pushed a pile of hay under the wagon, set it on fire, and departed. Choking and badly burned, the mother staggered out and scooped up the baby. The two older children died, shrieking, in the flames.

Two miles from the agency on the fort road lived David ter.[4] Their home was a spacious, well-furnished log house. Faribault with his wife, Nancy, and an eight-year-old daugh-Unlike many other mixed-bloods, the Faribaults were proud of their heritage. The young pair, handsome and vivacious, led the French and half-breed elements of the community. Formerly a trader, Faribault had intended to become a farmer and stockman, but resumed his former business when outraged by treatment the Indians received from traders. He refused to take part in the credit agreement of the Myricks and others.

Monday morning an ox-drawn wagon filled with frenzied fugitives reached the log house, the escapees begging for horses. David had only one team on hand, but gave it to replace the oxen. Left without mounts of their own, the Faribaults fled to the woods on foot, were surrounded, and taken captive.

'We are going to kill all the white people,' explained their captors, 'but will not hurt you because you have trusted us with goods.'[5] With their young daughter the captives were taken to Little Crow's village across the river. Their captivity was nerve-wracking. Each time Little Crow heard of other half-breeds helping whites, he threatened to exterminate all the mixed-bloods he was holding; but the Faribaults succeeded in persuading many Dakota acquaintances to modify their treatment of the settlers.

Near Beaver Creek, across from the agency and four miles upstream from the ferry, lived Patrick and Mary Hayden with their one-year-old child and Patrick's brother John.

Patrick started for the agency early Monday, encountered

a half-breed friend who warned him the Indians were crossing the river to kill the whites, and raced home to warn his family. The Haydens ran to the home of Benedict Juni,[6] their nearest neighbor.

Word was getting around, and the Zimmermans arrived a moment later. They had four children. The Junis had five.

All women and children climbed into Zimmerman's wagon. With Juni and his eleven-year-old son driving cattle at the rear and the two oldest Zimmerman boys following on foot, the party started for Fort Ridgely, seventeen miles away.

At the last instant Patrick and John Hayden decided Indian scares were foolish and turned to go home. Patrick's body was found near the river and John's at La Croix Creek.

Below the north end of the ferry screeching and whooping Indians surrounded the wagon. They shot Zimmerman, Juni, and the older boys, stripped the wagon, took the ox team and cattle, and made captives of all the survivors except Mary Hayden and her baby.

Mary jumped from the wagon into the woods above the road, reached the top of the bluffs, glimpsed the burning agency buildings, watched the looting of Magner's home, hid in the trees most of the day, and at one o'clock in the morning, her child safe in her arms, reached Fort Ridgely.

When word of danger swept over the prairie, neighbors instinctively congregated for group flight, but numbers meant no added strength. Instead, a large number of helpless people in a caravan merely provided the attackers with a convenient concentration of victims.

A larger group of fugitives than the one starting from the Juni cabin assembled early Monday at the Jonathan Earle home two miles farther north on the Beaver.

Jonathan, after graduating from the University of Vermont and teaching at 'select schools and academies' in western New York, had become a lawyer-farmer in Wisconsin, and served for a while in the state legislature.[7] In the spring of

1862 the Earles, with four sons and two daughters, succumbed to the appeal of free land in the west. Earle staked out a claim on Beaver Creek, built a frame house larger than the average homesteader's cabin, and planted fourteen acres of prairie to corn. Earle brought to his new home 'a good law, classical, medical, and family library of some twelve hundred volumes,' together with a melodeon and an assortment of other musical instruments, contributing quite an element of culture to the crude frontier.

Before breakfast on Monday four naked and painted Dakotas entered the Earle home, shook hands, and announced they were a war party chasing Chippewas. One of the Indians asked for Earle's gun, explaining he needed it to kill Chippewas.

'He made signs of taking it down' from its pegs on the wall, said Earle, 'and only desisted when sternly forbidden.' Leaving the house, the four painted visitors sat on a woodpile outside.[8]

Neighbors, having heard warnings, began to assemble after breakfast. Among the arrivals were Mr. and Mrs. S. R. Henderson with their two children and Mrs. Helen Carrothers, also with two. Mrs. Henderson was seriously ill with appendicitis. Mrs. Carrothers, whose husband had left the day before on a trip to another part of the state, had been taking care of Mrs. Henderson.

Having lived on Beaver Creek four years, the Carrothers had survived previous Indian scares. They had numerous friends among the Dakotas. Helen Carrothers felt sure the massacre rumor was untrue, objected to flight, and went to the Earle home only at the insistence of the Hendersons. Mrs. Henderson's appendicitis was so serious she was brought on a featherbed.

Including the Earle family, twenty-eight assembled for flight. Four were adult men: Earle, Henderson, a neighbor named Wegge, and Mrs. Carrother's brother-in-law, David.

Four were teen-age boys. Twenty were women and children.
Jonathan Earle and his fifteen-year-old son, Radner, had guns.
Radner's weapon was loaded with pebbles. The party had
three horse-drawn wagons for the Fort Ridgely trip.

Henderson's wagon contained his wife on her featherbed
and the Henderson children, a two-year-old daughter and
nine-months-old son. Except those who chose to walk along-
side, everyone rode in the other two wagons. As the party left,
the four Dakotas arose from the woodpile and followed.

Half a mile from the Earle house seventy mounted Indians
rode from the prairie and surrounded the wagons. Among
them Helen Carrothers recognized Medicine Man, a Dakota
friend in whose ability to provide medication she had great
confidence. She believed Medicine Man effected cures 'when
the wisdom of the white doctors and all other remedies failed,'
and had once summoned him to examine Mrs. Henderson.[9]
The Hendersons did not share Mrs. Carrothers' enthusiasm.
Henderson, in fact, had called Medicine Man 'a crazy old
humbug and fraud.'

Because of the size of the surrounding party, Helen Carrothers now knew the massacre rumors had substance.

'What do you want?' she demanded, speaking Dakota.

'We are going to kill all of you,' replied the nearest Indian.

The wagons halted and Helen stood up. She was the only
one among the settlers who spoke Dakota. 'You must not kill
us,' she said, facing the horsemen. 'Many of you are my friends
and often have been kind to me. We are your friends, also.
When have you ever come to our homes, wanting food, and
been turned away hungry? The Great Spirit would be very
angry with you if you killed your friends.'

'We would like to spare you,' said the Dakota slowly, in
English, 'but all whites must die.'

Reported Helen Carrothers: 'The women seemed speechless
with terror. The faces of the men wore a deathly pallor.'

Still in her wagon box, Mrs. Carrothers tried another appeal, again in Dakota. 'Since we are friends,' she said, 'all we have is yours. You have nothing to gain by killing your friends.'

This evoked a consultation. Leaving a dozen warriors as guards, the others briefly withdrew. Medicine Man was among the consultants.

'We will not kill you,' said the spokesman when they returned, 'but you must give us your horses.'

'Let us keep the end wagon. The woman in it is dying and cannot walk. She has two children too young to walk.'

'You may keep one wagon and pull it yourselves, but we must have the horses.'

After the horses had been unhitched the Indians rode away. Henderson and David Carrothers pulled, and Earle and Wegge pushed, the Henderson wagon. They had gone half a mile when about one-third of the mounted Dakotas reappeared from the rear, singing a monotonous, eerie chant as they came. It was the Dakota song of death.

Crackle of gunfire merged with the mournful chant, and three bullets thudded into the rear of the wagon, striking harmlessly between Wegge and Earle.

'Take my pillow case and wave it,' suggested Mrs. Henderson weakly from the wagon's interior.

Henderson and David Carrothers held the flag of truce aloft, but the attackers sweeping toward the wagon paid no attention. They shot off part of the hand with which Henderson clutched the pillow case.

Mrs. Henderson uttered a low moan and fainted. A shot struck Wegge; he fell behind the wagon, dead. David Carrothers began to run.

'Mr. Henderson cast one look of anguish and despair at his wife,' recalled Helen Carrothers, 'broke from his little girl who was clinging to him, and ran, leaping, crouching, and dodging the bullets which whistled after him.'[10]

If Medicine Man sought vengeance for having been called a fraud and humbug by Henderson he now received it, but Henderson was not present.

An Indian, reported Mrs. Carrothers, seized Henderson's daughter, 'sweet and pretty child of two, and beat her savagely over the head with a violin case, smashing her head horribly out of shape. Then he took her by her feet and dashed her brains out against the wheel of the wagon, spattering her mother with blood and brains. Another fiend took the nine-months-old boy, hacked off his limbs with a tomahawk, and threw the pieces at the mother. Then they made a big fire and tossed featherbed, woman, and mangled children into the flames.'[11]

Five more members of the party, altogether, including David Carrothers' two children, were killed.

Jonathan Earle fired at the attackers, and estimated thirty shots were fired at him in return. He thought he 'may have wounded or killed' an Indian, but there was no evidence that he had.

Radner fired pebbles at the faces of the attackers until two overtook and killed him.

'Noble boy!' mourned his father, 'He saved my life at the sacrifice of his own.'[12]

Of the twenty-eight starting from Earle's house only one, Ezmon Earle, got directly to the fort. Jonathan and his oldest son, Chalon, made a wide swing to the northeast and reached the fort twelve days later. Henderson likewise reached it after a long detour.

Earle's wife, his daughters, Helen Carrothers, and six others were made prisoners, their captors ceremoniously shaking hands with all before leading them away.

Carnage and plundering north of the river was concentrated in two additional sections on the opening day of the massacre. These were the La Croix and Sacred Heart Creek areas. At cabins on the La Croix, Indians from across the river killed

Peter Pereau, Frederick Closen, Andrew Bahlke, Henry Keartner, Mrs. William Vitt, and a dozen others.

Some of the most fearful atrocities of the massacre were committed by braves from Shakopee's and Red Middle Voice's bands near Patterson Rapids and at settlements on other parts of the Sacred Heart Creek. Children were trapped and burned to death in flaming cabins. Hands and feet were hacked off before death. Children were nailed to doors, spikes through their arms and legs, and swung back and forth until they died.[13] It was as though the Shakopee and Rice Creek braves forgot entirely they were Dakota warriors on serious business, and took time out to torture their victims as a matter of sport.

At one cabin a dozen braves killed the homesteader and two sons in a hayfield and murdered the settler's wife and his two youngest children in the house. Only a thirteen-year-old daughter remained alive. Her clothing was torn off and she was raped in turn by the twelve.

At another homestead on Sacred Heart Creek the raiders found John Schwandt repairing the roof of his cabin. He toppled to the ground, shot through the heart. Then the invaders killed Schwandt's wife, Christina, his pregnant daughter, Caroline, his sons, Christian and Frederick, Caroline's husband, John Waltz, and a hired man.

August, a twelve-year-old son, was tomahawked and thought dead. He retained consciousness, watched the murders of other members of the household, saw the Indians rip Caroline open with a knife, remove her unborn baby, and nail it to a tree.[14]

After the Indians departed August crawled and staggered to Fort Ridgely, hiding by day and traveling by night. He and his sister, Mary, hired girl at the Joseph Reynolds' home, were the only members of the Schwandt family to survive.

On the north side of the river, halfway between Sacred Heart Creek and the Upper Agency, was the 'great and elegant' stone house of Major Joseph R. Brown, former Sioux agent. Major Brown was away on business, but at home were his Wahpeton wife, his nine half-breed children, and his white son-in-law, Charley Blair. At four o'clock Tuesday morning a half-breed friend battered at the door, announced the whites at Yellow Medicine were being killed, and warned the family to flee. Oxen were hitched to a wagon and all occupants of the stone house went toward Fort Ridgely, Angus Brown and Charley Blair riding horseback.[15]

Five miles from home the party was surrounded. The Indians included Dewanea of Little Crow's band, Cut Nose, and Shakopee, 'three of the worst among the Lower Indians.'

Recognition of the Browns led to colloquy. Mrs. Brown, it was known, was a full-blood Upper Indian, and the children were half-breeds. In the absence of high-level authorization to murder mixed bloods, Blair was the only one who could be killed.

Angus Brown and Charley Blair, relieved of their mounts, were told to ride in the wagon. Angus was ordered to shoot white fugitives who appeared in other wagons, as evidence that his heart was with the Indians, 'but he refused to do so.'

After a pause at Rice Creek, the Browns were ordered to Little Crow's village on the threat that anyone trying to escape 'would be taken care of by the soldiers' lodge.'

Angus and Samuel Brown promptly called on Little Crow. The chief, as Samuel Brown recalled it, 'told us to bring our folks down here, and no one should hurt us. He was very kind to us, but he didn't believe he could keep Charley Blair alive until morning.'

If he protected all-white Charley or allowed him to escape, the chief explained, the younger Indians would kill Little Crow. Angus and Samuel thereupon reminded their host that their mother was a niece of Akipa, Wahpeton chief. If any harm befell Charley, the Upper Indians would be enraged.

It was a good enough argument to save Charley Blair's life. To avoid antagonizing the upper bands, Little Crow decided to risk the wrath of his own young men. He sent Blair under escort to the river, and from there Charley made his way to the fort.

Disagreement and disunity had begun to appear among the Lower Sioux. To make a move of elementary shrewdness, Little Crow needed to circumvent his own braves. The rift followed the line of cleavage shown in the pre-dawn council, and might easily grow wider and wider.

Few words of praise and no eagle feathers rewarded the young braves of most of the lower villages when they returned to tell of triumphs at Milford, Leavenworth, or north of the river. Instead, the returning warriors encountered the cold scorn of respected chiefs and tearful wails rather than applause from wives and mothers. Killing Chippewas meant eagle feathers; killing settlers meant ridicule. It was true that whites, unlike Chippewas, were easy to fool, did not try to keep out of sight, and seldom fought back. It was simple and not dangerous to kill settlers. Just the same, the contempt seemed a little unfair.

Bloody scalps brought back from the raids were rewarded by tongue lashings rather than scalp dances. Such chiefs as Wabasha and Wacouta tossed the scalps disdainfully into the fire.

'Only a coward shoots women and children,' sneered the chiefs.

'Soldiers and young men,' Little Crow had protested the day after the Lower Agency killings and first raids on the nearer settlements, 'you ought not to kill women and children. Your consciences will reproach you for it and make you weak in battle. You were too hasty in going into the country. You should have killed only those who have been robbing us so long. Hereafter, make war after the manner of white men.'[16]

There was talk of flight, of departure for the Red River, for British America, or for the western plains.

John Otherday, Wahpeton leader, sent a protest from Yel-

low Medicine when he heard of the murders. 'Some of you,' he
jeered, 'say you have horses and can escape to the plains, but
what, I ask you, will become of those who have no horses?'

'You say you can make a treaty with the British government,' scoffed Little Paul, another Upper Agency chief. 'That
is impossible. Have you not yet come to your senses? They are
also white men, and neighbors and friends to the soldiers.
They are ruled by a petticoat, and she has the heart of a squaw.
What will she do for men who have committed the murders
you have? I hear some of you talking very loud and boasting
you have killed so many women and children. That is not
brave; it is cowardly. Go and fight the soldiers! You dare not!
When you see their army coming on the plains you will throw
down your arms and fly in one direction and your women in
another, and this winter you will all starve.'[17]

Little Crow may not have called the young men cowards
and squaws, but even he did not sanction the killing of the
undefended. He accepted pillaged goods and divided the
spoils among the bands. He took custody of captives brought
to him, but it was known he turned some over to Sissetons and
Wahpetons, and believed he allowed others to get away. He
urged the upper bands to attack Yellow Medicine Agency. He
sent couriers to the Yanktons and elsewhere inviting participation, and a messenger to Selkirk reminding the British of
their ancient promise. Word went to White Lodge and Lean
Bear, the Sissetons south of the reservation. But when warriors
reported their triumphs among the settlers, Little Crow only
grunted. Always he talked of Fort Ridgely instead of more
raids on settlers.

Big Eagle and Mankato tried to keep their young men from
joining the raids. They succeeded most of the time, and so did
Wabasha and Wacouta. Mankato was a daring and able
leader. He, like Little Crow, talked constantly of military
strategy and the importance of attacking Fort Ridgely instead
of raiding undefended civilian settlements.

Of all the Lower Sioux leaders, it seemed to the soldiers'
lodge, only Shakopee[18] and Red Middle Voice appreciated
raids on the settlements. Only they fully realized how quickly
the killings of a few women and children would rid the whole
valley of whites.[19] Why, the young men wondered, did Little
Crow want them to make war after the manner of white men?
Why should one code of Sioux warfare apply to the Chippewas
and a different one to the whites?

THE CAPTIVE SAVED

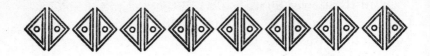

VII GOD IS THE REFUGE OF HIS SAINTS

At the Yellow Medicine Agency and in most of the upper part of the reservation all was serene during much of Monday, August 18.

Rumors of the Sunday murders at Acton began to circulate at Upper Agency[1] Monday noon. While not verified, they were tangible enough to impel Dr. Wakefield to send his wife and children below with George Gleason.

It was late afternoon before first whispers of the morning's killings at Redwood reached Yellow Medicine, and evening before the Upper Indians started to believe them. Then they called a council to consider their own course.[2]

Attending the council was a band of young Yanktonais, a fierce, envious clan, whose home was in Dakota Territory. The Yanktonais were not annuity Sioux, did not belong on the reservation, but were frequent visitors, not welcome to the agent. The band at the Monday evening council included some notorious agitators, present two weeks before at the warehouse raid. Now they formed the nucleus of a 'War Party,' advocating death for the whites and the looting of stores and warehouses.

Standing Buffalo and Red Iron, leading Sisseton and Wahpeton chiefs, lived too far away to be summoned to the hastily convened council. Their villages were represented, though, by warriors who had been in Yellow Medicine during the day and remained for the council, together with a sprinkling of their younger braves.

Present also were the Christian leaders of nearby Wahpeton villages, Simon Anawangmani, John Otherday, Akipa, the elderly and feeble Cloudman, and Paul Mazakutamane, brother of Cloudman and head speaker of the Wahpetons, better known as Little Paul. It was a heated and acrimonious council. The Christian leaders automatically constituted a 'Peace Party' and took a solid stand against attacks on the whites.

At first the Peace Party expressed disbelief in the Redwood reports. Later, when more details were brought by messengers who had to be believed, the Christians became violently indignant over the outrages reported.

Observers from Red Iron's and Standing Buffalo's villages at the start thought it impossible that the Lower Indians would begin war without first consulting the upper bands, or at least notifying them. After the reports had to be accepted, they voiced somber misgivings over the effects that acts of the lower bands would have on the Upper Indians.

To the Yanktonais and other advocates of war the abrupt action of the lower bands had been logical and necessary. If a Chippewa camp were to be raided, would the raiders give warning ahead of time? Of course not!

Now that the Lower Agency had been attacked, the upper bands would be punished when the soldiers came, whether they joined Little Crow or not. There seemed no very good reason to delay breaking into the stores of the traders. The provisions the stores and warehouses held really belonged to the Indians, and not to the dishonest, insolent whites.

The Wahpetons and Sissetons did not admire the whites any more than the Yanktonais did, said a Peace Party spokesman, but whether they liked the whites or not, they considered them necessary. Where else could they sell furs if the traders were driven out? Where else would they get ammunition? As long as the Chippewas traded for ammunition, the Sioux needed to do so, too, or they would surely die. If the whites were killed, the soldiers would come, take from the Dakotas everything they had, and drive them far away to a bad country.

Those who wanted war, suggested John Otherday,[3] could go down-river to where the whites were being killed.

Long before midnight it was evident the council could make no decision both factions would accept.

Red Iron's and Standing Buffalo's men left for their villages. The news they bore was far too momentous to wait until morning.

John Otherday, Simon, Little Paul, and other opponents of war knew immediate action was necessary to avert trouble comparable to the Lower Agency massacre.

The War Party made plans to attack the stores of the traders immediately.

Before midnight the council broke up, with no formal decision. Earlier Otherday, Little Paul, and Simon had left to make use of the time the war faction would spend looting the stores.

Warned by the whispers, and by friends slipping away from the council, over fifty frightened whites were huddled in the Upper Agency's main stone and brick warehouse. Otherday trotted from the council to the warehouse, told its occupants they would leave Yellow Medicine at the first sign of dawn, and warned against any departures from the stronghold before then.

Husband of a white woman and father of a half-breed child, John Otherday was a full-blood Wahpeton. He was forty-two years old, a comparatively recent convert to Christianity, and an advocate and practitioner of farming. Known to Upper and Lower bands alike as a tough-minded warrior, he was respected as a courageous fighter; none of his tribesmen dared jeer at his occupation or call him a 'Pataloon' or 'Cut-Hair.' In his youth Otherday had been a celebrated ruffian, renowned for having given Cut Nose his name by biting off his nose in a quarrel. Otherday's plan was to guide to safety the whites at the warehouse, and he used the time before dawn to send warnings to any who had not yet assembled.

Simon and Little Paul hurried to the Pajutazee and Hazelwood missions to warn Dr. Thomas Williamson, the Reverend Stephen Riggs, and their missionaries and teaching staffs.

Dr. Williamson and his wife refused to believe the Redwood reports and scoffed at the notion of flight.

Stephen and Mary Riggs were as hard to convince as the Williamsons when Little Paul first talked to them. But they had three young daughters; Little Paul emphasized the daughters as a particular hazard.

'Indian men would kill us to get possession of them,' said Stephen Riggs. 'Thus the case was stated by our neighbors!'[4]

At midnight Indian friends gathered at Hazelwood to pray. They sang, 'God is the Refuge of His Saints.'

To Stephen and Mary the Redwood news represented poignant personal tragedy. If true, the reports meant total collapse of the world they had spent a lifetime building. For years they had struggled to explain the sins and greed of fellow whites dealing with the Indians. For years they had proclaimed the principles of good citizenship and the Word of the white man's God. For a quarter of a century white Christians all over the land, responding to Riggs's appeals, had helped support his work among the Dakotas, at Lake Harriet, Lac qui Parle, Traverse des Sioux, and now at Hazelwood.

If the Redwood reports proved to be true, the failure of the missionaries was so total nothing could ever repair the damage. Skeptics and non-believers sometimes questioned the wisdom of efforts to Christianize the Sioux and predicted ultimate failure. The thought they may have been right was devastatingly bitter.

It was long after midnight before Stephen and Mary Riggs could bring themselves to spend the remainder of the night with their daughters on an island in the Minnesota River. Seventeen other teachers and trainees eagerly offered to accompany them.[5]

As soon as the Yellow Medicine council broke up, the war faction began its work of ridding the upper reservation of whites. There was a Myrick's store at Yellow Medicine, and as a matter of course the looting and shooting started here. In charge, living in quarters above the store, was Stewart Garvie. The raiders shot Garvie but did not kill him. Leaving a heavy trail of blood, he staggered to the stone warehouse.

Already in the warehouse, having fled before the council dissolved, were Duncan Kennedy and J. D. Boardman, clerks at Daily and Pratt's store, and the clerk from Louis Robert's trading house.

Peter Patoile, in charge of Francis Patoile's store, was shot but did not die.[6] Peter's uncle was the Yellow Medicine trader who had breakfasted that morning at the Joseph Reynolds' house and been killed later while escorting the Reynolds' hired girls and niece on their attempt to escape.

With Peter Patoile eliminated, all four Yellow Medicine stores were unattended and the war faction was free to pillage. When dawn came, plunderers were so absorbed that nobody noticed when John Otherday led sixty-two men, women, and children from the east end of the warehouse to the river crossing a mile away. In the party were Otherday's wife and child, Agent Galbraith's wife and three children, Sub-agent Nelson Givens, his wife, three children, and mother-in-law, Dr. Wakefield, the wounded Stewart Garvie, and most of the other white residents of the agency.

Otherday took his escapees north of the river to the Abercrombie 'military road,' and east to a branch of the trail leading to Cedar City. With the exception of Stewart Garvie the fugitives went from there to St. Paul. Garvie died at Cedar City, near Hutchinson.

One Yellow Medicine white who did not go with the Otherday party was Peter Patoile, too badly hurt to reach the warehouse. With blood spurting from his lungs at every gasp, Peter crawled into the bushes near his uncle's store. He hid there all day Tuesday, and during intervals of consciousness he watched the looting of the stores. After dark he crept to the ford across the Minnesota and crawled to the north side of the river.

For the next thirteen days, with only berries and roots to eat, much of the time uncertain what direction he went, plunging in and out of sloughs and soaked by the summer's heaviest rainfalls, Peter wandered over the prairie. Almost miraculously his wounds gradually stopped bleeding and began to mend.

Nearly two weeks after crawling away from Yellow Medicine, now able to stand erect, Patoile heard barking dogs in the distance. The sound might mean an Indian camp or a white settlement. Peter followed it to a cluster of cabins on the Upper Mississippi forty miles north of the present city of St. Cloud. In a direct line he was one hundred miles from Yellow Medicine; he had covered two hundred miles to reach the settlement.[7]

His saga nearly ended with his hanging. The settlers viewed him suspiciously and concluded he was an Indian. Peter had no means of identification, and his story could not be believed. But he did talk like a white man, and the settlers finally forwarded him to St. Paul, where the military would know what to do with him.

From his island near Hazelwood, still not wholly convinced the Indians were killing whites, the Reverend Stephen Riggs waded ashore Tuesday morning and walked to the Yellow Medicine agency. There he saw the sacking of the stores. The houses and other agency buildings were not burning. A friend explained the Indians intended to occupy them, and told of the dawn departure of Otherday and the whites. Riggs turned toward Hazelwood, at last convinced the mission needed to be evacuated.[8]

He stopped at Pajutazee to tell the Williamsons his painful decision. Dr. and Mrs. Williamson, starting to accept the Redwood massacre as fact, still maintained they were not personally in danger. They would stay, they said, at Pajutazee.

Before the Riggs's party left Hazelwood the group had grown to thirty-three. Instructors and trainees from both missions wanted to depart. Families of several sawmill employees waited to leave, together with most other whites still in the vicinity. Jonas Pettijohn and H. D. Cunningham, teachers, hurried down-river from Red Iron's village with wives and children.

One horse-drawn wagon and a few carts pulled by oxen were at hand to carry food and clothing. Most of the escapees would need to walk. The mission's cattle could follow the wagons. The mission's books and dishes were stacked in a hole and carefully covered. Except for a revolver worn by D. Wilson Moore of Fisslerville, New Jersey, the party was almost without defense.

Young Moore, a glass manufacturer, and his bride had gone to the Far West on a honeymoon trip three weeks before. In St. Paul the Moores attended a wedding at which Dr. Williamson officiated. When they told the clergyman they would like to see some Indians, he suggested Yellow Medicine. They were at Hazelwood when word of the massacre came, and gratefully accepted Stephen Riggs's invitation to leave with him.

There were two escape routes from Yellow Medicine. One would take the party ten miles directly north to the Fort Abercrombie trail. From there they could go east to Henderson or northeast to Cedar City, which would place them always at least five miles from the dangerous part of the reservation, and sometimes fifteen or twenty. The second route led southeast along the north bank of the river. Only the stream separated this route from the lower part of the reservation. Nearly opposite the mouth of the Redwood a branch of the trail veered northeast over the prairie to Hutchinson, but the main route continued along the river to Fort Ridgely, New Ulm, and eventually to St. Peter.

Although the second route was much the most hazardous, this was the way Riggs decided to go. Fort Ridgely, while dangerous to reach, offered the great attraction of being comparatively near. Besides, there was no trail to the Abercrombie road, and swampy land lay between. John Otherday had taken his party to the military road, but he knew where the marshes were and was skilled in steering a course by the sun and stars.

Tuesday night, refraining from building a fire which might attract Indians, the party camped near Hawk Creek, below the ford leading to Upper Agency.[9]

Wednesday afternoon four strangers armed with guns 'not of much account' joined the group. They wanted to go to New Ulm.

All afternoon a steady drizzle soaked the fugitives. Because oxen set a slow pace and nearly everyone was afoot, progress was sluggish. Food brought from Hazelwood would soon be gone. Everyone was cold and wet. Some of the children cried, and begged their mothers to take them home. Again it was considered inadvisable to build a fire, so nobody went to sleep warm and dry.

Really dangerous territory was reached Thursday. That night the refugees camped in a clump of trees almost directly opposite the mouth of Rice Creek and not far from Shakopee's village. By now everyone was hungry as well as wet and cold. This night the missionaries slaughtered a cow, built a fire, broiled meat, and baked bread.

Friday morning the party reached the fork where a northeast branch led away from the river. The right-hand fork, taken by the Hazelwood group, continued to skirt the reservation.

That noon the fugitives paused to eat and rest at the mouth of Birch Coulee. They were now only a few rods from Redwood Ferry, nearly opposite the Lower Agency, and within thirteen miles of Fort Ridgely. They met an Indian who urged them to 'hasten to the fort, as all the white people have been killed or have fled.'[10]

During the Birch Coulee pause an ox cart came clattering down the trail. It contained the Williamsons and three others. Their determination to stay at Pajutazee had evaporated on Wednesday when they learned that Amos Huggins had been killed the previous day at Lac qui Parle, thirty miles upstream from Yellow Medicine. Huggins, devoted teacher, beloved friend of missionaries and Christian Indians, had lived among Wahpetons all his life, but a young Wahpeton had killed him.

Counting the four men bound for New Ulm, the combined Riggs-Williamson party now numbered forty-two. Of this number, nearly thirty were women and children.

There was no telling what the situation would be at Fort Ridgely. Sharp cannonading sounded from the southeast during the latter part of the noonday pause. The fort must be under heavy attack. Thunder of artillery continued throughout the afternoon, growing louder and sharper as the fugitives neared their haven. Maybe the fort was held by whites and was being attacked by the Dakotas, or maybe it had fallen and the whites were trying to recover it.

Late in the afternoon a few flashes of light glowed briefly against blue banks of haze in the valley below. Was it light from the guns or were some of the fort's wooden buildings on fire? At sundown the cannonading stopped abruptly. Did darkness now conceal the besiegers, causing the artillerists to save their ammunition? Or had the fort capitulated? If so, who had been defending it, and to whom had it surrendered?

As the Yellow Medicine group advanced in the darkness its members stumbled, one after another, over a body. The body was clothed, so it could be guessed to be the corpse of a white man. Near the fort the wagons stopped and the men conferred in whispers.

Andrew Hunter, nephew of Dr. Williamson, volunteered to try entering the fort. If he did not return reasonably soon the refugees would know he had found the place held by Indians and had been captured or killed.

'He crawled into the garrison,' was the way Stephen Riggs described it. Every move he made, the volunteer felt sure, was watched by besiegers or defenders. The reason he was not shot at, he supposed, was that neither side wanted to reveal its position.

Andrew crawled back to report the fort held by whites but 'already crowded with women and children and scantily manned by soldiers.' The Hazelwood and Pajutazee refugees 'would be admitted,' but because space was limited all live-stock would need to be left outside the fortified area and assuredly would be stolen by the attackers.[11]

Another whispered conference was held. The fort was not the safe haven Riggs had anticipated, it appeared. The Reverend Stephen Riggs and Dr. Williamson 'decided not to go in, but to turn out and go around the fort and its beleaguering forces, if possible.'

Vehement objections were voiced by the four men bound for New Ulm. Aware that their own weapons were 'not of much account' and inadequate for the protection of themselves, to say nothing of thirty-eight women, children, and missionaries, they considered it needlessly foolhardy to continue. After a brief consultation of their own, they announced they would stay at the fort.

'But,' stated Stephen Riggs, 'we told them no one should leave us until we were past the danger. And to prevent any

desertion in this, our hour of trial, Mr. Moore cocked his revolver, prepared to shoot down any man who attempted to
leave.'

The threat, backed by the cocked revolver of the New
Jersey honeymooner, may not have been clerically correct,
but it worked. The fugitives turned left, seeking an old road
known to pass on the north side of the fort.

'The Lord guided us to the right place,' recalled the Hazelwood missionary, 'but while we were hunting in the willows
for the old unused road, there was a cry so much like a human
cry we were all quite startled. We thought it was the signal
of an attack by the Indians. Just then Dr. Williamson came to
me and said perhaps he had counseled wrongly, and that, if
we thought it best, he was quite willing to go back to the fort.
But I replied that we were now almost around it, and it would
be unwise to go back.' Later Riggs concluded the cry in the
willows 'probably was only the cry of a fox.'[12]

By dawn the escapees were well below the fort. The men
heading for New Ulm, nearing the end of their journey, were
released from further obligation to stay with the party. They
went ahead, and at some distance, still in view, entered a
wooded ravine. Shots reverberated from the trees. The former
trail mates had encountered an early-morning war party. All
four were dead.[13]

At the next fork in the trail Dr. Williamson kept his ox cart
on the main route, heading for St. Peter. He knew the hospitals
there would have need of a medical missionary.

Turning left, the main party reached the settlement of
Henderson a week after leaving Hazelwood. They were
greeted with cries of astonishment. By now the killing of the
entire party had been reported and accepted as inevitably
true.

'Surely, God led us and watched over us,' wrote Martha
Riggs, one of the daughters, to the Cincinnati *Christian
Herald*.

It would be difficult to prove anyone else watched over them; no Dakota claimed credit in this connection. But scouting and reconnoitering were highly developed accomplishments of the Indians. It is improbable that the noisy party, with children, livestock, and clattering ox carts, altogether escaped detection. Possibly it is significant that the four going to New Ulm were not molested while they were with the Hazelwood party, but were promptly killed after leaving its protection. Perhaps the record of the Hazelwood and Pajutazee evacuees for genuine friendship may have provided a special kind of watchfulness over gun-barrels, and kept Dakota fingers from pulling triggers. Certainly this possibility does not detract from the party's astounding audacity.

Nor is there reason to depreciate the group's courage because the Indians, who that day had subjected the fort to the heaviest attack of its history, had withdrawn to the south side of the river three hours before the missionaries reached the scene; neither the fugitives nor the fort's defenders could have been aware of the withdrawal.

In addition to the Yellow Medicine refugees thousands more jammed the trails of a wide area while the Hazelwood party rattled to Henderson. The exodus of some of the others was equally perilous. An impulse to flee seized thousands upon thousands of settlers throughout the frontier when they heard of the Redwood attack. The impulse produced action as more and grimmer details came out with the first escapees.

Residents of the Redwood, Sacred Heart, Creek and Beaver Creek areas who escaped death during the first few hours swarmed to Fort Ridgely for sanctuary.

Settlers from the country above New Ulm and the Cottonwood Valley hurried to New Ulm, children in arms and household possessions piled high on wagons. Some were overtaken and killed on the way. Rescue parties raced out from New Ulm and a score of would-be rescuers were slain.

Inhabitants of New Ulm fled to Mankato. Settlers from

the Henderson locality departed for Glencoe. Forest City and
Paynesville residents sought refuge in Hutchinson and St.
Cloud.

Residents of Mankato went to St. Peter. Those of St. Peter
left for Le Sueur. People from the lower valley formed melancholy processions clogging the trails to St. Paul, St. Anthony,
Minneapolis, and Hastings.

Minnesotans rushed across the Mississippi to Wisconsin.
Entire settlements were abandoned. Whole sections of the
state were deserted. Nearly forty thousand residents of an
area ten thousand square miles in extent were on the move and
most of the area was depopulated.[14]

There was panic, but panic grounded in reality. There was
terror, but terror induced by experience. There was fear
spurred by actuality. Ruthless and merciless attackers might
spring from behind familiar bushes at any moment with torch
and tomahawk poised. It was not a senseless fear and flight,
as hundreds had realized briefly after it was too late, and as
more were presently to learn. A new force, incredibly cruel,
wicked beyond anything ever known before, responsive to no
plea or logical persuasion, impossible to understand, was loose
upon the land. The only thing to do was to get out of its way.

Homesteads over which claimants had fought a few weeks
before suddenly were unimportant or undesirable. Cabins,
laboriously and carefully built, abruptly had become potential
death traps. Horses and wagons, means of flight, were possessions precious beyond price. Cattle, symbol of tomorrow's
prosperity, today might retard flight and were left without a
backward glance.

It was more important to escape the knife or hatchet than
to harvest oats or hay cherished since spring and now ready
for garnering.

Fertile countrysides, verdant in April, to be lived in forever,
had become hazardous wastelands unfit for habitation, to be
forsaken without a moment's delay.

VIII RIDGELY WAS IN NO SENSE A FORT

About the best that may be said for Fort Ridgely is that it was strategically located near the spot at which the Dakotas started their massacre.

'Ridgely was in no sense a fort,' wrote Judge Charles Flandrau. 'It was simply a collection of buildings, principally frame structures, facing in toward a parade ground. On one side was a long stone barrack and a stone commissary building, which was the only defensible part of it.'[1]

Ridgely was thirteen miles southeast of Redwood Agency, located on a hill across the river, about half a mile from the stream. Fort or no fort, it was the only buffer between six thousand Dakotas on the reservation and scores of thousands of settlers moving into land the Dakotas formerly possessed.

J. C. Dickinson, boarding-house keeper at the agency, reached the fort with his wagonload of women and children about ten o'clock the morning Redwood was attacked. At first nobody could quite believe his report of the slaughter from which he had fled. He appeared to be sober, however, and the girls, jabbering and wildly excited, insisted he was telling the absolute truth.

Almost immediately other fugitives began to arrive. Some were bleeding or had been blistered and seared by fire. Their stories matched.

Captain John Marsh, in command of the small garrison, listened carefully to the first arrivals and asked questions.

Then he quickly made up his mind. Within half an hour the captain, forty-six soldiers, and Patrick Quinn, elderly Indian interpreter, left for Redwood Agency.

Before leaving, Marsh sent a mounted messenger galloping over the prairie to find Lieutenant Timothy Sheehan and his men. They had been in the Yellow Medicine area during the previous month. Two days before, enroute to a new assignmen on the Upper Mississippi, they had paused at Fort Ridgely, and would still be within reach.

'The Indians are raising hell,' Marsh said in his message to Sheehan. He requested the lieutenant and his command to return to Ridgely at once.[2]

Lieutenant Thomas P. Gere, Marsh's second in command, was left in charge of Ridgely. Twenty-nine men, the post surgeon, the sutler, and the ordnance sergeant remained at the fort.

The customary thirteen-mile route to the ferry serving Redwood Agency led up-river on the north side of the stream. For them to reach the agency by a trail on the opposite side, the river would first need to be crossed. The stream was about ten rods wide. In a dry summer, with reasonable luck in his choice of a place to cross, a man might get over safely at a number of places between Ridgely and the agency.

The summer of 1862 was not dry. Heavy rains had fallen in the Upper Valley during the spring. The area had been blanketed by more snow than usual the previous winter. Consequently the river was high, even in mid-August, and the water had a resolute current. Only the Indians and a few old-timers knew where it was safe to go over.

Redwood Ferry was the proper place for anyone not an old-timer or an Indian to cross.

Captain John Marsh, acknowledging that neither he nor his forty-six men were old-timers or Indians, decided to use the ferry.

Captain Marsh was a young man of substantial leadership

capacity, great courage, and little experience fighting Indians. He had grown up at Fillmore, near the southeast corner of Minnesota. Prior to his assignment to Fort Ridgely, his military experience had consisted of ten months in a Wisconsin regiment which had seen action against the Confederates in Virginia. If Marsh had been less courageous or more suspicious, the day would have turned out differently.

Shortly after starting, Marsh's men began to meet terrified settlers fleeing toward the fort. Halfway to the agency they saw the first bodies of massacre victims. They were to see more than a dozen corpses before they reached the ferry. They saw burning houses in the ravines and on the river bottoms below the road.

Captain Marsh was impressed by the magnitude of it all, but was sure the destruction must be the work of a relatively small band of outlaws. Surely most of the Indians could not be involved. It was up to him to capture and subdue the renegades. The responsible chiefs of the Redwood villages most likely would help him.

The men encountered one or two highly excited and almost incoherent fugitives who talked wildly of having seen scores of Indians crossing to the north side above the ferry.[3] It was obviously true that some Indians had been north of the river. Otherwise, buildings on this side would not be burning and corpses would not be strewn along the road. Possibly a few remained, and maybe they continued to lurk somewhere in the vicinity. But the talk about scores of Indians crossing over undoubtedly must be wild exaggeration.

In reality, from the time the attacks started on the traders' stores, the soldiers' lodge leaders knew that all the troops Fort Ridgely could muster would reach the agency in three or four hours.

There had been little time to think about strategy, but almost certainly the Ridgely troops would approach along the north side of the river and cross on the ferry. This represented an opportunity to the lodge leaders. One hundred Indians promptly crossed the river a short distance above the ferry. At the moment Marsh was talking to the excited fugitives, the Dakotas were concealing themselves in the bottom-land shrubs and grass at the ferry's north end. There they quietly awaited the arrival of Marsh and his men.

To play safe, in case the soldiers crossed down-river and approached the agency along the south side, lookouts were posted on the hills and in the woods south of the river.

The only Indian visible from the north side would be Shon-ka-Sha, known to the soldiers as White Dog. A farmer Indian and one-time farming instructor at Redwood Agency, White Dog was considered quite civilized by the whites. He even had seemed philosophical when Agent Galbraith had given his job to Taopi, depriving White Dog of his regular government pay checks.

In the willows, hazel thickets, and tall grass at the crossing's south end were more than a hundred painted young warriors, invisible from north of the river. White Dog would divert the attention of the soldiers. His appearance would be reassuring. Altogether, he was an ideal lookout at the south end of the ferry.

For the Dakotas, the perfect situation would be if most of the soldiers boarded the ferry at one time. When the boat reached the middle of the stream, one hundred braves would arise from their hiding places on the north side. Another hundred would spring up at the south end. The surprised soldiers would know, for a brief moment, that the Sioux meant business. Then the troops would be helpless and amusing targets. Those who were not shot would be drowned.

It was not a particularly original ambush, and would surely have failed if Captain Marsh and Interpreter Quinn had thought it possible that most of the Lower Indians, instead of a handful of renegades, were on the war-path. As it was, they walked into the trap.

The trap did not spring exactly as planned, but it worked well enough.[4]

The troops reached the north end of the crossing at one-thirty in the afternoon. Interpreter Quinn recognized White Dog, waved a greeting, and shouted across the water. White Dog shouted back. Quinn reported to Marsh what he understood White Dog to say. White Dog seemed to be indicating all was well on the south side of the river. The Indians wanted to hold a council at the agency. Were the soldiers crossing over?[5]

The boat was on the north side, near the soldiers. There was no operator. The troops had passed Old Mauley's corpse but had not identified it. One of Marsh's men observed the ferry ropes were loose. Captain Marsh ordered his troops to the edge of the river. While the ropes were being tightened to the posts, the men lined up facing the water.

Now something went wrong. On the opposite side White Dog jumped back, firing his gun. This seemed to be a signal. Possibly it was premature.[6]

Scores of painted warriors leaped from the grass south of the river. A hundred others sprang whooping from the brush surrounding the ferry house at the rear of Marsh's men, or emerged from the ferry house itself.

All of the Indians had guns. All were yelling and shouting. They shot low enough to avoid any possibility of hitting Indians on the opposite bank. Most of the attackers were on higher ground than the edge of the river. Patrick Quinn and several more were killed by the first volley.

Captain Marsh ordered his troops to fall back from the water. There was no good place to go. Some headed for the ferry house, just now being vacated by some of the attackers. A brief, bloody, and one-sided battle followed. The only place not swarming with Indians was a thicket at the edge of the river. Captain Marsh and most of his survivors reached the thicket. Here the attackers needed to shoot at longer range,

and their fire was no longer as deadly. By four o'clock Marsh
and the remnant of his command had crawled to the far end
of the thicket, down-river from the ferry.

Crouching behind cover, dozens of warriors had got to a
point below the thicket. Marsh's way to the fort now was
blocked. The captain and his men were surrounded on three
sides by howling enemies, and on the fourth by the river.

Only the river, Marsh decided, offered a possible means of
escape. No Indians seemed to have followed along the south
bank. If Marsh and his survivors crossed the stream here, went
down its south side, and crossed again near the fort, they could
get back to Ridgely.

The captain was a strong swimmer but some of his men
were not. Maybe the river could be waded at this point, and
lower down; if the survivors got there before dark, perhaps
they would be fortunate enough to find one of the fords the
Indians and old-timers used.

Captain Marsh and some of his men waded into the stream,
weapons aloft. Some, including the non-swimmers, remained
on the north bank, keeping the Indians back and waiting for
the wading party to find a way across.

The water became too deep for wading. The captain and
some of the privates began to swim. They thought if they
found a comparatively narrow channel somewhere, the non-
swimmers could wade out as far as possible, and the swimmers
would then help them across to a point from which the others
could wade to the south bank.

'Cramp!' Marsh yelled suddenly.

His men could see he was in trouble. Three of the privates
hastily swam toward him. It was too late. By the time they
reached the swirl where they had seen him, he was no longer
there. They could not find him. They swam frantically back
and forth, sometimes under water. A drowning man was supposed to surface three times. Nobody saw John Marsh surface
even once. The current had carried his body downstream.[7]

Because there was nothing else to do, the survivors swam and waded back to the north bank. Sergeant John Bishop was now in charge. The command of forty-six men had dwindled to fifteen. Two of these were wounded, one so badly he needed to be carried.

When Marsh had started to cross the river, many of the Indians on the north bank gathered at the edge of the stream, laughing, jeering, and shouting. Most of those between the survivors and the fort crossed the stream lower down to intercept the fugitives as they fled along the south side toward the fort.

This was a break for the survivors. Hidden by an overhanging bank, they glided past the remaining Indians and stalked warily toward Ridgely. Those carrying the badly wounded man did not reach the fort until ten o'clock at night. Still later eight others, most of them wounded, straggled in. They had hidden until dark near the north end of the ferry.

Altogether, twenty-three survived. Twenty-five, including Captain Marsh and Interpreter Quinn, were dead.

One Indian, Towato of the Wahpekute band, had been killed at the battle of Redwood Ferry.

Monday had been a great day for the soldiers' lodge. The younger Indians had demonstrated that whites could be slaughtered safely and easily. Even the most hesitant had to agree that the battle at the ferry was a clear-cut victory.

The houses of the chiefs were filled with clothing, food, furniture, and other plunder from the warehouses, the traders' stores, and settlers' homes. In houses and in nearby tepees were scores of captive women and children who could be held as hostages or killed if it became desirable to get rid of them.

There was joyous whooping and triumphant dancing in Shakopee's village, the Rice Creek encampment, and in other villages near Lower Agency that night. Many knew of captive white girls who could be taken to vacant tepees. Everybody knew where there were cases of food to be eaten at will. Almost everyone knew where at least one bottle of whisky, taken earlier in the day from a settler's home or a trader's room, had been hidden away.

For Little Crow the day was long and not entirely satisfying. At the end of the pre-dawn council in his house, he flowed with the mob to Lower Agency. There he spent the forenoon 'on the ground directing operations.'[8] He grinned when he learned about Myrick and La Bathe, scowled when told of Prescott and Taylor, gave instructions, answered questions, and cautioned the young men to make captives of the women and children instead of killing them.

At noon he was informed that the first wagonloads of goods from the stores and warehouse had reached his village. He climbed the bluff to superintend unloading and to assign guards.

It was one-thirty in the afternoon before he started back to the agency. Peering toward the ferry, he saw a blue cloud of powder smoke hovering over the low ground at the far end of the crossing.

The soldiers' lodge, he was told, had ambushed the whites from the fort and killed all of them. The soldiers' lodge, he also learned, had made a camp just below the agency.

Near the agency Little Crow encountered Wabasha, mounted on a white horse. Wabasha wore his ceremonial costume. Eagle feathers adorned his head-dress. Eagle tails and wings hung down his back. Fringed buckskin draped his legs. Strings of beads and a belt of wampum were wound around his neck and waist.[9]

Little Crow asked whether Wabasha had led his own men in the attack. He received a curt answer, a denial the attack had been an act of war, a declaration he had not wanted any part of it, and reproaches for having yielded to the mob at the early morning council.

Wabasha guided his horse past Little Crow, staring coldly, and rode toward his own village. Little Crow went to the ruins of the agency, found little to do, and returned to his own house.

More wagonloads of plunder had been brought, and now captives began to arrive.

One of Wacouta's sons, a sixteen-year-old brave, came to Little Crow's house. He had been drinking and his face was flushed with excitement. His father, he explained, was very angry at him. He asked permission to stay at Little Crow's house for a while. Little Crow rebuked his caller for drinking the white man's devil water. Wacouta's son looked at the floor and changed the subject. He boasted gleefully of the hundreds of whites who had died at the agency, the neighboring settlements, and the ferry, while only one Dakota had been killed. When the other whites heard, he gloated, they would take warning and leave.

Little Crow glared at his visitor and remarked it would not be so easy to fool the whites now that they knew the Dakotas were at war. Today the soldiers had come with muskets. Next time they would bring wagon-guns.

The chief stalked outside. He would waste no more time talking to one so young and foolish.

Seated near a tepee was a sobbing young white girl, her face swollen and red. Little Crow ambled toward the captive. She watched him, holding her breath.[10] When he was a few feet away the chief jerked his tomahawk from his belt, swung it high above his head, and jumped toward the girl, whooping shrilly. The captive flattened herself against the ground, moaning. Little Crow brandished the weapon over her head a few times, laughed, thrust the ax back in his belt, and sauntered away, chuckling to himself.

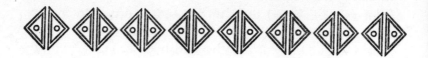

IX TWO HEAVY BOXES

When Captain Marsh and two-thirds of Fort Ridgely's troops marched to disaster Monday morning, only twenty-two soldiers were left in the garrison. Also remaining were Dr. Alfred Muller, Ordnance Sergeant John Jones, the post sutler Ben Randall, and seven men either sick or assigned to hospital duty. It was not much of a force of 'effectives' to be manning the only military establishment between the berserk Dakotas and the thousands of guileless settlers below. The next nearest military post was Fort Snelling, one hundred and sixty-five miles away by the shortest combination of cross-country trails.

In case of ordinary need, two days of hard riding were required for a mounted messenger to reach Snelling.

Lieutenant Thomas P. Gere was left in charge of Ridgely. Tom Gere was nineteen years old. This was the first time he had been in command of a fort.

Massacre fugitives, many of them cut, burned, or with bullet wounds, many carrying infants or clutching the hands of children, some gasping tales of horror, others mute with fright, poured into the fort all forenoon. In the first two hours more than sixty arrived.

By noon the little log hospital behind the stone barracks was full of seriously wounded. Post Surgeon Muller called for additional cots in his living quarters. The men assigned to hospital duty became frantically busy. Dr. Muller's wife took charge of the emergency ward in the living quarters and the doctor raced anxiously from quarters to hospital and back.

A majority of the refugees were women and children. When the first arrivals swarmed in, Lieutenant Gere had the uninjured escorted to a large frame building. The stone barracks, he realized, would be safer, but would be crowded when Captain Marsh came back with his men.

As the flood of fugitives swelled, some from the agency, others from the area between the fort and ferry or below the fort, Tom Gere began to think more than a handful of renegades must have been involved in the attack.

When a dozen half-breeds arrived, seeking sanctuary, the young officer felt a twinge of concern. The half-breeds he had met during his few weeks in Indian country seemed trustworthy, but the commander of a fort dared not take chances. Could any of those seeking admission be allies of the killers? Was there a risk in admitting everyone who came to the fort?

Tom Gere did not know, and none of his twenty-two men knew much more about the neighborhood residents than he did. Probably a little screening would do no harm. He assigned two men to the job, instructing them to admit at once the injured and those with children, but to route to a separate barracks any applicants who seemed even slightly questionable.

At noon a stage turned off the Henderson road, drove into the sally-port west of the parade ground, and came to a stop. A stranger climbed from the vehicle and started toward headquarters.[1] He asked for Captain Marsh.

A soldier who had moved toward the sally-port when the stage entered explained Marsh had gone to Redwood Agency. The newcomer frowned. The soldier explained the trouble at the agency was serious. A lot of whites had been killed there earlier in the day, he said, and people had been coming to the fort all morning in a steady stream. They came from the whole neighborhood as well as from the agency. Some of the fugitives, he added, were in bad shape.

The stranger scowled. Such loose talk would only make trouble for the Indian Office.

Almost as if it had been arranged, corroboration for the soldier's story came around a corner of the nearest building. A slim woman, ruddy-faced and bronzed, emerged on the parade ground. She was meagerly clad in a sack-like skirt and a torn, dirt-stained blouse. On one arm she carried a baby and over the other hung a rumpled shawl. She came hesitatingly, scanned the buildings uncertainly, and started for the structure behind the two men, inquiring for Dr. Muller. The soldier pointed toward the post surgeon's quarters.

From a distance there had been nothing unusual about the baby's appearance. The mother held him in a relaxed carrying position, her hand bracing the child's back. As she came closer it was apparent the baby was dead. His eyes were closed. A huge welt, red and shiny, covered half his head. The color of the skin on the other side was an unnatural blend of yellow and pallid blue. A streak of dry blood crossed part of the unbattered side and two dark red stripes were on a limp protruding leg. Murmuring gratitude, the mother continued toward the surgeon's quarters.

The stranger stared after her, his eyes round with horror. The soldier shrugged. He had been looking at horror all morning.[2]

No longer quite as brisk as he had been on entering the fort, the newcomer introduced himself and asked who was in charge of the post while Marsh was gone. The stranger's name was Wykoff, and he represented Superintendent Clark Thompson of the St. Paul Indian Office.

The soldier introduced himself, too. His name was Tom Gere, and he was in command during the captain's absence.

Wykoff stared. His face showed surprise and a little distrust. He stepped closer to Gere, and glanced around to be sure nobody else could hear. He and the four armed guards in the stage, he explained, had brought over $70,000 in gold, 'the long-expected annuity money.' [3]

Wykoff thought the stage should proceed with its cargo to Redwood Agency, but, explained Gere, it was 'of course, halted.' It would be safer, Gere felt, to await the captain's return with a report on conditions at the agency. There was room at the fort for the guards.

Lieutenant Gere led the way to a frame officers' quarters on the east side of the parade ground and opened a heavy oak door. The men, he explained, would keep the place clear of refugees, and would bring more bunks and blankets.

Wykoff went back to the stage. He and the guards lifted two heavy boxes from the rear of the vehicle and carried them across. The boxes contained $71,000 in gold, the annuity funds about which the Indians had been complaining.

Nobody at Fort Ridgely except Wykoff, Gere, and the four guards knew what the boxes contained. In St. Paul nobody knew but Indian Superintendent Clark Thompson, who had received the money from Washington Saturday morning, and the express company officials who had provided the guards and stage.

In the early afternoon during a brief lull between arrival of fugitives, Ben Randall, the post sutler, reported hearing gunfire from the direction of the agency. He and Tom Gere walked a few rods along the ferry road, west of the sally-port entrance. The pickets at the guard post had heard nothing, and now Ben could hear nothing. He wondered whether Johnny had rounded up the hell-raising Indians, and hoped maybe there was not much to the whole affair.

Refugees swarmed into the fortified area throughout the afternoon. Now they were starting to arrive from more distant places. Stragglers continued to come from the agency and the area between the fort and the ferry, dodging in from woods on the bluff or in the ravines, or from scrub growth on the river bottoms, where they had been hiding since morning. But whole wagonloads, drawn by plodding oxen, arrived from La Croix and Beaver Creeks, and even from as far away as Sacred Heart Creek, with tales of hot pursuits, narrow escapes, and of what had happened to others less fortunate.

To the men among the arrivals who had not been wounded and who looked as though they might know which end of a gun to point at an enemy, Lieutenant Gere issued muskets. The men were told they now were pickets.

Women who had not been wounded volunteered to help Dr. Muller at the little log hospital or Mrs. Muller at the emergency ward in the surgeon's quarters. Some prepared bandages, others helped dress wounds, and some learned to make cartridges, or busied themselves serving coffee and food.

It was a long, anxious afternoon. When refugees began to pour in from as far away as Sacred Heart Creek Lieutenant Gere knew positively that the outbreak was of major proportions and could not have been subdued by casual shooting at the agency. No word of any kind came back from Marsh during the afternoon. Fugitives reported encounters with hostile parties between the fort and the ferry. Maybe Johnny had crossed the river to Redwood Agency. Maybe he had followed the renegades over the prairie south of the river. Maybe he was chasing them over the north prairie country. Shakopee's young men on the Redwood and Red Middle Voice's band on Rice Creek were wilder and more inclined to act like hoodlums than the warriors from the bands of Wabasha, Little Crow, Big Eagle, and some of the other villages nearer the agency. Perhaps they were the ones who had caused the trouble, and possibly Johnny had been forced to go up the south side of the river to Redwood or Rice Creek.

After seven-thirty in the evening, when it was quite dark, word of the calamity at Redwood Ferry came to Lieutenant Gere. Two privates, sent ahead by Sergeant John Bishop, arrived to report that Bishop and twelve others, one wounded so badly he had to be carried, were on the way back. They brought the young officer 'the direful news of the slaughter of his comrades and death of his commander.' [4]

Gere arose from his headquarters table and walked to the door. The two privates followed to the door, went through, and closed it slowly behind them. Tom Gere walked back to the chair, put his arms on the table, lowered his head, and uttered a hoarse sob.

The door opened again. Ben Randall, his weathered face as white as it could get, stood in the doorway. Drowning, the sutler allowed gruffly, was not as bad as being burned or sliced up.

Later Lieutenant Gere could say proudly that he, 'without a moment's delay,' penned a dispatch calling for immediate reinforcements.[5] Then, because six hundred howling savages might swirl out of the night at any moment, he sent lookouts to the top of the barracks, stationed an extra sentry at the guard post, and put pickets on every side of the fort.

By eight o'clock Tom Gere had written a note to the Fort Snelling commander describing the day's events and asking for help. He requested the Snelling officer to relay word to Governor Ramsey.

Private William Sturgis, mounted on the 'best horse at Ridgely,' galloped away with the message, going by way of St. Peter, where he would notify the Renville Rangers, a company of Civil War recruits enroute to Snelling from Yellow Medicine. It was one hundred and sixty-five miles to Snelling, part of the way over dim cross-country trails. Private Sturgis rode all night and into the afternoon of the following day, making the trip in eighteen hours. His was one of the epic rides of frontier history. For it, the private was made a sergeant.

With one hundred and fifty more fugitives reaching the fort during the afternoon, the refugee population of the place was now more than two hundred. News of the fate of Marsh's command, 'in view of the possible result to the helpless and well-nigh unprotected mass of humanity, was sufficient to appall the stoutest heart.'[6]

After he knew Captain Marsh's company would not be coming back to occupy the stone barracks, Lieutenant Gere, more worried than ever about the hazards of fire in Indian warfare, ordered the women and children moved from their frame buildings to the barracks. Because scores of boisterous children were involved, the order was more readily issued than executed; but luck was on the young officer's side.

'One of the citizens on picket fired his gun and came running in crying "Indians!" Panic beyond description seized the refugees, who rushed frantically for the quarters. The alarm proved false, but good in effect.' [7]

The sentry's cry had swept the frame buildings clear of screaming and chattering children. They and their frantic mothers were now housed in the comparative safety of the stone barracks. No reward was given the sentry for his timely assistance. 'The picket was replaced,' reported Tom Gere.

Gere's twenty-two men, Marsh's survivors, the surgeon, sutler, ordnance sergeant, the citizen pickets, and two of the armed guards who had arrived in the stage were strung in thin lines around the fort's sides or perched on its roofs as lookouts. At any moment, out of any of the wooded ravines leading to every side of the fort, could come some or all of the six hundred Indians the young lieutenant estimated were now on the war-path.

Through the long darkness the sentries watched and listened. Any rustle in the bushes, snapping of a twig, or change in the night's coloration might mean that hundreds of painted savages, guns cocked, tomahawks raised, and mouths set to whoop were stealthily closing in on the fort.

In the post were six field pieces, half of them mobile, adaptable howitzers. A hundred yards northwest of the stone barracks were two magazines containing the most ample supply of munitions west of Snelling. About the same distance from headquarters stood a frame warehouse filled with blankets, cots, field tents, and other items potentially useful to warring Indians. Better protected, because in the stone commissary, were stocks of flour, sugar, and other food. Directly south of headquarters, across the New Ulm road, was a stable with two dozen horses; and in the nearby bottomlands grazed the fort's mules, oxen, and milk cows. And, in one of the frame buildings on the east side of the parade ground, was $71,000 in gold.

At any time during more than twenty-two hours Monday, the night of Monday, or the first half of Tuesday forenoon, a small fraction of six hundred warriors, with no difficulty at all and little danger to themselves, could have swarmed into the fort, slaughtered its handful of defenders, taken possession of its artillery, munitions, food, clothing, horses, and cattle, butchered two hundred women and children, and had $71,000 in gold to divide.

But the night slowly passed and no attack came. Tuesday's dawn revealed no massed warriors in any of the wooded ravines.

Of all the leaders at the villages near the agency, only Little Crow, Mankato, and Big Eagle recognized the possibilities and importance of an immediate attack on Ridgely and talked about it during the night. They did not know of the gold; if they had, perhaps their arguments for an attack on the fort might have been more persuasive.

Wabasha and Wacouta, still disapproving of the war, did not join in advocating capture of Ridgely.

The belief that New Ulm was entirely undefended swayed the young men of the soldiers' lodge. They were entranced by thoughts of the settlement's pretty young girls and the stores filled with goods. New Ulm, they were sure, was the most logical next objective; the fort could wait.

It was after eight Tuesday morning before lookouts on

Ridgely's buildings sighted Indians. Then, through a telescope atop the highest officers' quarters, they watched three hundred warriors, mounted, on foot, or in wagons, assemble on the prairies two miles west of the fort.

Choice of the prairie near the fort was not a matter of whim or an act of defiance. There were practical considerations. In the first place, the chiefs advocating an attack on Ridgely expected opposition from Shakopee and Red Middle Voice: the council site was more than twenty miles from their villages, and few members of their bands would be present. Secondly, the prairie site was on the same side of the river as Ridgely and within easy striking distance: from it the helpless fort should seem an attractive target.

Neither Shakopee nor Red Middle Voice attended the council. The former had been away from his village most of the night. With Cut Nose and a dozen other rowdies, mostly from his own or the Rice Creek band, he spent the night north of the river,[8] raiding settlements, setting fires, raping settlers' wives and daughters, plundering cabins, and intercepting wagons and ox carts filled with refugees trying frantically to get to the fort.

First to address the council was Little Crow. Dakota scouts, he observed, reported fifty soldiers approaching the fort from the northeast, about an hour away. Others reported more soldiers would come from St. Peter during the day, but they could not reach the fort until afternoon. At the moment there were no more than twenty-five soldiers at Ridgely. There were wagon-guns, but not enough men behind them to cause trouble. There were muskets, but how could twenty-five whites with muskets make trouble for twelve times as many Dakota warriors with guns just as good? There were dozens of blankets and tents in the fort, and more food than was found yesterday at all the agency stores. There were dozens of horses and cows, and hundreds of women and children. If the Dakotas acted at once they could have all the cannon and muskets, all the shot, powder, blankets, tents, flour, sugar, horses, cattle, and captives in the place. The twenty-five soldiers would fly like the wind when they saw the Dakotas come. Before the soldiers from the northeast could get near, the Dakotas would have the wagon-guns and the soldiers would be forced to stay away.[9]

Before Little Crow's plea was ended, Mazzawamnuna leaped to his feet. Mazzawamnuna was one of Shakopee's braves. He had remained overnight at the temporary soldiers' lodge near the agency, and was one of the few from Shakopee's village at the council.

Mazzawamnuna conceded the wisdom of every word Little Crow had spoken, but thought the words were even more true of New Ulm. In the stores at New Ulm were fifty blankets and bags of flour and sugar for every blanket or bag of supplies in the fort. There were a dozen women in New Ulm for each of those in the fort, and they were younger and prettier. At New Ulm there were not even twenty-five soldiers. If it were held, no soldiers could pass it to help the fort. The few who came from the northeast would be little more trouble than those now in the fort.

Sharp whoops of agreement applauded Mazzawamnuna's argument.

Next to face the council was Mankato. Great warrior though he was, he needed to wait for order before he could talk.

His braves would do what the council decided, said Mankato, but they had agreed not to torture women or kill babies. Mankato urged careful attention to the words of Little Crow, because he believed them to be wise. If the fort were taken before more soldiers came, the Dakotas would have cannon to keep other soldiers away and muskets to drive the whites from the land. Few muskets and no wagon-guns would be obtained at New Ulm. That was reason enough for taking the fort first.

Fourth to stand before the council was Rdainyanka, son-in-law of Wabasha. Unlike some of the other young men, he thought attacks on secluded cabins of settlers were pointless, but unlike his father-in-law, he did not favor peace.

At the ferry on the previous day, he recalled, the warriors had fought like brave Dakotas. They would fight the same way at New Ulm and Ridgely. Both places, he felt, could be taken without trouble if the braves acted at once. Probably it did not matter greatly which was taken first, since both were needed. If New Ulm was to be held first so no soldiers could reach the fort from the southeast, that might make it easier to hold the fort.

Again, as after Mazzawamnuna's talk, there were loud yells of approval.

A dozen other spokesmen, some advocating immediate attack on Ridgely, others arguing for a raid first on New Ulm, demanded to be heard. Two hours passed before the issue could be put to a vote.

Before then, Lieutenant Timothy Sheehan and his fifty men of Company C had swept into Ridgely from the northeast. Sheehan, vigorous, enthusiastic, and twenty-five years of age, had appropriate regard for the importance of speed and mobility in Indian warfare. His company had bivouacked near Glencoe on Monday night. When a messenger rode in with the note from Captain Marsh saying the Indians were raising hell, he at once ordered his men to break camp. Overnight, in nine and one-half hours, the command marched forty-two miles to Ridgely. They did not know what an acute emergency lay ahead of them until they had marched halfway to the fort; then they met a second messenger with Gere's report on the ambush at the ferry.

Two other units of reinforcements reached Ridgely later on Tuesday. From St. Peter came the Renville Rangers, the fifty Civil War volunteers Agent Galbraith had recruited and was escorting to Fort Snelling. Also from St. Peter came enough volunteer infantrymen to restore to a strength of fifty the company partly destroyed at the ferry.

As senior in length of service, Sheehan automatically became commander of Fort Ridgely on arrival. Probably no officer in all military history was more willing to relinquish command of a fort than Tom Gere, aged nineteen.

By Tuesday evening the garrison at Fort Ridgely had increased from twenty-two men to one hundred and eighty.[10] More than three hundred refugees were at the fort by now.[11]

Two-thirds of the Dakotas attending the council on the prairie west of Ridgely Tuesday morning voted to attack New Ulm that day. The remaining one hundred decided, after scouts reported reinforcements from the northeast had reached the fort, that they were not strong enough for an immediate attack, and they went home to their villages.

Little Crow's prestige had received another blow. It was not as serious as loss of the speakership election two weeks before, but damaging and painful.

Yesterday a howling mob had somehow induced the chief to sanction and lead a war he considered inadvisable and futile. Today a throng from which the chief hoodlums were absent voted decisively to ignore Little Crow's leadership and spurn his advice.

Red Middle Voice and Shakopee did not need to be present at the council on the prairie. Their soldiers' lodge won readily enough without them.

Dimly Little Crow had begun to perceive the nature of his internal problem and the enormity and finality of his error in yielding to the howls of the mob the previous morning.

X   SURELY HELP IS ON THE WAY

As a result of Tuesday's dissension among the Dakotas, three days elapsed before Little Crow and the soldiers' lodge collaborated in all-out attacks on either Fort Ridgely or New Ulm. At the end of three days the fort and the settlement were better prepared for attack than they had been Tuesday morning.

Meanwhile minor attempts were made to take both objectives, and independent raids continued far from the fort or town. There was a Tuesday raid on New Ulm, as the council had voted there should be, followed by a first attack on Ridgely the next day. Both efforts were half-hearted. To the Indians they proved that neither the settlement nor fort could be taken as easily as speakers at the council had asserted, and that unified action of Little Crow's faction and the soldiers' lodge would be needed.

New Ulm, much the largest settlement near the reservation, was on the river sixteen miles below the fort. It had been founded two years after the Dakotas moved to their new reservation. Started by members of the Chicago Land Verein who were soon joined by an organization of Cincinnati Germans called the Colonization Society of North America, in seven years New Ulm had attracted a population of nearly one thousand.[1]

Most of its residents were newly arrived immigrants. Few could speak English. To Dakotas most of them were 'Dutchmen' who could not converse in Sioux, but jabbered among themselves in a language nobody else knew.

South of the Minnesota valley at varying distances of fifteen to twenty-five miles was the flat, wide valley of the Cottonwood, a small stream from the western part of the state which joined the Minnesota two miles below New Ulm. Land in both valleys had been pre-empted by scores of Germans. It was in these valleys, at Milford and Leavenworth, that dozens of cabins were raided and scores of settlers slaughtered Monday afternoon. Farther west on the Cottonwood were other cabins not yet raided, whose occupants were probably ignorant of Monday's occurrences.

After the Tuesday council broke up, soldiers' lodge runners visited all Dakota villages near Redwood Agency to announce that New Ulm was to be attacked that afternoon.

More than two hundred warriors, some mounted and others afoot, assembled to go to New Ulm. Less than half got there, and it was three in the afternoon before they arrived.

Most of the others went south to the Cottonwood valley. There they found dozens of untouched cabins to raid; barns, haystacks, and fields of grain to set on fire; cattle and horses to round up; unwarned settlers to murder; and captives to take.

Those who got to New Ulm accomplished little. For two hours they carried on a shotgun battle. A white girl thirteen years of age was killed.[2] At four-thirty black rain clouds swept the town. Sheriff L. M. Boardman and sixteen armed men rode in from the direction of St. Peter. When it stopped raining the Dakotas were gone. They had taken no captives and had made off with no loot. The soldiers' lodge attack on New Ulm was considered a failure.

That evening a council, smaller and less formal than the morning's assemblage, met near Redwood Agency. No great defense had been encountered at New Ulm, but what sense did it make for one hundred young braves to try taking the town by themselves? Maybe the older chiefs could be of use in mustering more men. Maybe they could help keep the forces from scattering. It even seemed possible now that Little

Crow might have been right in wanting the Tuesday attack to be on Fort Ridgely.

Very well, Little Crow could have his attack on Wednesday, and the soldiers' lodge would do what it could to help him.

According to Little Crow's calculations, there were now about one hundred and seventy-five soldiers in Ridgely. If the three hundred Dakotas who had been at the Tuesday council, with a hundred more recruited from the lower villages, joined in a Wednesday attack, they still would outnumber the fort's defenders more than two to one. Little Crow was consulted respectfully, and agreed to serve as commander in chief for the occasion.

His Wednesday plan was simple. He would create a diversion across the road west of Ridgely. Meanwhile, two hundred Dakotas would assemble east of the fort and capture the place in a rush. If this effort failed, which seemed improbable, it would be followed by a massive attack from the ravine leading to the fort from the southwest. This could not possibly fail.

There would be more than two Dakota warriors for each white man in the fort. Ridgely and everything in it would belong to the Sioux before dark.

Shortly after noon the chief with three companions, all mounted, appeared just out of firing range west of the fort. Each waved something unidentifiable. They rode back and forth. From the top of the officers' quarters and the commissary building the performance was watched with puzzled interest.

Little Crow was 'apparently inviting conference.' Sergeant John F. Bishop, survivor of the ferry ambush, tried to induce 'the chief's nearer approach, but without success.'[3]

One of the Dakotas raised a hand in acknowledgement, but shook his head. The pony parade continued.

'Here they come!' a sentinel yelled suddenly from the roof of the stone barracks. 'The ravine is full of 'em!'

The northeast ravine was a wooded gully leading to one end of the barracks. Some of the painted warriors pouring out of it were within a few yards of the frame buildings forming the east side of the parade ground before they were seen.

Lieutenant Tom Gere and thirty-five men of Company B, all with muskets, were on the parade ground. They flew to the northeast corner and poured a heavy barrage into the ravine. The Indians who had neared the buildings quickly disappeared into the trees. All visible warriors in the gully fell back.

During the forenoon two men had started to carry munitions from the magazines northwest of the fortified area to the stone commissary building. They were still at it, and now needed to be covered.

One of the howitzers was wheeled to the northwest corner, and James McGrew, while covering the activities of the munitions carriers with it, also kept attackers from approaching the west or north sides of the area.[4]

Two of Ordnance Sergeant John Jones's other howitzers were wheeled into action. J. C. Whipple, 'an artillerist of experience during the Mexican War,' who had escaped from Redwood Agency and was now one of the fort's citizen soldiers, took charge of a twelve-pounder at the northeast corner and helped the infantry clear the ravine.

Sergeant Jones manned a third wagon-gun at the southwest corner.[5] It was from a ravine leading to this corner that Little Crow intended to launch his massive attack if the first rush failed. The ravine promptly filled with 'savages swarming to easy musket range,' compelling Jones 'to deliver his fire under the most trying circumstances,' but the ordnance sergeant held his corner.[6]

For five hours a heavy fire was poured on the fort, and from it. At sundown the Dakotas went home. They had captured none of the wagon-guns and had not killed or wounded the artillerists. They withdrew without having taken any captives, blankets, or tents. They had gained no munitions, food, or livestock. The $71,000 in gold, about which nobody knew remained in the fort.

The first attack on Ridgely had been no more successful than the first raid on New Ulm. Musket fire spoiled the rush from the northeast ravine; three wagon-guns badly frightened the attackers, and one of them, the howitzer at the southwest corner, broke up the massive attack Little Crow had thought could not fail.

That evening a heavy rain began to fall on Ridgely. It continued all day Thursday, giving both the defenders and attackers a chance to prepare for the greater attack that was sure to follow.[7]

At the fort Sheehan fretted about fire. A fire-arrow had landed on the roof of one of the officers' quarters on Wednesday; it might have burned the building if a sentinel had not seen it. The steady rain was, of course, soaking the shingles; if the next attack came soon the buildings would be less vulnerable.

Sheehan worried about great gaps between buildings on the south and east sides of the parade ground. This was something he could partly correct. Work details spent much of Thursday filling the gaps with barricades made of bagged oats, cordwood, rocks, and hastily felled trees.

The greatest worry of all, though, concerned the three hundred or more civilians now crowding the fort.[8] Over one hundred were adult women. They were of all ages and states of mind and health. Some had seen their homes destroyed. Some had been badly wounded. Others had seen husbands or children die agonizing deaths a few days before. Some, haunted day and night by horrors recently seen or experienced, were near insanity. The elderly ones did not expect to emerge from the fort alive, and did not much care. One was totally blind. Some were pregnant; they worried and wailed because their husbands were dead.

Nearly two hundred of the inmates were children. Tiring

quickly of the restrictions imposed by life in a fort, they raced noisily from one hazard to another. They locked themselves or each other in the root cellars and ice houses. They became lost in the ravines leading to the hill on which Ridgely stood, in woods on adjacent bluffs, or in bottomland marshes. They found live cartridges and bags of powder to use as toys. Only during the Wednesday attack did they behave as refugees should.

With three hundred extra residents at the fort and no supply wagons coming through, provisions in the commissary and warehouse dwindled. When they were gone there would be starvation. Everyone went on half-rations.

Sanitation was a distressing problem; the fort had no plumbing.

Medical and surgical supplies ran low or became non-existent.

Crowded quarters meant a constant threat of epidemics. If an epidemic broke out there would be little chance to control it; a hundred women and children might perish.

A hundred might burn to death if fire-arrows ignited the roofs of the buildings; probably all three hundred would be butchered if the Indians overwhelmed the fort's defenders.

Troops could not be spared from the hundred and eighty defenders to evacuate the refugees to the settlements. There was nothing to do but hope reinforcements would come before the Indians attacked in overwhelming force.

Again and again Tim Sheehan asked about the message Tom Gere had sent Monday night to Fort Snelling, requesting it be relayed to the governor. What could be the matter? Hadn't the governor received the message? Hadn't he believed it? Hadn't he known it was urgent?

In half the time that had elapsed since Monday, reinforcements could have come from Fort Snelling. Tim Sheehan and his fifty men had made it from Glencoe in one night. Surely help was on the way and would reach the fort at any moment.

Surely the governor cared about the lives of the three hundred women and children. Surely he did not expect one hundred and eighty men to hold the fort against the whole Sioux nation.

Little Crow, meanwhile, also worried about reinforcements. If Ridgely was to be captured the job would need to be done before more white soldiers arrived, and by more than the four hundred Indians he and the soldiers' lodge had been able to muster Wednesday.

Neither Shakopee nor Red Middle Voice had been present at the Wednesday attack. No more members of their bands had taken part than Little Crow could count on his fingers. They had wanted war with the whites, but now stayed away from the fighting.

Why was that? Maybe they were angry because the Tuesday council had been held far from their villages. But more likely it was because Shakopee, Red Middle Voice, and their young men had been raiding distant settlements. Whatever the reason, the time for tough talk had come. Shakopee had more warriors than any other chief of the lower bands. He and Red Middle Voice could, if they wanted to, send two hundred braves for a big attack on the fort. They might not listen to Little Crow, but maybe they would heed the soldiers' lodge.

In Little Crow's own and neighboring villages were dozens of young men who seemed to have some connection with the Rice Creek soldiers' lodge. Little Crow summoned them. Red Middle Voice and Shakopee, he complained, did not act as Dakotas should act. They wanted war, but when the fighting started they and their warriors were absent. He asked the young men to say Ridgely was to be captured Friday, and to tell Shakopee and his uncle to send for their braves if the braves were away on raids.

Three chiefs of the upper bands had expressed interest in Little Crow's war. They were Sleepy Eyes of the Wahpetons, and two Sisseton leaders, White Lodge and Lean Bear. To all three Little Crow sent word of the plans for Friday. Also, although he suspected it might be futile, he invited Standing Buffalo, Red Iron, and other Sisseton and Wahpeton leaders to bring warriors.

By now it had become somewhat difficult to find settlers who had not fled after the Monday attack, or settlements which had not established defenses. War parties from the bands of Red Middle Voice, Sleepy Eyes, and Shakopee solved the problem, however, by going farther and farther afield. Consequently, neither the Wednesday attack on Ridgely, nor Thursday's rain, produced any respite for settlers within many miles of the reservation.

Wednesday noon at West Lake, fifty miles north of Redwood Agency, a party of warriors visited the home of Andreas Broberg, a Norwegian immigrant.[9] After shaking hands with everyone in the Broberg household, the braves shot Andreas, his sons, aged fifteen and eleven, and his brother, John. Then they turned to Broberg's wife and his sixteen-year-old daughter, Ernestina. Mrs. Broberg's screams and struggles created enough diversion to permit Ernestina to escape. The mother was then beaten to death.[10]

Near the home of Andreas was the cabin of his brother, Daniel. The war party visited it next and murdered the brother and his wife. Of the two Broberg families, Ernestina was the only survivor.

Nearby lived a Swedish family named Lomberg. Three of the family's five sons were killed, and a fourth wounded. The fifth, John, escaped and carried his wounded brother to safety.

Altogether, twenty-two were murdered in the West Lake vicinity. The clothing of victims in this locality was set on fire in most cases and burned from the corpses.

Near the northwestern end of the reservation, forming part of Dakota Territory's boundary, was Big Stone Lake. At the south end of the lake, adjoining the present site of Ortonville, were stores of Myrick, Forbes, and other traders, located to serve Sissetons and Wahpetons. They were nearly one hundred miles from Redwood Agency.

These stores were looted Thursday. Four clerks, half-breed and French, were killed.[11]

In the bottoms south of the lake, George Loth and four men from New Ulm, hired by Agent Galbraith to harvest hay, were surprised Thursday morning by a band of Yanktonais. The Indians carried guns wrapped in blankets, whipped out the weapons, and shot Loth and three of his workmen. Only Anton Manderfeld[12] escaped. He raced eastward across the prairie. Hungry and exhausted, he looked for food in cabins on the way, found nothing in them but corpses, wandered in the Big Woods, was lost, and presently reached St. Peter.

Far to the east near Eagle Lake, also on Thursday, four Dakotas entered the cabin of Lars Endreson. They shook hands with the family, then shot Lars to death and wounded his youngest son. Guri, wife of Lars, hid in the cellar with her youngest daughter, aged three.

When the attackers left they took along as captives two older Endreson girls. On the way from the cabin they killed the oldest son as he ran up to learn what was happening.

After dark, Guri and her daughter crept from the cellar. Inside the house they found the wounded younger son alive, but 'crazy with fear and pain.'[13] Guri found a sled, put her surviving children in it, and pulled them five miles to the cabin of her son-in-law. Two men, critically wounded, were inside. Nearby, overlooked by the attackers, was a wagon and team.

After transferring her children to the wagon and loading the men on it, Guri drove thirty miles to Forest City, stopping occasionally to bathe and bandage the wounds of the injured.

XI EVERYONE'S FRIEND

Redwood Agency was forty-five miles northeast of a lake-strewn country which gives birth to most of southern Minnesota's principal rivers. North and east from the lakes flow the Cottonwood, Redwood, Yellow Medicine, Lac qui Parle, and Watonwan. South, into Iowa, flow the Rock and Des Moines rivers. Largest of the area's bodies of water is Lake Shetek, one of the headwaters of the Des Moines.[1]

Thirty-five miles west of Lake Shetek, near the edge of Dakota Territory, were the villages of White Lodge and Lean Bear, the Sisseton chiefs who chose to locate south of the reservation. Both chiefs heartily detested white settlers. When word of Little Crow's war reached them Monday night they sent a message to the Medewakanton chief expressing interest and offering co-operation; to them Little Crow sent expressions of appreciation. Wednesday night he sent messengers with invitations to participate in the Friday assault on Ridgely.

Near Lake Shetek eleven families, mostly with three or more children, had pre-empted land in the late 1850's. To White Lodge and Lean Bear, it seemed that the whites were building cabins uncomfortably near.

On the prairies east of the lake were, among others, the claims of the Everetts, Eastlicks, Duleys, Irelands, Wrights, Smiths, a recently arrived bachelor named Rhodes, and Charlie Hatch, unmarried younger brother of Mrs. Everett. Near the lake's outlet were the Koch and Hurd homesteads.

A thick stand of oaks, elms, and maples formed a woodland

around the lake. Just outside the woods was the shanty of Charlie Hatch. Early Wednesday Charlie saw smoke billowing from a neighboring claim. He leaped on his horse and galloped to offer help. A stack of hay was blazing. Outside the cabin lay the neighbor, dead.[2]

Charlie dismounted. Kneeling beside his neighbor's body, he paused to consider. It could be the work of Indians, although those in the vicinity seemed friendly. If it was Indians, probably they were still in the neighborhood. If they were, anyone clattering around on a horse would be in deadly peril. Just the same, everyone needed to be told. Straightening up on his knees, Charlie murmured a prayer. Then he arose and ran from shanty to shanty, dodging through trees and low places, to report what he had seen.

Two miles east of the lake's wooded border stood the cabin of John Wright, a two-story structure of heavy logs. It was larger and more sturdy than any other building in the neighborhood, and here the occupants of the sod shanties instinctively assembled. More than thirty men, women, and children streamed toward it, wondering whether there really was danger.

In a clearing near the Wright place gleamed two yellow and white tepees. From them swarmed Dakotas who were known to all the settlers.

Old Pawn, everyone's friend, was among them. He seemed worried, told what had happened at Lower Agency and Redwood Ferry, and said three hundred 'bad Indians' were roaming the Shetek neighborhood.[3]

Mrs. Koch, wet to her waist and sobbing hysterically, was one of the arrivals. The grave-faced neighbors gathered around her. She trembled and her teeth chattered so violently it was hard to understand what she tried to say.

What she said was that the Indians had taken Andrew's gun from the house and shot him with it. 'She said she could not stand it, for her husband lay in the barnyard with his face

in the mud.'⁴ She had waded the shallows to warn residents
at the far end of the lake, had seen Indians at the Hurd home,
and had run back.⁵

Pawn and some of his companions disappeared toward the
tepees. They returned naked, with stripes and swirls of colored
clay on their chests and faces.

William Duley, his round face reddened with anger, glared
at Pawn.

The bad Indians, Pawn explained, would not kill him and
his comrades if they dressed like warring Dakotas, 'but we will
fight for you when the time comes.'

Duley, Smith, Ireland, and Wright each had a gun. Eastlick
had two. He gave one to Rhodes, who had brought no weapon.
Pawn urged the whites to shoot off their guns

'That will scare the bad Indians. They will be afraid to
come near.'

'Do you think we are fools?' snapped a settler. 'We will
keep our guns loaded and cocked.'

Pawn said he would go to the Koch barnyard to get Andrew's body if one of the whites accompanied him. The offer
was declined.

A party of painted strangers on ponies appeared in a meadow south of the cabin. Pawn and two others from the tepees
rode out to consult with the strangers.

'The three hundred are nearly here,' said Pawn when he got
back. 'We had better go to the woods. When the bad Indians
come they will set the cabin on fire and kill everybody.'

It was two miles to the timber bordering the lake. Between
lay a great slough, three hundred acres in extent, marshy in
early summer but passable in August.⁶

Some of the women and many of the men argued against
leaving the cabin. Chinking had been knocked, here and there,
from the outside walls. It would be simple to see and shoot
invaders. Upstairs was a reassuring pile of clubs and axes.
Sacks of shot and a keg of powder were at hand. There would

be a good chance to stand off attacks and prevent attempts
to burn the cabin.

But Pawn was persuasive. The attackers, he argued, would
outnumber the cabin's defenders ten to one. Most of the defenders were women and children. In the woods there would
be individual hiding places. At least some would survive in
the timber. If they stayed in the cabin all would certainly be
hacked or burned to death.

Pawn's arguments finally won. There was one team and
wagon. The younger children and some of the women climbed
into it. Everyone else walked.

A mile from the cabin, at the edge of the slough, a dozen
mounted Indians, whooping and howling, bore down on the
wagon. Pawn was with them. Behind were as many more, also
on ponies. All waved guns and yelled shrilly.

Rhodes, clutching the gun he had received from Eastlick,
plunged toward the slough. Smith also ran from the wagon.

'My husband commanded Mr. Rhodes to come back and
bring his rifle, as he had the best one among them,' said Mrs.
Eastlick, 'but nothing would stop them.' [7]

Two or three Indian ponies darted ahead, too late to turn
Smith and Rhodes from their course. Sophia Smith whimpered
forlornly.

By now the first wave of Indians had stopped the wagon.
The second dozen swept nearer, yelping and shooting.

'Head for the grass,' hissed one of the men in a whisper.

With the first party of attackers already ahead of the wagon,
the second would complete the encirclement. Gunfire crackled
steadily as the second line approached. From one side of the
wagon it was only a long jump to the nearest patch of slough.
Everyone made it, but not before shots tore into the shoulders
of the two oldest Duley children. The youngest Ireland child
received a leg wound. A bullet nicked one of Lavina Eastlick's
heels.

Rhodes and Smith had run west toward the main part of the

slough, not to the patch near the wagon. At the edge of the grass the men with guns spun around and fired. Duley and Ireland aimed at a horseman threatening to ride between the fugitives and the grass. The attacker fell howling to the ground. He was Lean Bear, one of the Sisseton chiefs. Duley was credited with having killed him, but some felt the credit belonged to Ireland.[8]

Circling nearer, half the Indians rode along a ridge east of the whites. The attackers whooped triumphantly. Between the patch in which the fugitives were concealed and the main slough was a wide stretch almost barren of grass. With some of the attackers on top of the ridge and others patrolling the bare area leading to the main slough, the whites were snugly surrounded. There was no way they could escape. Careful planning could not have produced a more perfect trap.

On the ridge White Lodge, Pawn, and a dozen others dismounted, squatted behind wild plum trees with guns across their knees, and began a patient watching.

Grass and rushes seven feet high filled the trap in which the whites were hidden. There was no water at the base of the rushes; there were only parched hummocks, painful to sit or lie on for any length of time.

Movements in the grass and reeds told the watchers where to direct their shots. Gunfire poured steadily from the ridge and from warriors on ponies. Any movement in the slough drew a sharp barrage.

None of the crouching whites could see each other or their assailants. They could see only a curtain of brown rushes, swaying in the small breezes that sighed over the slough. Rustling of the parched reeds, barking of guns, and a whining hiss when balls cut close through the grass was all they could hear for a while.

Then somebody groaned. It was a loud, nearby sound.

'Who is shot?' quavered someone.

'I am,' said Charlie Hatch.

'Bad, Charlie?' asked his sister.

'I don't think so.'

'Where are you, Charlie?'

'Keep still!' said Charlie. 'Don't move!'

Sarah Ireland screamed, abruptly and piercingly. She had been hit in the bowels. Her mother began a strangled lamentation.

A shot grazed Lavina Eastlick's side. Another thumped into her head. She felt blood trickling past one ear.

'John,' she called softly, 'I have been shot.'

'I'm coming, Vinny.'

'Don't! Stay where you are.'

William Everett's voice cried out in surprise and agony.

'Billy! Billy! Tell me where you are,' begged Almira Everett.

'Mirie, we better both keep still. They will know where you are.'

Mirie felt a thud on her neck and then a sharp pain. Blood poured down, soaking her dress.

'I think we both have to die, Billy. Hadn't I better pray?'

'Yes,' said Everett.

Mirie slumped on the sharp hummocks and prayed. When she opened her eyes she saw only tall spikes of grass quivering against a cloudy sky. Dusty, parched smells filled the air. The dust was thick near the hummocks and made her thirsty. It was a blessing, at least, that clouds covered the sky, to keep the heat down.

Someone groaned sharply two times and then was silent.

'John! John!' cried Lavina Eastlick.

There was no answer. Slamming of guns and snarling of balls through the grass were the only sounds. Lavina's heel and head wounds hurt terribly. Her head ached with a violence she had never known before.

'John is dead,' said Mrs. Koch flatly.

'I am coming,' moaned Lavina.

'It will do no good,' Mrs. Koch said. 'I am sure he is dead.'

Four of the five Eastlick children were near their mother. Merton, the oldest, was eleven. Freddy, Frank, and Johnny were the others who were near. Johnny, the baby, was fifteen months old. Mrs. Eastlick clung tightly to him. She did not know what had become of Giles. She called his name but Giles did not answer.

'Is daddy dead?' the other boys kept asking.

'You must keep still!' cried Mrs. Eastlick. 'If you don't, the Indians will know where you are.'

It was becoming oppressively warm in the tall grass. Even the small breeze had died down. Now only when a ball slashed through the reeds was there a rustling. Lower clouds moved across the sky. Thunder growled in the west. The guns did not seem to bark quite so often. Maybe the attackers were running out of ammunition.

Sophia Smith shrieked loudly and suddenly. A shot had struck her hip.

'Henry! Henry!' she pleaded in agony. But Henry did not hear. He and Rhodes were in the main slough.

Sophia screamed again and again. Each shriek was answered by a burst of strident laughter from the ridge. Guttural sounds of conversation drifted down.

'Come on out,' yelled Pawn. 'Nobody will hurt the women and children.'

There was no response from the slough.

'Come on!' Pawn called again.

'Can you come here, Pawn?' asked Everett.

'No. You must come out.'

'I can't. I am almost dead.'

'You are a liar,' retorted Pawn.

Two more shots sounded from the ridge.

'I'm just about done for,' Everett whispered hoarsely. 'Somebody else talk to him. Tell him I'm dead.'

Almira Everett got to her feet, waving one arm above her head, and stood wobblingly on a low mound.

'Pawn,' she called, 'that last shot killed Billy.'

'Come out. I want you and Julia Wright for my wives.'

'Guess you better, Mirie,' whispered Everett.

'Only if Lavina will go along.' Almira swayed on the mound, almost unable to stand. Blood continued to stream from her neck wound.

'He asked for Julia,' said Lavina. 'I don't think Julia has been shot, but I have.'

Julia Wright was silent for a long moment.

'No,' she finally said, 'I have not been wounded. We would all be better off if we had stayed in the cabin.'

'Don't talk about that, now.'

'Stop talking!' shouted Pawn. 'Come out! Bring the guns.'

Almira Everett and Julia Wright, followed by their children, walked and crawled to the base of the ridge.

'Make them come up here,' ordered White Lodge.

'Up here!' barked Pawn. 'Don't be so slow.'

Almira's dress was a mat of caked blood. She could no longer stand, and was unable to climb the ridge. Her children and Julia Wright tugged and pushed. Near the top of the ridge she died.

When the children reached the crest of the ridge Pawn raised one of them to his bare shoulder. 'See,' he called to anyone who might be able to observe him from the patch, 'we will not kill women and children. Hurry out, or we will set the grass on fire.'

'They could do it, too,' muttered Thomas Ireland. 'Wish it would rain.'

'You girls better go,' said William Duley. 'Take the young ones. Maybe they will be spared.'

'Maybe,' growled Ireland.

Lavina Eastlick, Sophia Smith, Laura Duley, and Sophia Ireland, with most of their children, lurched to their feet. Lavina, carrying Johnny, limped in the direction from which she had last heard her husband's voice. He lay on his left side.

She felt his face and knew he was dead. She and Johnny knelt beside the body. Lavina kissed her husband's face.[9] Merton had followed and now tried to help his mother toward the ridge.

Huddled at the crest were those who had emerged. Near them, leaning on guns, were the Indians. Two squaws were with them. Eight or nine ponies, tied to nearby plum trees, stamped restlessly to rid their legs of flies.

Lavina turned at the foot of the ridge, looking for her other children. She saw Freddy, the four-year-old, come from the grass. One of the squaws saw him, too, and jumped down the ridge in long strides. Lavina felt a momentary surge of hope; then the squaw picked up a gnarled piece of wood and swung it at the boy's head. Freddy's face was streaming blood when he staggered, screaming and unknowing, past his mother.

Giles was not in sight, but Lavina saw Frank. He was on his knees at the edge of the patch and another squaw was clubbing him. Blood spurted from his mouth. He called 'Mother! Mother!' Lavina started toward him. A warrior blocked her way, swinging a gun at Johnny.

'Up there!' he snarled, pointing at the ridge.

With Merton's help and with Johnny still in her arms, Lavina staggered to the top of the rise.

Now a black line of clouds had swept across the sky, and the thunder cracked nearer. A sheet of rain pounded across the slough.

Mrs. Koch and several others had already reached the top of the ridge. On the crest White Lodge grabbed Mrs. Koch's hands and pulled her toward a path leading eastward. Two of his companions tugged at the arms of the two oldest Ireland girls, Rosa and Ellen. Another jerked at Julia Wright's hands.

Sophia Smith and Sophia Ireland began to crawl up the ridge on their hands and knees. Mrs. Ireland had tried to carry the wounded Sarah and was covered with blood. Two Indians at the top watched for a moment. Then they laughed harshly, pointed their guns, and killed the two mothers.

Pawn and another warrior, huge and black, eyed Lavina Eastlick and Laura Duley as they lurched to the crest. Johnny was still in his mother's arms.

'Hurry along!' commanded Pawn, prodding Lavina sharply.

A few steps ahead a young Indian pointed his gun at ten-year-old Bill Duley and shot him dead. Laura Duley screamed hysterically.

'You said you would not kill women and children,' shrilled Lavina.

Pawn peered at Lavina contemptuously. He backed away, loaded his gun, and leveled the weapon at her. Lavina jumped and turned. The ball stung into her back, tore out above the hip, and pierced her right arm. She fell to the ground. Pawn stalked away. Merton jumped to his mother's side. She had not lost consciousness.

'Carry Johnny, Merton. I think my back is broken.'

Merton picked up the baby and walked away, stopping at every step for an anxious backward look until the pathway turned and low trees cut him from view.

Julia Wright reappeared, shoved by her captor.

'There are five guns, or maybe more,' rasped her guard. 'Get them.' His push sent Julia plunging toward the slough. After a long absence she returned with one defective weapon. Her captor snorted indignantly and hurled the gun to the ground. It landed on the path near Lavina.

Pelted by the downpour, the ponies tethered to the plum trees snuffled and jumped restlessly. Lavina heard them and was beset by a fear they might step on her if she remained on the trail. She tried moving, found she could twist her body, and rolled into the grass at the side of the path.

A young Indian saw her move. He bounded toward her, picked up the useless gun, clubbed her head and shoulders, and then returned to the ponies.

Hours later, when consciousness returned to Lavina, it was very dark. The only sound on the ridge was the steady pouring of rain. Lavina could not stand or walk but discovered she could crawl. Blood continued to trickle from her wounds and she had little strength.

Inch by inch she dragged herself to the place where the women and children had climbed from the slough. She crept to the bodies of Sophia Smith, Sophia Ireland, five-year-old Willie Everett, Belle Duley, and her own boy, Frank. She also found her son, Freddy, Charlie Everett, and Julianne Ireland with her head against her dead mother's breast.

By dawn Lavina had crawled to the far side of a low rise. Here she slumped, unable to move, agonized by the fear that sparks of life remained in some of the children.

She thought the Indians had come back when the sun broke through a low crust of clouds in the east. During most of the day she thought she heard tortured children scream and sob. Late in the afternoon she heard three shots; then the sobbing and screaming stopped.

Because she could only crawl and lost consciousness from time to time, it took Lavina three days to reach the road, a rough trail leading seventy miles northeast to New Ulm. It came the same distance from the southwest, from Sioux Falls, in Dakota Territory.

August Garzene, a mail carrier driving a one-horse sulky toward New Ulm, saw her near the trail. Garzene, having come from Sioux Falls, had not heard of the agency or Shetek attacks, but knew he needed to get Lavina to a doctor.

Later in the day the sulky overtook Thomas Ireland, wounded eight times but able to creep slowly out of the slough. On the following day the party picked up Alomina Hurd and her sons, one year and three years of age.[10] The attackers had killed Alomina's husband, Phineas, before he reached home, but Alomina and her boys had escaped.

Fifty miles from Shetek the refugees sighted a small figure

on the road ahead, carrying what seemed to be a ragged bundle. As they drew nearer Lavina saw it was her son, Merton, still carrying his baby brother.[11] More than two weeks after the attack Lavina and her sons reached Mankato and Lavina's wounds at last could be dressed.

Nobody knows, or can know, exactly how many died at Lake Shetek. Fourteen months after the killings a burial party removed a dozen bodies from the slough. Forty-two years later fourteen were reburied in a common grave on a knoll near the lake. Other bodies were buried in unmarked graves on ridges east of the slough. Plowing has since erased all trace of the unmarked graves.[12] Victims not trapped in the slough were buried separately from the fourteen on the knoll; not all of those killed in the slough are in the common grave.

Other men in addition to Thomas Ireland got out of the patch alive. William Everett and Charlie Hatch, both severely wounded, reached New Ulm. William Duley waited at Mankato, hoping Laura and the surviving children might be released from captivity.[13]

A higher proportion of men than of women and children in the slough lived. This was not what the attackers had planned, but the heavy rain had made it impossible to set the grass on fire.

Rhodes and Smith, the two who ran when the Dakotas neared the wagon, escaped alive. Smith returned to the Shetek vicinity after the Civil War, married and was divorced from Lavina Eastlick, and moved to Washington Territory. Rhodes did not return to the lake. With Smith he enlisted for Civil War service. His former neighbors said he deserted from the Union cause and fled to Canada.[14]

Three women and five children, taken captive by White Lodge, were released three hundred miles away in Dakota Territory as the year drew to a close. Laura Duley and her surviving children were among them.

XII .THAT GUN WAS TERRIBLE

Fort Ridgely contained no well or cistern. Its water source was a spring-fed reservoir in a ravine a quarter of a mile southeast of the parade ground.[1] Ordinarily, with only the garrison present, Sutler Ben Randall kept the barracks' tanks abundantly full by making an occasional trip to the reservoir. But three hundred refugees could use an astonishing quantity of water in a short time.

Early Friday Lieutenants Sheehan and Gere were horrified to discover that the tanks were almost empty. Sutler Randall, with an armed wagon party, left for the ravine at once.

When they got there, they found no springs or reservoir. They found jumbled clay where the catch basin had been, puddles of mud instead of springs, and a slow trickle of dirty water.

'Quick! Fetch shovels and spades!'

Wednesday's attackers had kicked the reservoir walls apart, and filled the springs with earth and rocks. Cattle and mules from the nearby stables, trampling in search of water, had completed the demolition.

When the spades and shovels arrived the wagon party dug out the springs, rebuilt the catch basin, and returned with a supply large enough to last four or five days.

Replenishment of the water tanks was the chief occurrence at the fort Friday morning; much larger events took place across the river below the wrecked agency. On the river bottoms warriors from far and near assembled for the 'grand affair,' the final attack on Ridgely.[2]

Little Crow, Mankato, and Big Eagle were present in person. Each brought a column of eager braves from his own band. Many dozens of young men from the villages of Wabasha, Wacouta, Traveling Hail, and other peace-inclined chiefs arrived to take part, free to do so since Friday's events were to be strictly military. Some of them were led by head-soldiers of their own choosing; others were led by leaders designated by their chiefs. Shakopee and Red Middle Voice failed to appear personally, but scores of their young men came, chanting songs of war. Altogether, five hundred warriors of the lower bands gathered for the attack.

From the upper bands three hundred Sisseton and Wahpeton young men, defying protests of Standing Buffalo, Red Iron, and the Christian chiefs, arrived to offer their services. Missing were the two Sisseton chiefs with villages south of the reservation; Lean Bear had been killed at Shetek and White Lodge had herded his captives far south and west of the fort.

By mid-forenoon eight hundred braves had assembled. The meadows south of the river were 'alive with Indians, all in high spirits and confident of taking Fort Ridgely. They were either over-dressed or not dressed at all. Their horses were covered with ribbons, feathers, or bells, jingling and tinkling as the Indians rode along singing their war songs.' [3]

The leaders shared the confidence and high spirits of the warriors. No reinforcements had arrived at the fort. Scouts had seen none coming from the north or east. There continued to be fewer than two hundred troops holding the place. This time there would be twice as many attackers as on Wednesday. They could outnumber the defenders four to one.[4]

Little Crow regretted the absence of Lean Bear and White Lodge; it was a shame they would miss the spectacle's start, but maybe they would arrive in time for the pay-off. The non-appearance of Shakopee, Red Middle Voice, Red Iron, Standing Buffalo, and others was deplorable, but it was good to see so many of their young men ride in. Actually, eight hundred Dakotas would be able to take the fort without a great deal of guidance; Little Crow, Mankato, and Big Eagle easily could provide all the leadership needed, of this Little Crow felt sure.

Mankato would lead the assault at the southwest corner. Little Crow would direct the charge from the northeast ravine. Big Eagle would supervise the south and east sides in general, and jump in anywhere the attack might falter.

The fort's artillery seemed the only possible source of trouble. It was necessary to take into account that some of the men in the Wednesday attack had been a little afraid of the howitzers. For this reason the chiefs devoted much of their pre-battle exhortation to the subject.

True, the whites had wagon-guns, but what could two hundred whites do against four or five times as many brave Dakotas? For every wagon-gun there would be at least two hundred Dakotas. The few men behind the guns could easily be killed, and then the wagon-guns would belong to the Dakotas. After that, no white soldier would dare to come up the valley.

Wagon-guns could shoot in only one direction, and were slow to turn. With hundreds of Dakotas jumping on the gunners from all sides, there was nothing to fear. The men at the guns would all be dead before even one of them could shoot. Each warrior who killed a gunner would be awarded an eagle's tail feather to show his bravery, promised Little Crow.

Victory seemed so certain that the chiefs ordered a train of empty wagons to a clearing south of the river opposite the fort. There the wagons would wait for the loads of munitions, food, blankets, and other plunder the attack was sure to yield.[5]

Along the river bottoms, out of the fort's sight, rode the multitude of attackers, dismounting within a mile of their objective. Respectfully behind them followed a horde of squaws with extra ponies and dogs. The squaws could guard the horses from which the warriors dismounted. All would be needed to carry or drive back the loot, captives, and livestock the braves would obtain.

Most of the Dakotas had muskets. Some carried tomahawks, bows, or knives in addition. As they neared the fort the warriors inserted clumps of grass, clusters of golden rod, or branches of leaves in their headbands. The purpose was disguise, but the effect was partly ornamental; the mass converging on the fort had a festive, jaunty air, but the weapons they all bore showed their purpose was grimly serious.

Before one o'clock hundreds of braves packed the wooded ravines leading to the fort. Some wore gaudy costumes; some were naked except for breech cloths; and nearly all were smeared with red, blue, yellow, or black clay, sometimes with stripes of white between.

As before, the plan of attack called for a rushing charge. This time, since enough Dakotas were present to do it, all sides of the fort would be rushed at once.

If the charge was not an immediate success, the attackers would pour a heavy and continuous fire into the place from all directions. While this was going on Mankato would launch an all-out assault from the southwest corner and finish off the exhausted garrison. The continued firing would help cover Mankato's preparations, and compel the whites to use up such small-arms ammunition as they had left. Since no reinforcements or supply trains had reached them, they must be running low. With luck, there would not be many muskets in operation by the time of Mankato's assault.

No diversion like the mysterious parade preceding the Wednesday attack was staged this time. It would not work, and did not seem necessary. Consequently, the sentries knew when the first Dakota entered the nearest ravine, and presently everyone in all the buildings expected a simultaneous charge from all sides of the place.

Behind every door and window facing the woods, and behind the barricades between the buildings, the men of Companies B and C and the Renville Rangers, all with muskets and a little ammunition, quietly took their places.

Field pieces in addition to the three howitzers used during the previous attack already had been wheeled to the parade ground. As before, veteran Artillerist Whipple manned a howitzer in the northeast corner. Sergeant James McGrew again was at the northwest gun, and Ordnance Sergeant John Jones, this time shielded by barricades, was in the southwest corner. The major addition was a huge twenty-four-pounder, tentatively placed on the west side near the sally-port entrance. There were also two twelve-pounders, to be used if necessary, and to be manned by any survivor who felt qualified to handle a wagon-gun.

By one o'clock at least half the eight hundred attackers, many behind trees or bushes, were within a few yards of all sides of the fort. Not a shot had been fired. Not a fire-arrow had flown toward any buildings. Every gun was loaded and cocked. Every bow was strung. In each ravine fire-arrows smoldered in readiness. Now Little Crow gave the signal and Big Eagle relayed it to Mankato.

Blood-freezing whoops sounded all around, dreadfully near at hand. Bullets filled the air like hail. Muskets barked and slammed on every side. Ordinary arrows and fire-arrows whizzed in a steady stream. Their whistling was punctuated by shrill cries of triumph whenever one sailed extra high or far. A dense cloud of powder-smoke drifted into the parade ground from the surrounding woods and out of the buildings, blue, pungent, and irritating to the eyes.

A dozen fire-arrows landed on every roof, but the shingles were wet from Thursday's rain; the flames sputtered and died. No defender needed to leave his post to help fight fire.

Charge after charge started out of each ravine, but each time a rush began muskets barked from every outward-facing window and door of the nearer buildings and from the barricades. No rush broke through a barricade and no attacker gained the shelter of any building. The musket fire of the defenders, as heavy and well-aimed as the fire of the attackers, forced each thrust back to the cover of the trees. From the ravines came the excited, vehement voices of the chiefs, wheedling, berating, angry.[6]

Presently the attackers could only continue pouring bullets and fire-arrows into the parade ground and on the buildings. For a time the answering fire from the garrison became less intense; the small-arms ammunition was almost gone. Already Tim Sheehan had barked a sharp order. Already a crew of non-combatants, both men and women, had removed balls from some of the artillery's spherical case shot, collected and recast balls fired into the parade ground, and started to improvise musket ammunition.

Thus far the wagon-guns had not spoken. No Dakota had come within jumping distance of a gun crew. White muskets had forced back all attackers who had tried to shoot at the gunners. Now the time had come for Mankato's final drive.

Southwest of the fort were hayricks, the granary, vast woodpiles, the sutler's house and store, and the warehouse. Directly south were the stables. Most distant, beyond effective firing range, was the hay. Most of the stacks had remained dry through the Thursday rain. A huge tower of flame roared abruptly into the sky when one of Mankato's warriors dropped a torch at the base of the middle rick. The nearer woodpiles began to blaze a moment later.

Swirling clouds of dense yellow smoke covered some of Mankato's men as they darted inside the stables and sutler's store. Here, they were only three hundred feet from the post headquarters and one officers' quarters building, and could riddle the wooden structures with musketry fire.

One charge after another, each protected by the guns in the stables and store, and each nearer the fort than the previous one, swept up the southwest ravine. 'The fire in front of Jones' gun became so hot and accurate,' said Lieutenant Gere, 'as to splinter every lineal foot of timber along the top of his barricades.'

Seargeant John Jones provided his own relief. He had used his howitzer to place shells far down the ravine to break up the charges originating there; now he lowered the gun and dropped shells on the stables and store.[7] This set the buildings on fire, dislodged the snipers, and forced the ravine column to fall back.

Heavier than before came an attack from the northeast ravine. It was an effort to divert defenders from the southwest corner, but it failed; Whipple's howitzer and Gere's musketeers repulsed the new threat without calling for aid.

From the northwest corner McGrew watched masses of attackers swing wide around him to join the forces in the southwest corner. They detoured out of range, but he ran his howitzer out and delivered two or three volleys of canister after them, just to show the northwest corner had protection.

Then McGrew hopped to the twenty-four-pounder on the parade ground, helped wheel it next to Jones's howitzer, and waited. Jones double-charged his piece with canister and also reserved fire for a moment.

When the reinforcements reached a point between the main column Mankato was forming and the party of squaws and ponies farther out, both gunners fired.

The canister from Jones's howitzer tore into the main body of warriors. The shell from the twenty-four-pounder landed between the reinforcements and the main party, preventing their convergence.

According to Tom Gere, the 'ponderous reverberations' of
the big gun 'echoed up the valley as though twenty guns had
opened, and the frightful explosion struck terror to the
savages.'

Nobody tried to reorganize the assault column in the
ravine; nobody could have done so. The attackers fled across
the river in panic.

After six hours of what Tim Sheehan described as 'one of
the most determined attacks ever made by Indians on a
military post,'[8] the fiery battle, sometimes lit by the flames of
burning buildings, sometimes almost smothered by heavy
clouds of yellow smoke, had ended.

Little Crow was not present for Mankato's attempted final
charge, did not see the retreat, and heard the twenty-four-
pounder from across the river. During the final diversionary
attack from the northeast, a shell from Whipple's howitzer
had crashed near him. The chief needed to be helped from
the field.

One white citizen, Joseph Vanosse, was killed when the
buildings at the south end of the fort were strafed. Seven
wounded whites reported to Dr. Muller for bandaging.

Most of the fort's out-buildings were destroyed. Those
surrounding the parade ground stood, badly damaged but
not quite in ruins.

During the conflict Ridgely's horses, cattle, mules, and oxen
were driven across the river by the squaws. They were the
day's only plunder. Not a single wagon-gun had been captured. There were no stacks of munitions, flour, pork, blankets,
or tents to load on the wagons in the clearing. The wagons
went back empty.

Intact in a wooden building on the parade ground's east
side was $71,000 in gold about which no Dakota knew.

Not one of the refugees was herded back as a captive.

None of the eight hundred Dakotas had earned a new eagle
tail feather; not one gunner had been killed.

Mankato and Big Eagle rode back together, the last to claim their horses and head glumly across the river.

There seemed no hope. Tomorrow more whites would surely come. If the Dakotas could not take the fort today with eight hundred braves, probably they never would be able to do so. After today's failure, the Winnebagoes and Yanktons no longer could be counted as possible allies.

'That gun the soldiers used at the end was terrible,' one of the chiefs said.

'With a few guns like that, the Dakotas could rule the earth,' mused the other.

Hours later the missionaries and teachers led by the Reverend Stephen Riggs and Dr. Williamson came to the fort from up-river, discussed stopping, decided not to, and continued their journey.

It was now five days since the Lower Agency slaughter. Four more days the fort's distraught occupants waited, sure that the attack might be renewed at any moment.

On the fourth day one hundred and seventy-five citizen horsemen arrived. They were greeted by wild cheers. They announced that twelve hundred infantrymen were on the way, and made camp near the fort to wait until the others arrived.

A day later, eight days after departure from Fort Snelling, Colonel Henry Hastings Sibley reached Ridgely with the infantry.

Of tributes paid to the men of Company B, Company C, the Renville Rangers, and Lieutenants Tom Gere and Tim Sheehan, the most impressive came from a leader of the attacking forces.

'We thought the fort was the door to the valley as far as St. Paul,' said Big Eagle, 'and if we got through the door nothing could stop us this side of the Mississippi. But the defenders of the fort were very brave and kept the door shut.' [9]

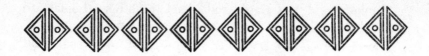

XIII A VERY FINE SPECTACLE

In valley towns below Fort Ridgely the attack on Redwood Agency was recognized immediately as signifying a major emergency.

Men of the valley acted instantly to meet the threat. Starting Monday, and during the next two days, companies of 'citizen soldiers' were formed at New Ulm, Henderson, St. Peter, Mankato, Traverse des Sioux,[1] South Bend, Le Sueur, and elsewhere. They gave themselves such names at St. Peter Frontier Guards, Mankato Volunteers, Brown County Militia, and Le Sueur Tigers.[2]

Those who had guns carried their own weapons from home, knowing they would have no other source of arms. Since the largest game for which they ordinarily needed guns was wild geese, rabbits, ducks, and squirrels, few had weapons other than single-barrel shotguns.

New Ulm, everyone knew, would be the first settlement subjected to Indian attack. It was the largest place near the reservation, and notoriously devoid of defense.

The citizen soldiers headed for New Ulm at once. Most were on foot. Many had no shoes. Some had no weapons excepting pitchforks or clubs.

Most left wives and children behind and worried lest Indians butcher their families while they were gone. Many left crops ripening in the August sunshine or herds of cattle grazing in remote meadows. They feared fields might be set on fire or unguarded cattle driven off. Nevertheless, they con-

verged on New Ulm. Part of the St. Peter Frontier Guards
and some of the Le Sueur Tigers got there on Tuesday almost
as the first attack was ending.[3] At New Ulm they formed a
large company under Captain John Belm's command.

At New Ulm the citizen soldiers chose Judge Charles E.
Flandrau of St. Peter to be their commander in chief. The
judge was a brilliant lawyer, thirty-five years of age, and
experienced in Indian affairs, having at one time served as
Sioux agent. He was a native of New York. His father had
been a law partner of Aaron Burr. A term in the navy and
two years as a mahogany cutter had convinced young Charles
he should study law and go to the Far West. After serving as
a member of Minnesota's state constitutional convention,
Flandrau had become an associate justice of the new state's
Supreme Court. He had been one of the organizers of the
St. Peter Frontier Guards. Athletic, eloquent, an alert,
respected, and intelligent leader, he had great natural aptitude for the responsibilities to which the citizen soldiers
elected him.

With the volunteers came Dr. Asa W. Daniels of St. Peter,
Dr. W. R. McMahon of Mankato and Dr. Ayer and Dr. William W. Mayo of Le Sueur, bearing surgical kits and medical
supplies. They knew hundreds of mangled and burned refugees were pouring into New Ulm. The need for medical care,
they were sure, was greater than could be met by Dr. Weschke
alone.[4]

Later Dr. Mayo's sons, William and Charles, would develop
a world-renowned medical center at Rochester, Minnesota.

From the standpoint of natural defenses, New Ulm was as
unfortunately located as any frontier town could be. It was
strung along the south side of the river, in the lowest part of
the valley. The valley was about two miles wide at this point.
Wooded bluffs along its south edge afforded perfect cover
for enemies to approach unobserved. Between the town and
bluffs the land rose in a series of wide shelves which provided

additional cover and natural platforms from which enemies might launch attacks.

Most of the houses of the town's German settlers were made of wood. Five in the up-river end of town had been burned during the Tuesday attack. Virtually nothing could be done to make this section defensible.

Six blocks down-river was New Ulm's business district. Here many buildings, including houses, were constructed of brick.

Barricades, improvised of wagons, logs, and rocks, had been erected in the business district before the Tuesday attack. Parts of six square blocks, altogether, were barricaded, and here the populace took refuge. If a last-ditch stand had to be made, it necessarily would be made in this section.

Hundreds of residents had fled to Mankato and St. Peter on Monday when word of the Redwood massacre arrived. Hundreds of refugees, however, including many who were wounded, had streamed into New Ulm from all sides, even as residents were departing. Consequently the town, without counting the citizen soldiers, continued to have a population of about one thousand.

Citizen soldiers poured into New Ulm on Wednesday, Thursday, and Friday. There were no Indian attacks during these three days.

Commander Flandrau detailed some of his volunteers to strengthen the barricades. He sent others, in small detachments, to search ravines and swamps for wounded fugitives unable to reach safety. The search parties buried dozens of mutilated corpses found along the trails or near settlers' cabins, and brought in a few living refugees.

Detachments which returned on Friday evening reported having heard heavy cannonading in the northwest all afternoon. At sundown the sound ended. Fort Ridgely had been under attack. Maybe it had withstood the Indians; maybe it had fallen.[5]

By Friday afternoon over three hundred citizen soldiers had trooped into New Ulm. Nearly one-third were without guns. Neither the town nor the volunteers could supply them. Even if there had been weapons, shortage of ammunition was beginning to worry the defenders.

A rumor swept the settlement that Colonel Henry Hastings Sibley, with hundreds of troops dispatched by Governor Ramsey, was approaching the vicinity.

Commander Flandrau sent messengers to find the colonel. They bore notes pleading for a few of the troops reported to be with him. The notes added, 'Bring powder, lead, and caps. We are short.' [6]

Another rumor flashing through town before daybreak Saturday deprived Flandrau of part of his command. This report said that Winnebago Indians were joining the Dakota revolt. The Winnebago reservation was only a few miles from South Bend, a hamlet near Mankato. If the story was true, the hamlet's women and children were in deadly peril. The South Bend contingent left for home at dawn.

A little later on Saturday morning Commander Flandrau's lookouts reported great pillars of smoke rising far to the northwest across the river. The commander hurried outside to see for himself. Becoming more and more numerous, the pillars billowed nearer and nearer, some on both sides of the valley.

It was soon evident that hundreds of Indians were sweeping toward New Ulm, setting fire to cabins, haystacks, barns, and fields of grain as they advanced.

At nine o'clock a great mass of Indians swarmed out of the woods two miles above town and assembled on an upper shelf. Flandrau quickly posted his forces outside New Ulm, in the direction from which the attack would come.

At ten the mass of Dakotas began to move toward the whites. It was a dramatic sight.

'Their advance upon the sloping prairie was a very fine

spectacle,' said Flandrau, 'and to such inexperienced soldiers as we all were, intensely exciting. When within about one mile and a half of us, the mass began to expand like a fan and increase in the velocity of its approach, and continued this movement until within about double rifle-shot, when it had covered our entire front. Then the savages uttered a terrific yell and came down upon us like the wind.' [7]

The yell had the effect it was intended to have. Most of the citizen soldiers never before had needed to cope with anything more formidable than a temperamental horse. They yielded ground. They fell back beyond some of the outlying houses. This was an error, and one of which the attackers took immediate advantage.

Every house promptly became a fort sheltering as many as ten Indians. From his unexpected shelter each poured a deadly fire.

The citizen soldiers may not have been skilled Indian fighters at the start of the morning, but they learned fast. They could yell, too, and they did. They could occupy houses, too—and there were many waiting to be used as forts.

About twenty Le Sueur Tigers took possession of a huge partly enclosed windmill three blocks south of the barricaded area. They were accomplished snipers, and fought back all attempts to dislodge them.[8] Their location was strategic. It controlled the main approaches to the barricaded business district. Another party of white marksmen occupied the brick post office a block southwest of the barricades.

But the Indians were also adaptable. They saw opportunity in the abandoned lower part of New Ulm.

A brisk breeze whipped through town from the southeast. The Sioux took quick advantage of this circumstance.

While much of the action was still concentrated in the up-river area, a party of Dakotas stole quietly into the southeast area and set fire to its wooden buildings.

Presently much of the lower section was in flames. Dense

clouds of acrid smoke poured into the main part of town, blinding and choking the defenders. Blazing embers fell nearer and nearer the barricades.

Nobody could take time to fight fire; there were too many Indians. The combat pattern set early in the day continued. The conflict moved through most of the town, literally from house to house. Control of whole blocks or entire sections of town might depend on who reached a strategically located building first. The fighting and fires raged all morning and half the afternoon.

At three o'clock sixty Indians gathered at the rear of downtown buildings along the river, near the ferry landing. Commander Flandrau and his officers realized that an assault was taking form.[9] Sixty citizen soldiers charged around a corner squarely into the enemy concentration, yelling and howling as fiendishly as Dakotas. All had guns and all were shooting. A volley from the barricaded area added to the effect. The suddenness of the charge scattered the Indians. They did not reassemble. Two whites were killed in the attack.

This did not quite end the day's battle. Fighting continued until dark, but there was no major assault. At sundown most of the Indians went home. Despite their superiority in numbers and weapons, they had been unable, after the first morning charge, to force the citizen soldiers back. When the Dakotas headed home Saturday night, they knew another door to the valley had been kept shut.

The force attacking the settlement numbered six hundred and fifty, the second largest the Dakotas were to assemble at one time.

Most of the upper and lower bands were represented. With or without the sanction of their chiefs, young braves were present from the villages of Lean Bear, White Lodge, Red Iron, Standing Buffalo, and others. From the lower villages came Big Eagle, Wacouta, Mankato, and numerous other chiefs, personally leading bands of their braves. Little Crow, nursing his wounds of the previous day, was not present. His head soldier, Gray Bird, came with a party of Little Crow's warriors.

Not over two hundred citizen soldiers took part in the fighting. More were present but did not have guns. No reinforcements or ammunition arrived from Sibley during the day.

Thirty-two whites, including non-combatants, were killed at New Ulm and more than sixty were wounded. This was a large number of casualties in relation to the number engaged. Seven of the dead were members of New Ulm's own company of citizen soldiers.

Little plunder was taken, but one-third of the town was destroyed. One hundred and ninety houses, including the forty buildings fired by Flandrau to prevent their use as Indian forts, were in ashes.

At noon the next day troops under Captain E. St. Julien Cox arrived. They were heralded as reinforcements from Colonel Sibley, but were not. They were another company of citizen soldiers called the St. Peter Frontier Avengers,[10] which had organized the previous day.

On Sunday Commander Flandrau and the city fathers took stock of the situation and decided to evacuate the town's residents to Mankato the next day. Flandrau needed ammunition badly. If the Indians assaulted the town again, a thousand non-combatants and refugees might be slaughtered. Not much more than a few pitchforks would be on hand to prevent it.

For five days and nights, and in some cases for six, the non-combatants lived inside the barricades, the women and children 'huddled in cellars and close rooms like sheep in a cattle car.'[11]

The food supply was almost gone, and no more food was reaching the town. The only thing coming in was more refugees. Despite the efforts of the volunteer doctors, they could

not be given adequate care, and certainly could not be properly housed, fed, or defended.

Mankato was a little more than thirty miles down-river.
Evacuation was risky, but not as hazardous as staying in New
Ulm. One hundred and fifty-three wagons, loaded with women, children, wounded refugees, and household goods, accompanied by two hundred men on foot, departed for Mankato on Monday.

Tentatively, Flandrau planned to return to guard the ruins
of New Ulm with one hundred and fifty citizen soldiers and
the little ammunition remaining. But the men were barefoot,
weary, and desperately worried about their families. They
wanted to get home as quickly as possible, and could not be
persuaded to go back to New Ulm.

'I did not blame them,' commented Flandrau.[12]

The citizen soldiers had been where they were needed and
when.

Commander Flandrau returned to St. Peter that day.
Camped nearby he found Colonel Henry Hastings Sibley with
hundreds upon hundreds of troops. The colonel had what
seemed like tremendous quantities of ammunition and supplies but was waiting for more.

XIV   WITH UTMOST PROMPTITUDE

Because Private William Sturgis rode all night, he was able to deliver Tom Gere's message to Fort Snelling on Tuesday afternoon. Word reached Governor Alexander Ramsey eighteen hours after Lieutenant Gere heard that Marsh's command had been ambushed at the ferry.

Immediately Ramsey ordered four companies of Fort Snelling troops 'to move to the scene with the utmost promptitude.'[1] Ex-Governor Sibley was made a militia colonel for the occasion and asked to command the troops.

Henry Hastings Sibley, a stately and dignified country gentleman, lived in a baronial mansion at Mendota. His home, below Fort Snelling, was near the confluence of the Minnesota and Mississippi rivers.

Born fifty-one years before to a middle-class Detroit family, Sibley at the age of eighteen had gone to Mackinac as a clerk for the American Fur Company.[2] The young clerk prospered. Within six years, at the age of twenty-four, now a partner in the firm and head factor on the upper Mississippi, he moved to Mendota. He received one thousand dollars salary a year and five per cent of the fur company's profits from operations in the area. At Mendota he ordered his manor house built, 'had horses and dogs, retainers to do his bidding, and a French cook of the finest skill.' Eight years later he acquired a wife, who presently bore him nine children.[3]

Although he had announced retirement from the fur trade

in 1853, Sibley retained enough interest in the affairs of the American Fur Company to enter claims after the Sioux treaties for a total of $157,000 in his own and the company's behalf. Except for trips to treaty councils, to New York, and to Washington, he rarely had gone far from Mendota in recent years.

General Zachary Taylor, familiar with the ways of fur traders during his tenure in frontier army posts, called the American Fur Company 'the greatest set of scoundrels the world ever knew.'[4] But few fur company stains marred Sibley's escutcheon. He had a reputation for 'purity of character,' and was considered an 'honest, scrupulous, incorruptible, public-spirited' citizen.[5]

He had served as Minnesota's first governor. After the new state's election a canvassing board announced his victory over Alexander Ramsey, the Republican candidate, by a vote margin of two hundred and forty. Enemies sneered suspiciously at five hundred and fifty-four votes from the Pembina and Cass districts. The only residents of these districts were Indians, 'captive customers' of the American Fur Company. Every one of their votes had gone to Sibley. Ramsey supporters muttered charges of fraud, and protested that Indian votes were not valid.[6] The canvassing board thought otherwise, protecting the Sibley escutcheon from possible political blemish.

Sibley did not seek re-election. He preferred 'the peace and quiet of private life to the thorny path of public office.' Alexander Ramsey ran again and, this time, was elected.

Some citizens considered it astonishing that the governor selected his former political opponent as the man to subdue the Dakotas. They could only assume it was because Sibley was well-known and his appointment might reassure some of the thousands fleeing in panic because of the massacre.

Unquestionably, Henry Hastings Sibley[7] had been successful in his trading relations with Indians. He was an outdoors enthusiast, knew how to handle a shotgun, and loved to hunt wild fowl. He spoke French and had a trader's comprehension of the Sioux language. He was personally acquainted with some Indians and half-breeds and had been given an Indian name, Wah-ze-o-man-zee, which meant Walker in the Pines. He possessed, it was claimed, 'a profound knowledge of Indian character and habits.' He had been one of the early whites in the area. He was well read. He had courtly manners and was a gracious host.

But could he fight Indians? He was without military experience. He did not seem a natural-born Indian fighter.

To fight Indians effectively, a man had to move with lightning speed. He needed the same kind of scouting sense the Indians had, in order to quickly and accurately appraise every shred of information he received, and know at least as much about the foe as the enemy knew about him. He needed, in addition, enough imagination and resourcefulness to keep the opponents in a state of uncertainty and bewilderment. And, perhaps, above all, he needed to be adjustable. Conditions of warfare in the Indian country were rarely ideal; a good Indian fighter was one who could adapt readily to whatever conditions he found and make the most of such means as he had.

Mobility, scouting aptitude, imagination, and adaptability were not known to be traits of the new colonel. In fact, critics called him lethargic, conservative, and staid. But perhaps his handling of the Sioux campaign would prove how wrong critics could be, and maybe the criticism was politically inspired.

Sibley's start was not auspicious. It took the new colonel a day to get away from Snelling. Before leaving, he wrote to the governor complaining about the ammunition, tents, and camping gear with which he had been supplied.[8] The Austrian musket, in his opinion, was 'a very poor affair'; he would greatly have preferred Springfield rifles.

At Belle Plaine, a day out, he found the populace 'absolutely crazy with excitement,' and encountered wave after wave of settlers surging down the valley.

There were small family groups, and huge cavalcades composed of the entire population of whole settlements.

Some fugitives were afoot, limping and stumbling. Some were in farm wagons piled high with bedding, implements, furniture, grain, and crates of live poultry. When they saw the troops, some cheered; others sobbed in relief and gratitude. All told tales of horror to anyone who would pause to listen. Some had been hurt; others carried wounded companions. All, including those who had fled before the Indians came near, were sick with terror and despair.

Sibley's men commandeered wagons and teams, giving the drivers scraps of paper showing the date and the piece which had been impressed into service. Then they unloaded the wagons, turned them around, and drove away. Long after the troops had passed, stunned refugees stood at the roadside, staring at piles of belongings, and wondering what to do next.

Two hundred and twenty-five men were with Sibley. Others were to meet him at St. Peter. One company, led by Captain Hiram Grant, had veered westward through the woods. When they reached the Glencoe trail they would go south to Fort Ridgely and meet Sibley there.

Out of Belle Plaine on Thursday the colonel was told 'some or all' of Fort Ridgely had been burned. The report was not true; the flaming final onslaught, in which hayricks, outbuildings, and stacks of wood were burned, would not take place until the next day.

Sibley's response to the report was astonishing. He did not speed his two hundred and twenty-five men to Ridgely to save its refugees or what might remain of its garrison. He did not send a messenger asking Grant to rush his company to the rescue on the double. Instead, he ordered Grant to avoid Fort Ridgely and head for St. Peter, forty miles east of the fort.[9]

Part of Sibley's route between Fort Snelling and St. Peter

led through the eastern edge of the Big Woods. By frontier standards the road was considered good. The trip over it often was made between dawn and nightfall, but it took the colonel two and one-half days. When he reached St. Peter, Sibley wrote it had been a fatiguing trip, because 'the roads are execrable.'

Colonel Sibley had not organized any scouting service to keep himself posted regarding the enemy's strength and movements. He had thought about it. But when he got to St. Peter he decided he would not need such a service after all, because at St. Peter he encountered Jack Frazer.[10]

Frazer, a half-breed, partly Sioux, had long been an acquaintance of Sibley's. He had avoided capture at Redwood Agency, knew all about the lower bands, and was eager to tell his old friend whatever the colonel might want to know.

Thirsting for knowledge, Sibley listened attentively. Over seven thousand Dakotas, Frazer estimated, were already engaged in the revolt. They had fifteen hundred warriors, mounted and well armed. Probably the whole Sioux nation was rising, Yanktons, Yanktonais, and all.[11] There were at least twenty-five thousand Sioux between Ridgely and the Missouri. They could muster at least five thousand warriors.[12]

On leaving Fort Snelling, Sibley had been satisfied to have four companies of troops; if he needed more, he would be able to recruit them locally.[13]

After his talk with Frazer, though, the colonel called for 'five hundred additional troops officered by the best men and armed with Springfield rifles, and a goodly supply of fixed ammunition.'[14]

With fifteen hundred warriors to fight against, or possibly five thousand, Sibley thought it would be madness to take four companies of foot soldiers into the Sioux country. Austrian muskets now seemed more inadequate than ever. Infantry began to seem unsuitable; since the Indians were mounted, a man would need cavalry to catch them.

Not even Jack Frazer knew for sure whether any soldiers or civilians survived at Fort Ridgely. If there were survivors, they needed to be given up as lost. No troops or ammunition could be sent in an effort to rescue or evacuate them.

Flandrau's appeal from New Ulm arrived Friday evening, but the colonel felt obliged to ignore it. Men and munitions could have reached the town readily overnight, and have been there before the Saturday attack, but Sibley felt he could not spare them. Had he felt differently, one-third of the settlement might not have been destroyed the next day.

Trained and dependable scouts might have corrected the estimate that fifteen hundred warriors, mounted and armed, were already at war, and that the number soon might be five thousand. They could have learned and reported that Yanktons and Yanktonais had not joined the revolt and that even most Wahpetons and Sissetons had declined to take part. They might have told the colonel that eight hundred braves was the most that Little Crow could muster, and that his usual strength was far less than that.

An accurate scouting service might have told Sibley he could afford to help save New Ulm.

Reliable scouts might have informed him that it would be safe to rescue the women, children, and handful of troops awaiting his arrival at Ridgely.

But Sibley had no dependable scouts. His conversation with Frazer caused a four-day delay at St. Peter while he awaited the five hundred additional troops and the Springfield rifles he had ordered.

He did not wait in vain. From Fort Snelling, diverted from Civil War duty, came six companies of infantry, all armed with Springfield rifles. Three hundred mounted troops also arrived, as did a great train of wagons laden with ammunition and subsistence.

By August 26 Sibley's force had swelled to nearly fifteen hundred. Now the colonel felt he dared start toward Fort

Ridgely. But first he got off a note to Governor Ramsey complaining he had seen no newspapers for days; he 'would like to have late papers' sent to him by messenger. In two more days the army had reached Ridgely, and now, thought Sibley, the action could start.

'The war of races,' proclaimed the colonel, 'has begun, renewed in its old and simplest form.'[15]

In reality, the war had begun long before Sibley arrived; as far as Fort Ridgely, New Ulm, West Lake, Lake Shetek, and many other places were concerned, the war had been fought during the eight days the colonel had spent reaching the scene.

When Governor Ramsey's messenger arrived with the newspapers, Sibley was horrified by some of the things he read about himself.

'The state undertaker with his company of gravediggers,' the St. Cloud *Democrat* called him.

'A snail who falls back on his authority and assumed dignity and refuses to march,' hooted the Hastings *Independent*.

More horrifying to Sibley, had he been able to see them, would have been comments flowing to the desk of the governor who had requested the new colonel to move to the massacre scene 'with the utmost promptitude.'

'Send us an earnest young man to take command,' begged Sheriff Roos of New Ulm. 'Such a man will do more with the present force than Sibley ever would do with ten or fifteen thousand troops. He is, in my mind, a coward.'

Horace Austin, St. Peter attorney, injected a political note into his protest to the governor. 'That a man who defrauded you out of the executive chair on the strength of Indian votes is continued in power while murder, rapine, and plunder surround his imbecility,' wrote Austin, 'staggers us all.'

Few editorial writers or authors of letters to the governor appeared to think the colonel showed much promise as an Indian fighter.[16]

The distance between Snelling and Ridgely had been covered in a night and part of a day by Private William Sturgis. Yellow Medicine missionaries, afoot, with children and driving oxen, had covered more distance in seven days than Sibley had covered in eight.

It was hard to believe that anyone could spend eight days getting to Ridgely. And, since hundreds of women and children at New Ulm and Ridgely had been in deadly peril every moment of the eight days, it was hard to forgive.

No doubt the roads were execrable. But Tim Sheehan and Company C, over more execrable roads, had sped forty-two miles in one night when they heard the Indians were raising hell.

Did it really matter whether Springfield rifles were better than Austrian muskets? The citizen soldiers had neither. They defended New Ulm with squirrel guns.

If Sibley's appointment had been for the purpose of reassuring settlers fleeing in panic, it had failed in its purpose. Those who had abandoned their homes continued to flee, feeling as fully unprotected as ever.

XV NO CALAMITY RECIEVED LESS ATTENTION

No calamity in the nation's frontier history affected as many civilians or exceeded in horror the massacre engineered by Red Middle Voice. None received less attention when it occurred or was more quickly and totally forgotten.

Compelling and understandable reasons kept the outbreak from attracting much notice at the time. Foremost among them was the fact that it took place during the Civil War's second year.

Quick Confederate successes had marked the previous year. During the spring of 1862 the North reversed the tide. In early summer the Federals held Kentucky, most of Tennessee, parts of Alabama, and Mississippi. In Virginia, they seemed about to capture Richmond.

Then, in late June, less than two months before the Sioux arose, General Robert E. Lee launched a great counter-offensive and Stonewall Jackson began to sweep the Shenandoah Valley clean. Presently Northern troops no longer threatened Richmond. John Hunt Morgan invented modern guerilla warfare for the Rebels in Kentucky and Tennessee.[1] The North yielded Virginia. Now Washington, rather than Richmond, began to look doomed.

Northerners stopped taking it for granted that the Secessionists would be crushed, and began weighing the possible effects of a Confederate victory. By August there were more important things to worry about than Indian troubles in the Far West.

A second reason the Sioux massacre was not taken more seriously was the incredible scope and viciousness of the attacks. Six months after the outbreak Jane Grey Swisshelm, lecturing in the East, complained that everyone 'totally disbelieves the story of the outrages committed. People cannot and will not believe it possible that any set of savages committed the outrages we say they did on the people of a civilized state.'[2]

A third reason was that many of the outbreak's victims were strangers in the land. They were newly arrived immigrants with few or no acquaintances in North America. In Norway, Germany, Sweden, or Switzerland, a mother or brother, hearing dim rumors, might shake a head and murmur, 'I warned Hans (or Guri, Jacob, or Marie) about those wild Indians in America.' Some, never hearing details, might spend a lifetime wondering why no word ever came from those gone to the new world.

Nearly as important a reason as the war was the lack of communications and reporting facilities in the border country. Telegraph wires had not linked St. Paul with the nation's news centers until two years before. Not until years later did rows of telegraph poles march into the upper valley. A decade and a half would elapse before the telephone would be invented. Messages on the frontier were sent by mounted couriers or stage lines; the time it took to send them had to be reckoned in days.

Telegraph or telephone lines to and from Redwood Agency, Ridgely, Lake Shetek, and New Ulm would have been a great convenience. They would have saved many lives. But even they might have made little difference in the reporting of the massacre as news.

Most skilled newspaper correspondents and magazine writers in 1862 were preoccupied with the Civil War. Most of those remaining near the frontier lacked experience in weaving accurate and coherent accounts out of scattered and fragmentary reports.

No press associations had correspondents in or near the Sioux country. Pictorial journalism had not been invented; only a few photographers even experimented with cameras on Civil War battlefields.

There were four daily newspapers in the new state, all in St. Paul. Newswriters on the four papers gathered what massacre information they could. Much of it seemed too fantastic to be useable. There had been previous Indian scares, but this one topped them all. Yarns about Indians needed to be handled with caution. If the killings had only taken place at Winona, Madison, Milwaukee, or some other place where it would be possible to check, or if only Yellow Medicine or Ridgely had telegraph offices, maybe the stuff could be used as it came through. As it was, the stories could be treated in only one way.

Such phrases as 'unconfirmed rumors' and 'probably exaggerated reports' hedged all the early accounts. In its first report of the killings at Acton, the St. Paul *Pioneer and Democrat* prudently ascribed the story to Mr. Whitcomb, county treasurer, well known as a gentleman of truth.'[3]

By Wednesday refugees, eye-witnesses, and a few wounded survivors began to reach St. Paul. Reputable citizens who had talked with other survivors at such outposts as Glencoe, Mankato, or St. Cloud also began to arrive.

Often it was impossible to extract facts from the refugees. Many settlers could speak little English even when calm; now they had seen mates beheaded or children nailed to cabin doors, and were wildly excited. No doubt they had stories to tell; too bad they were so incoherent.

Conflicting accounts were another problem. Yet another was that some of the stories were disproved as soon as they got into print. There was, for example, a solemn report that

LITTLE CROW:
'Dakota chiefs do not fear to die. They will do what is best for their people.'
(FROM A PAINTING BY T. W. WOOD.)

SACRED HEART CREEK *(chapter 6)*
Of 28 starting, only one got directly to the fort.

BIRCH COULEE *(chapter 18)*
Dozens squatted just out of range, sliding ahead when they wanted to shoot.

NEW ULM *(chapter 13)*
Nobody could take time to fight fire; there were too many Indians.

SOUTH BEND *(chapter 24)*
Some recalled Little Crow's words, and thought they had been fools to surrender.

This group of Sioux chiefs and warriors made the treaty with the Government in 1858. The two figures are (left) Big Eagle and (right) Traveling Hail.

This photograph of the 1858 treaty group includes the white representatives as well as the Sioux. The Indians are (left) Mankato and (right) Wabasha.

all the missionaries at Hazelwood and Pajutazee had been murdered. The story was complete, with details that seemed authentic. 'All of the Farmer Indians,' it seemed, 'gathered at Rev. Riggs's home, but were overpowered.' The day after this story had been published in St. Paul and distributed on the nation's press wires, the Riggs group reached safety at Henderson and Dr. Williamson's party emerged alive at St. Peter.

Estimates of the number of whites killed varied so remarkably that nobody knew what to believe. An average of the estimates made no sense whatever.

One report said a thousand deaths was an 'absurd exaggeration' and declared fifty was the 'authentic toll.' Others said more than two hundred had been killed at Lower Agency and across the river on Beaver Creek and Sacred Heart Creek. There was reason to think that four times fifty had died at Milford, Leavenworth, and Lake Shetek. The 'authentic toll' of fifty probably would apply to West Lake alone, ignoring hundreds killed elsewhere.

Estimates of property damage were just as unsatisfactory. Ten days after the massacre's start a report said seventeen houses had been burned at New Ulm. Next day the number was officially announced as one hundred and ninety.

Queried routinely by wire, news editors everywhere denied interest in details of a fanciful yarn from an obscure part of the Far West. Too much news of absolute authenticity and top importance poured in from elsewhere. The Rebel Congress finally was ready to hold its first session. Who cared about distant Sioux when Lee, Jackson, and Bragg were much nearer and alarmingly active? For those who wanted news of the Far West, there was a Kansas City dispatch about the defeat of fifteen hundred Northern troops.

It was August 23, six days after the Redwood Agency massacre, before a believable story of the Dakota outbreak chattered on the press wires from St. Paul.[4]

During the unreported six days, hundreds of settlers had been hacked to death or cremated in blazing cabins, two hundred and seventy women and children had been carried away to captivity, Captain Marsh's command had been ambushed, Ridgely and New Ulm had each withstood two attacks, half a dozen settlements had been wholly destroyed, and over thirty thousand pioneers had abandoned their homesteads in terror.

While accurate, the press dispatch of the 23rd conveyed only a fractional account of the catastrophe befalling the frontier. It confirmed reports of an uprising at Lower Agency, mentioned Marsh's encounter at Redwood Ferry without saying what its outcome had been, said that refugees poured into Fort Ridgely, and stated that roads in New Ulm's vicinity were lined with bodies of murdered settlers. Governor Ramsey, the dispatch added, had received letters saying that hundreds were known to have been killed; it was thought the final count might be in the thousands.

Seven days after the massacre the Chicago *Tribune* reported refugees fleeing from New Ulm and said Captain Marsh's command had been attacked. The captain's death was reported, but 'not confirmed.'

A second dispatch, less accurate than that of the 23rd, went out from St. Paul the following day. This report said that two scouts, Antoine Frenier and an interpreter named Fletcher,[5] 'had gone through the Indian lines to reconnoiter.' Their reconnaissance may have included a conversation with Jack Frazer, the source of Sibley's information, but the dispatch did not say so.

Frenier reported Fort Ridgely surrounded by two thousand warriors, or two and one-half times as many as ever attacked it.

Fletcher declared 'everyone' at Yellow Medicine dead, with bodies littering doorsteps and yards. He said he had personally seen the corpses of all members of Major Joseph

Brown's family. In reality, almost everyone at Yellow Medicine had been led to safety by John Otherday or the missionaries, and the Browns were safely up-river with Wahpeton relatives by this time.

Included in the dispatch was the news that residents of Glencoe and the vicinity were alarmed over the 'immense damage' being done to their crops by fleeing settlers.

Newspapers in some of the nearer cities had begun, by now, to voice editorial indignation over the outbreak. 'That the secession sympathizers and agents have been instrumental in causing the difficulty with the Indians is evident,' asserted the St. Paul *Daily Free Press.*

The Sioux, according to the Chicago *Tribune,* 'were induced to commit these outrages by Indians from Missouri and secession traders from that state.'

Northern spokesmen quickly took up the charge of Confederate complicity. Henry M. Rice, formerly Territorial Delegate, declared, 'The Sioux Indians were induced by rebels and traitors to make war upon our people.'[6] Caleb Smith, Secretary of the Interior, reworded the charge, but made it semi-official. The outbreak's cause, he told Congress, 'is to be found in the insurrection of the southern states.'[7]

No evidence confirmed these suspicions. Partly refuting them was the fact that nearly three hundred Northern infantrymen, captured at Murfreesboro, Tennessee, were released by the Confederates on a basis which left them free to fight the Sioux. The parolees joined Sibley at Fort Ridgely.[8]

By August 25, newspapers announced Sibley had 'arrived to relieve the beleaguered settlements.' Sibley had, in fact, reached St. Peter. At no time was St. Peter beleaguered, but Sibley's appointment convinced editors, at least in distant news rooms, that everything had been brought under control.

Now the massacre story was more than a week old and clearly no longer news. Readers who had been aware of the Sioux disturbance need be distracted no longer. They could again give full attention to the Civil War. Before the end of August came important developments to claim their interest.

For one day Northern papers proclaimed 'General Pope's Victory Avenging Bull Run.' The next day their readers learned the terrifying truth: Pope jubilantly but mistakenly had told Washington the enemy was in retreat. Almost before the joyful news reached the Northern public, thirty thousand seasoned Confederates shredded Pope's flank, sent his army reeling toward Washington, and started Pope to an oblivion especially made for a discredited general.

Within a week thereafter, Secretary of War Edwin M. Stanton created a Military Department of the Northwest and sent Pope to fight Indians. A trifle subdued, but with most of his energy and bombast intact, General John Pope immediately ordered Colonel Sibley to 'take such prompt and vigorous measures as shall quell the hostilities.'[9]

By now few newspapers outside the Northwest could pay any attention whatever either to the hostile Sioux or to General Pope. Greater events and generals dominated the full attention of both North and South.

On September 17 the forces of Generals George B. McClellan and Robert E. Lee collided at Sharpsburg on Antietam Creek. Southern casualties amounted to ten thousand. The North's were twelve, with three thousand killed or fatally wounded.

In comparison, Indian troubles in the Far West were of no consequence whatever.

XVI   KILL, IF INDIAN

Three days after his army reached Fort Ridgely, Colonel Sibley sent an expeditionary force up-river to Redwood Ferry.

Its purpose was to bury dead at the ferry, the agency, and north of the river. In addition, the men were instructed to learn all they could concerning the whereabouts of the Lower Agency Indians.

Sibley placed Captain Hiram P. Grant in charge of the mission. Grant's forces included Company A, Sixth Volunteer Infantry, and a company of mounted rangers led by Captain Joseph Anderson. Altogether, there were one hundred and fifty troops.[1]

A number of worried citizens, seeking word of relatives who had been at Redwood Agency or elsewhere on the reservation the first day of the attack, accompanied the expedition.

Included in the citizens' brigade was Major Joseph R. Brown, former Indian agent and long-time resident of the area. Because his wife was an Indian, Brown did not believe Interpreter Fletcher's report of having seen the corpses of his wife and children. On the other hand, he had failed to hear any positive report of their escape.

Also among the worried citizens were Agent Galbraith and Trader Nathan Myrick. The latter understood Andrew, his brother, had been killed. Galbraith was unaware that his family had escaped in John Otherday's party.

Another member of the citizens' brigade was Joseph De-

Camp, operator of the Redwood sawmill, absent the day of the massacre, and subsequently unable to learn what had happened to his wife and children.

Also present was S. R. Henderson, Beaver Creek settler. On the massacre's first day he had broken away from his two-year-old daughter, 'cast a look of anguish and despair' at his dying wife, and fled when his party of fugitives was surrounded. He did not seek word of his family's fate. He had watched from a distance while Dakotas made a blazing pyre of his wife's featherbed; his only hope now was to help bury the remains.

A scout with the company was Ezmon Earle, another former resident of the Beaver Creek neighborhood.[2]

At the north end of the ferry, Captain Grant's men found the bodies of Interpreter Patrick Quinn and nineteen other members of Captain Marsh's command. On the way from the fort they had buried the mangled corpse of Old Mauley, the ferry operator, the remains of a dozen settlers who had not made it to safety, and the body of the agency barber. After interring Marsh's men, the party returned a few miles toward the fort and camped for the night.

In the morning Captain Anderson's rangers, accompanied by DeCamp, Galbraith, Brown, and most of the other anxious citizens, crossed at the ferry to the south side of the river. There they were to explore the Indian villages and agency ruins in an effort to find out whatever they could regarding the foe.

Captain Hiram Grant's company remained north of the river. Henderson accompanied them, and so did Ezmon Earle. They proceeded upstream toward Beaver Creek, 'occasionally halting to bury whole families.' Henderson identified one mass of charred bones as the remains of his wife and two children. Ezmon recognized, by the clothing, the decomposed body of his brother, Radner. About mid-forenoon they saw what Captain Grant took to be an Indian.

'I halted the command,' said the captain, 'and sent a force of twenty men to surround what I had seen; to capture, if white, but to kill if Indian.'[3]

What Captain Grant's men surrounded was not an Indian. It was what remained of Justina Krieger, twenty-eight years old, who, before the massacre, had lived in a settlement on Sacred Heart Creek. It took the captain's men a long moment to figure out what they had surrounded.[4]

Justina's first husband had died five years before, leaving her with two young sons and a daughter. Subsequently she married Frederick Krieger, who also had three children by a previous marriage. He and Justina produced three daughters. In the spring of 1862 the family moved to a homestead in the Sacred Heart vicinity. Here Frederick built a large cabin of logs and boards; the usual sod shanty would not have provided enough space for a family of nine children and two adults.

During the late afternoon of the 18th Justina had thought she detected a peculiar odor. She mentioned it to Frederick when he returned from the fields near sundown.

Frederick pointed through the cabin door. On the horizon flickered a line of yellow and red. Krieger supposed it was a grass fire, and was happy he had plowed a fire-break around the house a few days before.

Running footsteps sounded suddenly on the loose boards leading to the cabin. A neighbor, August Fross, stood in the doorway, breathlessly reporting that he had found the bodies of a woman and two children a mile away on the road.

At almost the same moment another neighbor, Eckmel Groundman, stood panting in the door. His voice quivering with excitement, he told of finding the whole Busby family killed. John Busby and his wife and children, said Eckmel, were dead in their cabin, and at the Monweiler's cabin all the doors and windows had been smashed.

Within an hour thirteen families had gathered at the cabin of Justina's brother, Paul Kitzman. The older children ran to warn surviving neighbors. Groundman and Fross sprinted away to get their own families.

An hour after dark the thirteen families, in eleven wagons and buggies, started for Fort Ridgely, twenty-seven miles distant. They passed the bodies August Fross had found, three dark shapes on the road.

During the night the refugees traveled fourteen miles, a little over half way to the fort. Chances were excellent, the men thought, that they could reach Ridgely by noon.

Soon after dawn eight mounted Indians appeared. Some were bare and others wore blankets. All had painted faces and carried guns. At first they rode slowly, parallel to the wagons, inspecting the whites. Then they began to draw nearer, guns poised.

Paul Kitzman recognized several of them. One repeatedly had eaten at the Kitzman home. Paul sometimes had gone fishing with him.

When the Dakotas first neared the wagon train several advocated firing on them. A lively argument followed in German. One problem was that less than half the men were armed.

A few yards from the wagons the approaching Indians lowered their guns. It was a gesture of reassurance. Paul's fishing companion slid from his horse and walked casually toward the wagons. Paul stopped his team and alighted. His friend greeted him effusively, throwing an arm over Paul's shoulder and kissing him resoundingly.

'Judas-like, he betrayed us with a kiss,' reflected Justina.[5]

Paul's friend sauntered the length of the wagon train, his shotgun pointed toward the ground. He shook hands with everyone, remarking how early it was for them to be so far from home.

'We are going to the fort,' explained Paul. 'Indians have been killing everyone in the neighborhood.'

'Chippewas did it,' said Paul's friend. 'Dakotas do not kill anybody.'[6]

One of the settlers, speaking English, asked the Indians where they were going.

Paul's friend answered. 'We are after the Chippewas, to kill them.'

There were Chippewas near the fort, the Dakotas declared, and the settlers would be killed if they went ahead.

'All of the men at one time, except Paul Kitzman, were determined to fire' on the Indians, recalled Justina, but Paul persuaded them not to.

Now all the Indians had come nearer. More of them dismounted and shook hands with the settlers and their wives. Some of the children, frightened by the painted faces of the strangers, began to cry.

'Tell them not to cry,' said a Dakota. 'We will not hurt anyone. Turn around. We will guard you until you get home.'

'The Indians put up their guns,' Justina remembered. 'All now joined in a friendly meal of bread and milk.'

Everybody climbed from the wagons and buggies. The vehicles were kept headed toward the fort. Blankets were spread on the ground. During the meal, the Indians peered constantly toward the southeast, the direction of the fort. They blustered about what they would do to the Chippewas.

The settlers decided to unyoke the teams and let them feed.

'Have you got anything more for us to eat?' one of the Dakotas asked while the horses and oxen were grazing. Some bread remained. Several families contributed home-grown watermelons. The Indians withdrew a short distance to eat by themselves.

After the teams had fed briefly, the settlers brought them back. Most of the men carrying weapons placed them in a single wagon while hitching their teams. Some neglected to take the guns to their own wagons later.

'We have decided we will not leave you,' one of the Indians announced when they returned. 'Turn the wagons around. We will protect you until you get home.'

'The cat plays with the mouse before it pounces,' growled one of the settlers in German.

Several were reluctant, but a majority, persuaded by Kitzman, finally agreed to turn the wagons around. The Indians accompanied the settlers while they backtracked much of the distance they had come during the night.

At first nobody objected that the whites rode surrounded, three Indians on each side of the train, one ahead, and one behind. Justina's husband noticed, and became uneasy.

Paul Kitzman, watching the escort, gradually began to share the apprehensions of the others. He remembered unhappily that at least half of the few weapons of the whites were in one wagon.

If the Indians wanted to, he observed, they could kill every white man with one volley. With one exception, the Dakotas had double-barreled guns. They carried their guns, loaded and cocked, in their hands. The eight Dakotas could fire fifteen shots without reloading. This would be more than enough to kill the thirteen white men.

When the wagons approached the dead woman and children lying sprawled on the road, Paul suggested the bodies be buried.

In taking spades and shovels out of the wagons the whites would have a chance to get their guns without arousing suspicion.

The idea came too late. Before the wagons stopped, the Dakotas had drawn up in a line at the rear.

'We have brought you almost home,' said one of the Indians coldly. 'Now give us your money.'

The whites were startled. Some were not sure they understood the meaning of the demand. Those who had been suspicious wondered whether, perhaps, they would be allowed to live after all.

Some of the whites climbed from the wagons. There was

nothing to do but take up a collection. Frederick was designated to gather the money. When he came to Justina, he handed her his pocket knife.

'What is this for?' asked Justina.

'A rememberance,' her husband answered. 'I think they will kill all the men.'

One of the Indians advanced to take the money from Frederick. The others remained in line, guns leveled, but did not follow when the wagons started again.

Two white men, killed since the previous evening, were on the road almost in front of the Krieger cabin. The wagons halted. At last a few of the men got their guns.

As the wagons stopped fourteen naked Indians rode up whooping, surrounded the whites, and opened fire. None of the eight escorts was among them. Most of the fourteen were Rice Creekers or members of Shakopee's band. They included Young Shakopee, Dewanea, and Cut Nose, a trio active in many events north of the river.

The first shots were aimed at the men, some of whom grabbed frantically, but in vain, for weapons. Of the men, only Frederick Krieger, John Fross, and Gottlieb Zable survived the first volley.[7] Paul Kitzman and nine others lay dead or writhing on the ground. Frederick stood between his oxen, dazed and motionless.

'The Indians then asked the women if they would go along with them,' reported Justina, 'promising to save all that would go, and threatening all who refused with instant death.'

Two or three of the thirteen women took a faltering step forward. Justina remained in the wagon, distractedly fumbling with an end of the blanket covering her nine children and step-children.

'My husband,' she said, 'urged me to go with them, telling me they would probably not kill me and that I could perhaps, get away in a short time. I refused, preferring to die with him and the children. One of the women who had started off with the Indians turned around, hallooed at me to come with them, and taking a few steps toward me, was shot dead.'[8]

Five other women and two more men were killed at the same time. Frederick, the only man still alive, continued to stand between the oxen. His hands gripped the hames and his eyes flashed from side to side.

In a whisper Justina urged the children to slip from the wagon's back end. Children had already jumped from some of the other wagons. Three Indians ran among them, clubbing with gun butts. Eight of Justina's children and step-children slid unobserved from the wagon and crawled into a thicket.

The ninth, one of Justina's younger daughters, the last to leave the protection of the blanket, was seen. An Indian jumped at her, swinging his gun butt and shouting. Justina saw her daughter die, blood gushing from her mouth.

Another Indian discovered Frederick still alive, and moved up behind him, gun leveled. He fired and Frederick slumped between the oxen.

Many of the children who had been clubbed huddled in a terrified group near one of the buggies. Blood streamed from the faces of most of them. Some writhed in agony, shrieking and sobbing. Others lay still, already dead.

Justina tried to leap to the ground. One of the attackers fired at her. She fell from the wagon box, her back torn by seventeen buckshot pellets.

She lost consciousness and lay on the ground many hours. At night, partly conscious, she heard two Indians return to search the bodies of victims for overlooked valuables. They felt Justina's pulse and concluded she was dead. One of them slashed off her dress with a sharp knife. In doing so he cut a four-inch gash in her abdomen. Then the two moved to the cluster of clubbed children.

'I saw one of these inhuman savages seize Wilhelmina Kitzman, my niece,' said Justina, 'hold her up by her foot, her head downward, her clothes falling over her head. While holding her with one hand, in the other he grasped a knife, with which he cut the flesh around one of the legs, close to the body. Then, by twisting and wrenching, he broke the ligaments and bone, until the limb was entirely severed from the body. The child screamed frantically, "Oh, God! Oh, God!" When the limb was off the child was thrown on the ground, stripped of her clothing, and left to die.'[9]

Of the eight Krieger children who crawled into the woods, one died of starvation. Seven eventually got to Fort Ridgely. They were among the three hundred refugees housed in the stone barracks, awaiting Colonel Sibley's arrival.

Seven other fugitives, most of them under four years of age, did not start for the fort. They remained hidden in the thicket that night. The parents of all seven had been killed or taken captive. In the morning the youngsters took refuge in the Krieger cabin. They were there when Indians came to the cabin, looted it, and set it on fire. All seven died in the flames.

Before morning Justina's mind was almost faded. She was greatly weakened from loss of blood. With no food excepting a few berries and roots, and nearly without clothing, she crawled toward Fort Ridgely for twelve days. Then Captain Hiram Grant's men surrounded her.

A soldier wrapped her in a blanket. Another lined a wagon box with grass and made a bed for her. Grant detached members of the burial party to guard her during the day.

Grant's company continued toward Beaver Creek. They found and buried 'more than eighty' bodies during the day.[10]

Then they turned back in the direction of Fort Ridgely. On the way the wagon in which Justina had spent the day was added to their train.

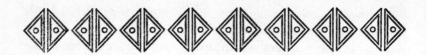

XVII THE CAPTORS WERE ANNOYED

After their major attacks on Ridgely and New Ulm had failed, the lower tribes had to decide whether to abandon their villages.

Scouts reported Sibley at St. Peter with 'two or three miles of soldiers.' Sibley moved slowly, the scouts said, but it seemed impossible he would spend much more than another day reaching Fort Ridgely.

For Little Crow it was a momentous and melancholy decision. His attempt and the efforts of Mankato and Big Eagle to weld the Dakotas into a cohesive force had been futile. With more than four times as many men as the whites, they had not captured Fort Ridgely's wagon-guns.

Shakopee and his outlaw uncle, Red Middle Voice, had done nothing to help win the war they had helped bring about. They and the Rice Creek soldiers' lodge were only killers, undependable as warriors. They had created the revolt that made hundreds of others as guilty as the four Acton murderers. Now they chased around to remote settlements looking for unarmed whites to kill, and kept away from the fighting, pretending it was none of their concern.

Wabasha, Wacouta, and Traveling Hail, opposed to war in the first place, talked only of peace. Big Eagle had not wanted war, either, but now at least helped in the fighting. He was a true Dakota chief, one of the few, it seemed to Little Crow.

Standing Buffalo, Red Iron, and most other Sisseton and

Wahpeton leaders took no part in the war; they tried to keep their young men out of it.[1]

No help had come from Yanktons, Winnebagoes, Chippewas, or the British. Every day it was more certain that none was coming.

Some of the braves boasted the war had been a success, but Little Crow did not think so. It was true, as the braves pointed out, that the Sioux now had dozens of horses, milk cows, oxen, and mules they had not possessed before. It was true that the warriors brought in vast piles of provisions every time they went on a raid. They had taken hundreds of captives and killed many hundreds of whites. Lean Bear was the only chief killed, and Little Crow's injury at Ridgely had proved to be nothing more than a mild concussion. Considering the numbers engaged at the ferry, Ridgely, and New Ulm, relatively few Dakota warriors had died in battle.

But without Ridgely's wagon-guns, Little Crow did not believe the gains of the first week could be held, at least not from the lower villages. At the start there had been talk of withdrawal to Red River, to British America, or across the Missouri; since Ridgely and New Ulm the talk had grown louder. But if the Dakotas fled out of the upper valley the whites would have everything they ever had asked for, and the war's result for the Sioux would be loss of such land as they still had. Before fleeing, the Dakotas might at least try for the kind of settlement the Sauks and Foxes had got out of Black Hawk's war.

Perhaps the villages near Lower Agency needed to be vacated, but at present, at least, there was no reason for flight from the valley. If two or three miles of troops were coming, the lower villages might readily be surrounded. But if the lower bands moved above the Yellow Medicine, or maybe to the prairie opposite the mouth of the Chippewa,[2] they would be able to protect the livestock, provisions, and captives they had taken.

In addition, they would be in an improved position to continue the war. Trails along either side of the river afforded the only way a white army could move against the Dakotas if they went upstream. Very possibly, if white troops tried to follow, there would be opportunities to ambush and destroy them.

As soon as the second battle of New Ulm was lost, the head men of the lower bands gathered in council to discuss withdrawal. The arguments for moving above the Yellow Medicine were convincing. It would be complex and difficult, but no serious opposition to the idea was voiced.

Packing took most of the following day; there were great heaps of plunder to stow on all possible vehicles. But by dawn of the second day processions from each village merged in a great stream of wagons, carts, and buggies which flowed up the south side of the river. Captives, some in wagons and more on foot, were taken along.

To one of the captives it looked as if the moving stream was 'five miles in length and one mile wide.' The procession was composed of 'every kind of vehicle that was ever manufactured. Nice coaches . . . ox carts, chaises, bakers' carts, peddlers' wagons. . . . Sometimes a cow with poles tied to her back, Indian-style.'

The Dakotas wore 'all kinds of finery, the more ridiculous the better . . . women's bonnets, considered great ornaments, were worn by men altogether. White crepe shawls were wound around their black heads; gold watches were tied around their ankles, the watches clattering as they rode. The squaws were dressed in silk gowns, with earrings and breastpins taken from the whites. . . . It was hard to keep from smiling to see how they were used by these poor savage creatures; they looked more like a troop of monkeys than anything human.' [3]

From the train came a confused and deafening medley of sounds, with 'mules braying, cows lowing, horses neighing, dogs barking and yelping as they were trodden upon, children crying, kittens mewing, . . . and musical instruments accompanied by the Indians singing the everlasting Hi! Hi!'

Warriors rode on both sides of the cavalcade to keep captives from escaping. Long lines of cattle were driven ahead of each band. Scores of children raced excitedly from one segment of the caravan to another.[4]

At Rice Creek, upstream from Redwood River and halfway between the lowest villages and the Yellow Medicine, the procession halted for the night. Some of its units remained there several days; most of them went the next day beyond the Yellow Medicine, some as far as the Chippewa River.

Red Iron, cold-faced and grim, met the arrivals at the Yellow Medicine, determined to prevent any effort to force the upper bands into the war.[5]

The Wahpetons and Sissetons, Little Crow was told, had formed a soldiers' lodge of their own. He must put his tepees where he was told, and in no other place. If he tried to escape over Sisseton land when the white men came, Standing Buffalo's men would kill him.

Under the direction of Red Iron's men, most of the new encampments near the Yellow Medicine were placed between the villages of Cloudman and Akipa, two of the Christian chiefs. Those opposite the mouth of the Chippewa were downstream from Red Iron's village, where any attempt to flee over the Sisseton part of the reservation would be reported at once to Standing Buffalo.

Little Crow was far from a prisoner. He could not go upriver over Sisseton lands, but was free to move north, south, or downstream any time he saw fit.

As soon as the new villages had been established, Little Crow led one hundred and fifty Lower band warriors north over the Minnesota and headed for the Big Woods.[6] There, according to plan, they would intercept reinforcements trying to reach Fort Ridgely from the northeast. While they were in the vicinity they would undertake raids on Forest City and Hutchinson.

Some of the warriors rode ponies. Others walked. Little Crow made the trip by wagon. Joe Campbell, half-breed prisoner, drove the chief's team.

Joe could read and write; Little Crow could not. Consequently, Campbell was to serve as the chief's private secretary as well as his driver. Bucketing across the prairie in the wagon, Little Crow told Joe what he wanted him to write.[7]

Regardless of what the young men said, Little Crow was convinced the war was going badly.

True, there had been a quick and satisfying victory at Redwood Ferry, but the success had been due to surprise. Now that the whites knew the Dakotas were on the warpath, surprise would never again be as easy.

Against one success there had been four failures, the two attacks on the fort and the two on New Ulm.

All four failures were the result of the young braves' being more interested in robbery, rape, and murder than in fighting. This was the one most important reason why the future of the war did not look bright. It was the reason, Little Crow felt, that Fort Ridgely was not now held by Dakotas.

To be sure, raiders had been successful in attacks on settlers. But most of those attacks were against unarmed farmers who did not even try to resist or escape. The attacks were not tests of skill or courage; they were unworthy of Dakota warriors.

It was true that one of the objectives of the war was to drive whites from the valley. Thousands had fled, the scouts reported, since the first attacks. But the Dakotas, by themselves, could not keep the valley clear of whites very long.

Except for Little Priest and a dozen Winnebago warriors at Redwood Agency when the attack started, no help whatever had come from that band.

Even worse, comparatively few Upper Indians had joined

the war. Many Sissetons and Wahpetons had gone with the Yanktonais on their summer buffalo hunt. They at least had a little excuse. But there was no excuse whatever for hundreds of warriors in the villages of Red Iron, Standing Buffalo, and others, who refused to have anything to do with the war.

Everybody seemed to be waiting for the Lower Indians to prove the whites could be beaten. Nobody thought the Fort Ridgely and New Ulm performances were impressive. Clearly, there would not be a general uprising, with Little Crow its leader.

By now everyone knew hundreds of soldiers were on the way up the valley. Now it was too late to hope for allies of any importance.

Dejectedly, Little Crow dictated a note to Joe Campbell. He told Joe to make two copies, one addressed to Governor Ramsey and one to Sibley.

The note requested a cessation of hostilities and a treaty of settlement.[8] Maybe the whites would offer terms the Dakotas could not turn down.

When the letter was written Little Crow asked Joe to read it aloud to the warriors.

It provoked such violent objections and derisive hooting that both copies of the note had to be destroyed.

With them were destroyed much of Little Crow's prestige and most of his authority over the hundred and fifty braves.

This became apparent the following morning. Tumultuous disagreement broke out among the warriors, and the chief could do nothing to quell it. More than one hundred of his men flatly refused to go to the Big Woods.

Hutchinson and Forest City were nearer, and could be plundered with ease. The whites were cowards and would not put up much of a fight. Besides, many settlers had fled, leaving much unprotected loot in their cabins and sheds.

Little Crow argued that the expedition's first job was to cut

off reinforcements trying to reach Ridgely through the Big
Woods. Hutchinson and Forest City could be picked off on
the way home.

Few even listened to the chief's argument. More than two-
thirds of his command withdrew from his leadership. Walker
Among Sacred Stones was chosen head of the mutinous
faction.[9]

This left Little Crow with only thirty-seven men, far short
of the number required for a successful Big Woods operation.
He turned over command of the remnant to his half-brother,
White Spider.

Separation of the two groups lasted overnight, with the
factions camping several miles apart.

Also camped in the neighborhood were seventy-five white
soldiers commanded by Captain Richard Strout.

Early Wednesday morning White Spider's braves, and sixty
mounted warriors under Walker Among Sacred Stones, closed
in on Strout's command two miles south of the late Robinson
Jones's 'public house' at Acton.

Strout's men, outnumbered and mostly without horses,
fought through White Spider's line. Pursued by the warriors
of White Spider and Walker Among Sacred Stones, they
reached Hutchinson by mid-afternoon.[10]

Five whites were killed or mortally wounded and seventeen
others were injured. One Indian was killed and three were
hurt. The Battle of Acton could be considered an Indian
victory, but not one for which Little Crow could take credit.
He had fought, not as a chief, but as a private in White
Spider's ranks.

The reunited Indian forces went into camp near Cedar
Mills, northwest of Hutchinson. There they divided into two
segments, one group to attack Forest City and the other to
raid Hutchinson. By now Little Crow had given up hope for
an excursion to the Big Woods. He joined the Hutchinson
party, but not as its leader.

Stockades had been built at both settlements since the start of the massacre. Most inhabitants sought protection in the stockades at night. This saved lives, but simplified looting and destruction of property.

Settlers who had failed to take refuge in the stockades fared badly when the attack parties fanned out from Cedar Mills.

Near Forest City braves led by Sacred Rattle raided the cabin of Jack Adams. After murdering Adams, the attackers took his wife and baby boy captive. The boy annoyed his captors by crying. Sacred Rattle grabbed the baby's feet and dashed his brains out against a rock.[11]

At Forest City the attack started about three o'clock in the morning. Part of the attacking band rode into the center of town, whooping loudly and shooting. This served to keep everyone inside the stockade. The rest of the band pillaged and set fire to five buildings.

Events at Hutchinson followed a similar pattern. The chief difference was that more buildings were destroyed and more spoils obtained. Over twenty houses were looted and burned. Hutchinson Academy, pride of the frontier, was demolished.

Hundreds of horses, oxen, and wagons were taken from the two towns. All were needed to transport booty to the encampments above the Yellow Medicine. Atop one of the wagons rode Little Crow. Near the Yellow Medicine camp, a messenger met him with a letter from Henry Hastings Sibley. Scouts had found and brought it in. The chief asked Joe to read it.

'If Little Crow has any proposition to make,' read Campbell, 'let him send a half-breed to me, and he shall be protected in and out of camp.'[12]

Little Crow thoughtfully stared at the note, pretending to read it. Then he chuckled mirthlessly. Sibley seemed to think Little Crow could make any decisions and offer whatever propositions he chose to. Probably he blamed Little Crow for all that had happened. Possibly he would not be satisfied until he had killed him. In a way, he was right, but war was not a one-man decision, and neither was peace, as the hooting braves had reminded Little Crow four days before.

At least the letter invited a proposition for peace, and should be answered. This time the braves could not hoot at Little Crow; the suggestion for a settlement had come from the whites. Wabasha, Mankato, Big Eagle, Traveling Hail, and the rest would have a voice in the answer.

XVIII   MY MOTHER'S PEOPLE

Soon after Little Crow had led his warriors north of the river toward the Big Woods, scouts reached Yellow Medicine with word that New Ulm was evacuated and almost unguarded. This, it seemed to the braves on the south side, meant a chance for great gain at little risk.

Gray Bird, Little Crow's head soldier, met with Mankato, Big Eagle, and the rest to consider what might be done. The strategy they developed was simple. It dovetailed nicely with Little Crow's excursion and would supplement his activities.

Not counting any casual help Shakopee and Red Middle Voice might contribute, three hundred and fifty braves remained south of the river. They would go to New Ulm, load up with loot, and cross the river below Fort Ridgely.[1] There they would cut off reinforcements approaching Sibley from the southeast, while Little Crow blocked any help trying to get to the fort from the northeast.

Having made a plan, the chiefs decided to execute it at once. Their braves moved south to the prairie, turned east, and tramped down-river toward New Ulm. Ahead of the main body, through the wooded fringe of the bluffs, moved keen-eyed young scouts. Behind the troops, to cook for the warriors, followed a party of squaws.

As they neared their former home locality, one of the scouting parties detoured for a look at the recently abandoned villages. There they found evidence that the area had been visited earlier in the day by whites.

The Sioux scouts moved higher on the bluffs, hoping to get a broad view of the valley. Standing motionless near the top, they saw a sight which sent some of the scouts running to summon the chiefs. High on the northern bluffs, outlined in the light of the late afternoon sun and clearly visible to the watchers on the river's south rim, crawled a party of troops and wagons. The column moved slowly in the direction of Fort Ridgely.

The troops and wagons were Captain Hiram Grant's, homeward bound from Beaver Creek. Captain Grant was regretting that it was too late to return all the way to the fort. The burial party would be expected back that night, but the fort was probably three or four hours away. Grant had begun to look for a camp-site offering wood and water.[2]

The nearest good site was at the head of the gulch known as Birch Coulee. Leading from the prairie to the river bottoms, the coulee was thirteen miles from the fort. It was about six miles from the point at which the party had added the wagon in which Justina Krieger lay on her bed of grass.

Birch Coulee was almost directly across the river from the ruins of the Lower Agency. It was here that Captain Joseph Anderson's rangers had parted from Grant's troops earlier in the day to start their explorations south of the river. If they had not already returned, they could be intercepted here and invited to share the camp-site.

Captain Grant selected for his camp a flat space on the prairie, a short distance from the head of the ravine. A clear stream of cold water flowed through the coulee. The ravine's timber would provide convenient firewood.

West of the camp-site and a little above it was a grassy meadow. To the north stretched miles of open country. Near the north edge of the site was a low 'roll' in the prairie. At the south edge were trees.

Grant's men arranged the wagons, end to end in the form of a horseshoe, to surround the tents. Then they stretched ropes from wagon to wagon on which to picket the horses. Since nobody knew whether Captain Anderson's rangers were still south of the river, and, if they were, whether they would want to stay or proceed to Ridgely, enough room was allowed on the picket ropes to accommodate their horses, just in case.

Captain Anderson and his rangers rode up while Grant's men were placing the wagons. They quickly accepted the invitation to share the camp-site. With them were Joseph Brown, Agent Galbraith, Joseph DeCamp, and others who had come along to seek missing relatives.

Several of the citizen soldiers, including Nathan Myrick, who had found the corpse of his brother during the day, had decided against riding to the top of the coulee and were already on the way to the fort.

Anderson reported that his rangers had found and buried two dozen bodies at Lower Agency. Some of the men had climbed the south bluffs to inspect the Indian villages. They found the houses and tepees entirely vacant. Joseph Brown and other veterans of the Indian country had gone up-river beyond the mouth of the Redwood. They had seen no current sign of Indians in any part of the area, and theorized that the Sioux had gone far west to the James River in Dakota Territory.[3]

Brown viewed Grant's camp-site without enthusiasm. It was a little near the timber, he thought, and he did not like the roll north of the camp. If there were any Indians within thirty miles, that hump in the prairie would give them perfect cover for an attack on the camp.

Captain Grant knew Joe Brown had lived in Sioux country most of his life and was an Indian scout of renown. If Joe had been more emphatic in his objections, the captain would have asked him to suggest a safer site.

But Brown's explorations of the Redwood area had convinced him that few Indians remained below the Yellow Medicine. He had been among those who had visited the empty villages and estimated they had been vacated four days before. Anderson's and Grant's men had been riding horses or wielding spades and picks all day and were tired and hungry.[4] All things considered, the captain's choice of a camp-site did not seem bad enough to call for a big disturbance and selection of a different place.

Anderson's men fastened their horses to the lines between the wagons. Captain Grant established ten picket posts at equal intervals around the camp. Since there were ten posts, each could be safely distant from the tents. Each was manned by three soldiers, so thirty would always be on guard.

Soon everyone had eaten and all but the men on picket duty had fallen asleep, some in tents and some beneath the wagons.

On the southern bluffs the Indian chiefs summoned by the advance party had come to see for themselves. Quickly they sent scouts to learn all they could about the camp that was taking form near the upper end of Birch Coulee. Then they smoked quietly, and waited for the scouts to return.

After dark the scouts came back with information that at least one company had camped at the head of the coulee. They estimated that seventy-five men were in the camp,[5] and described the location as perfect for a surprise attack.

Big Eagle, Mankato, and Gray Bird sent two hundred warriors across the valley to surround the camp, and kept the other hundred and fifty south of the river.

An hour before sunrise one of the pickets thought he detected a movement in the grass. He eyed the spot carefully. It was nearly the end of his watch. He wondered whether the long vigil had made him spooky.

Again the grass stirred. This time there was unmistakably a movement. The sentry thought it might be caused by a wolf or possibly by one of the dogs or wild hogs he had seen near the camp at dusk. Since it was four o'clock, everyone would be rolling out in a short while, anyway. There could be little harm in firing.

The picket fired, and heard the ball whine sharply across the prairie. An Indian's head appeared. Then another, and then two more. Two other guards fired, one merely because he thought it would be amusing to give the men a scare. Now the whole camp was awake.

It had not been part of the attack plan to arouse the sleeping camp with a roar of gunfire. The Indians snaking near the sentry posts carried no guns. Armed only with bows and arrows, they expected to kill the pickets quietly, without alerting anyone else. Then a second line of attackers would close in with guns, shooting sleep-dazed soldiers emerging from the tents. A rush from all sides would finish off any survivors.

Three shots from the picket posts, though, were enough to rouse the camp. In each tent fifteen or twenty hands grabbed guns. From beneath the wagons crawled scores of others, awake and armed.

'Come on boys, don't be afraid!' shouted Sergeant Bob Baxter in the tent where Ezmon Earle had been sleeping. He started for the entrance. As he groped in the faint light for the entry flap a bullet cracked through the canvas.

'My God, boys, I'm shot!' cried Baxter. With a bullet through his chest, the 'big, noble fellow' crumpled to the ground, dead, knocking Ezmon down as he fell.[6]

By now Dakotas with muskets and rifles had swarmed near all sides of the camp-site, stridently whooping 'Ho-Ho! Ho-Ho-Ho!' Since the plan of attack had miscarried, they made their rush immediately, before the soldiers were wider awake.

For a moment all was confusion. Guns roared on every side, some in the camp and some in the area surrounding it.

Wounded cried out in surprise and pain. From the half-light came the shrill yells of the attackers. On the ropes between the wagons terrified horses plunged and snorted. Every officer in the camp-site shouted at once; there was no mistaking the urgency and excitement in their voices, but it was hard to hear what they said.

'Fall down!' shouted one. To dozens emerging from tents
and crawling from underneath wagons it sounded as though
he had ordered 'Fall in!' Many of those springing to obey died
at once.

'Lie low!' cried another. 'Hug the ground! Take good aim
before you shoot!' [7]

'Get behind the wagons!' yelled Captain Grant. 'Turn them
over!'

Darting from wagon to wagon, half a dozen started to do
so. They came to the wagon holding Justina Krieger.

'Not that one!' cried a soldier. 'There's a sick woman inside.'[8] Justina's wagon was the only one to remain upright.

In the first few moments, long before full daylight, twenty-
two men lay dead or mortally wounded. Sixty more were
wounded seriously but not fatally. Most of the remainder also
had wounds, many of them painful but not crippling or deadly. Eighty-five of the eighty-seven horses on the picket lines
were dead.

The survivors hurdled into the horseshoe of overturned
wagons, or crawled behind dead horses. From here they shot
steadily and accurately enough to force the attackers back a
little.

Inside the horseshoe were a few shovels the burial details
had carried. Tough prairie sod was not easy for a man hugging
the ground to cut, but the shovels and a few pocket knives
helped loosen it. Then, by jabbing with bayonets, scooping
with mess kits, or clawing with bare hands, some of the
survivors surrounded themselves with low mounds of earth,
or burrowed into the ground. Others, crouching behind the
wagons, dug a trench long enough for part of one company.
To both sides of it, darting in the shelter of the overturned
wagons, they dragged bodies of horses, corpses of comrades,
saddles, boards, and rocks for meager breastworks.[9]

From the trees at the south, the low ridge on the northern

edge, the grass on the east, and the slightly elevated area west of the camp-site, came a steady barrage of gunfire. Indians by the score lay on the far side of the roll in the prairie. Dozens of others squatted in the grass, just out of range, sliding ahead whenever they wanted to shoot.

During the first rush, even before he got out of his tent, Bob Boyd's face was struck by a charge. Another pierced his right thigh. A bullet entered the front of his right shoulder, passed through the shoulder blade, and lodged at the rear in a mass of bone fragments. Unable to crawl to a sturdier shelter, Bob remained in the tent.

He was joined by Henry Rolleau, a wounded half-breed.

'Where are you hit?' wheezed Bob.

'In my eye. I'll have to die. I never thought my mother's people would kill me. Are you hurt bad?'

'Oh, a little,' said Bob.

Another bullet tore through Henry's hand.

'It was,' declared Boyd, 'the most terrible sound I have ever heard.' [10]

Henry began to cry like a child, but gradually sank into a coma.

From the start the attackers realized they were up against more than seventy-five soldiers. When the defenders behind wagons and horses forced the first line of Dakotas to fall back, one of the marksmen left the group in the trees at the coulee's head. He raced across the valley to get reinforcements. The one hundred and fifty braves on the south side started at once for the coulee. Behind them, carrying pots and kettles, trailed the squaws.

With more than half the whites dead or seriously wounded, and with only two Dakotas killed during the opening attack, the sixty-five or seventy defenders still able to shoot were outnumbered five to one when the enemy's reinforcements arrived.

The whites were solidly surrounded. There was no chance

to send a messenger to Fort Ridgely for help. At one point
Corporal James Auge, French half-breed and head interpreter,
offered, if a horse were provided, to dash through the lines
in an effort to reach the fort. Of the two horses remaining
alive only one could possibly have made the trip, but this
horse was shot before Auge could mount him.

'The attempt would have meant certain death, anyway,'
reflected Private Boyd.

A stifling cloud of battle smoke, trapped in the dead air
between the trees and the high ground on two sides of the
camp-site, hovered over the survivors. There was only one
small bucket of water inside the horseshoe, and no way to get
more. The dying and wounded moaned for relief from thirst.
From hand to hand passed the bucket, with word that each
man might have one swallow.

One head of cabbage was all the food inside the ring of
wagons and dead horses. All other provisions were in a wagon
left on the prairie, which no man could hope to reach alive.

'A small piece of cabbage leaf was all I had,' said Ezmon
Earle. 'It was delicious.'

Thirst and hunger did not bother the attackers. To them
the affair took on some of the aspects of a picnic.

Whenever a warrior became thirsty he crawled through
the grass to the trees at the top of the coulee.[11] Then he arose
and walked to a place where the ravine's stream ran deep
and cold.

In the coulee the squaws set up an outdoor kitchen. Here
they served roasted corn and broiled beef to warriors who got
hungry.

If he was fatigued or sleepy, a brave could take a nap on
a bed of moss in the ravine, confident that nearly three hundred and fifty warriors could keep less than seventy whites
securely trapped.

During the afternoon some of the survivors thought they
heard artillery east of the coulee. For a while there was hope

that a relief party might be approaching. No more sounds of shelling were heard, however. Nightfall came, but no relief had arrived.

After dark the weapons of the dead or severely wounded were distributed among the combatants. Now each defender had two guns, but his ammunition was nearly gone. Only men guarding vital approaches were permitted to fire. When night came the attacking barrage diminished, but 'fitful firing continued all night.'

An Indian bearing a white flag approached at sunrise. He carried no gun, and stood within a few yards of the survivors, waving his flag.

'Find out what he wants, Jim,' called Captain Grant.

Corporal Auge, the half-breed interpreter, barked a few questions in guttural Sioux. Squinting watchfully and shifting the white banner from hand to hand, the caller made a long, arm-waving reply.

'He says,' translated Jim Auge, 'the Indians were reinforced during the night, with many Sissetons and Wahpetons coming to join them. He says there are now as many Indians as there are leaves on the trees. They are going to charge, he says. They will take no prisoners. They will kill everybody; but if the half-breeds do not shoot during the charge they will not be killed.' [12]

In Grant's company were nine others, in addition to Jim, 'with some Indian blood.' Many had acquaintances among the attackers. During the previous day they had been targets of special jeers, taunts, and threats from the foes.

'What do you men say?' asked Grant. 'Do you trust them?'

A brief, tense discussion in Sioux followed among the half-breeds. Presently Jim spoke again.

'I will tell him the half-breeds are just like white men. We all came here to fight side-by-side,' called Jim. 'I will ask him why they stay so far away if they think they can whip us. If they are so brave, let them charge.'

'That is good,' Captain Grant called. 'Ask him, if there are as many Indians as there are leaves on the trees, why they wait. If there are so many, why do they want to keep the half-breeds from shooting?' [13]

Jim delivered the message in Sioux, his voice heavy with sarcasm.

The caller shrugged slightly, raised the pole from which the white flag fluttered, wheeled around, and stalked into the trees.

All the camp-site's defenders, half-breed and white, knew that not enough ammunition remained to fight off a charge if one came.

Even if there was no rush by the enemy, few of the badly wounded could survive a second day. After another day without water, food, or sleep, many of the remaining combatants would be too weak to continue fighting.

Only a strong party from Ridgely could drive the attackers away. Had the sounds of yesterday's battles carried the thirteen miles to the fort? If the men at the fort heard the firing, why hadn't they come?

XIX REMEMBER BIRCH COULEE!

Almost as soon as the Battle of Birch Coulee began the shooting was heard at Fort Ridgely. Listeners concluded Captain Grant's expeditionary force was in trouble.

A detachment set out to provide relief but 'soon returned because, after they had gone a short distance, they could hear nothing.' Until the first relief party ceased to hear anything, reverberations caused by the hills led its members to believe the conflict was within eight miles of the fort.[1]

On Ridgely's hilltops soldiers continued to hear firing. Doubters went to listen and returned convinced. The rumble of gunfire was muffled by distance, but nobody who heard it doubted what it was. If a man put his ear to a bare spot on the ground, the sound seemed to come more clearly.

The sustained shooting indicated that much more than a skirmish with a scouting party was going on.

As far as anyone knew, Captain Grant may have found thousands of Sioux warriors in the Redwood area. Even a few hundred could be more than a match for one hundred and fifty whites with little or no experience in fighting Indians. Even a handful of enemies could do a tremendous amount of damage if they caught the soldiers scattered in small burial parties.

When the men left two days before, they had intended to be away only one night. Why hadn't they returned? Why did the firing sound so clear and yet so distant? Why was nothing being done?

For all anyone knew, the men might be out in the open, cut off from cover. The persistent shooting might mean the Indians were wiping them out.

More reinforcements had arrived at the fort. Nearly fifteen hundred men were camped near it. If Grant was in trouble, there were plenty of men to go to his aid. The troops were restless. Many criticized Sibley. Some made remarks bordering on insubordination. If he knew so much about fighting the Sioux, let him prove it.

Colonel Sibley agreed to ride to a nearby hilltop to listen. Two of his officers, William Crooks and Samuel McPhail, accompanied him. The three dismounted and stood away from their horses.

The sound of gunfire was faint, but unmistakable. It was puzzling that the members of the first relief party had been unable to hear it when they got a few rods from the fort.

Sam McPhail advanced a theory. He recalled that the relief party had gone into the valley. If the shooting was on the prairie above, the sound might be dimmed by the hills.

The officers agreed that the sound seemed to come from the direction of the agency and from the fort side of the valley.

Sibley directed McPhail to order out fifty mounted rangers and three companies of infantry and 'proceed to the relief of Captain Grant's command.' [2]

Crooks suggested a howitzer or two might join the operations.

If Tim Sheehan, Tom Gere, or John Jones had been assigned to lead the second rescue party, they might have found and relieved the survivors before noon, within eight hours of the start of the attack.

Sam McPhail, who had learned about Indian fighting from Colonel Sibley, did not.

It was nearly noon before the second rescue party got away. They swung out on the prairie northwest of the fort. Here the sounds of the conflict became increasingly clear. This confirmed the supposition that the battle was on the north side of the river.

Three miles from Ridgely the infantry and two teams, one wheeling a six-pounder and the other a howitzer, caught up with McPhail's horsemen. There were now more than two hundred men and two wagon-guns in the column.[3]

After being joined by the infantry, the rescue party proceeded seven miles toward the sound of the firing. This brought the column within three miles of the coulee. Then there was an interruption.

'A large force of Indians made their appearance,' said McPhail.[4]

It was now the latter part of the afternoon. The survivors at the coulee had been under attack twelve hours. McPhail ordered his column to halt.

'By this time,' reported Colonel McPhail, 'the enemy had almost completely surrounded my command. As it was impossible to ascertain the location of Captain Grant's command, I did not deem it prudent to advance further, and ordered the column to retire to a commanding position, where we corralled and awaited reinforcements.'

That was Sam McPhail's interpretation of events. The Indian version differed.

According to Big Eagle's account, when Sioux scouts reported a large body of reinforcements coming from Fort Ridgely Mankato borrowed fifty warriors from the coulee.

'He scattered them out,' said Big Eagle, 'and they all yelled and made such a noise the whites must have thought there were a great many more.'[5]

If the Indians ever actually surrounded McPhail's command, they did not stay long. McPhail's men fired two or three artillery shots. These were the shots which gave temporary hope to the men trapped at the coulee.

'When the Indians returned to the coulee they were laughing at the way they had deceived the white men, and we were all glad the whites had not pushed forward and driven us away,' gloated Big Eagle.

From the 'commanding position' to which he had retired, the prudent McPhail sent two messengers to Fort Ridgely appealing for help.

The third relief party left the fort during the evening with the dual assignment of rescuing McPhail's column and Captain Grant's command.

This party consisted of over a thousand men. Like McPhail's relief party, they wheeled two wagon-guns along. Only enough men were retained at Ridgely to hold the fort against attack. The rescuers reached McPhail, who was camped three miles from the coulee, about midnight.

By that time the surrounded men at the coulee had been under attack twenty hours. Two more of the wounded had died. The living were thirsty, hungry, and nearly dead with fatigue. Half the living were faint from loss of blood and moaning with agonizing wounds.

At daybreak Sioux scouts reported that 'three miles of troops'[6] had merged with McPhail's column and were heading for the coulee.

They were only three miles away, but it took them eight hours, 'from three o'clock until eleven, to make the three miles.' [7]

The rescuers arrived thirty-one hours after Captain Grant's party had first been attacked, and twenty-eight hours from the time that battle sounds were first heard at Ridgely. From the fort to the coulee it was 'an easy march in five hours.' Compared to the forty-two miles Lieutenant Sheehan's company made overnight when told about the Indian raids, the Birch Coulee rescue was not impressive. It did nothing to enhance Sibley's reputation as an Indian fighter.

As the three miles of troops and four wagon-guns approached the coulee, 'the Sioux, perceiving themselves outnumbered, delivered some harmless parting shots into the camp and disappeared at about eleven o'clock. No pursuit was attempted.' [8]

Two dozen lay dead or mortally wounded at the coulee. Between fifty and sixty more had disabling wounds. Nearly all the others were somewhat injured.

Eighty-seven horses were dead. Their carcasses, and the bodies of soldiers which had served as breastworks, had been punctured repeatedly by bullets.[9] From them a heavy stench hung in the air. Surrounding the survivors were the overturned wagons, the sides and floors of their boxes ripped to splinters by gunfire.

From behind and between the shattered wagons and bloated carcasses crawled pallid, blood-streaked men. Some croaked feeble cheers when the relief party arrived. Most of them were coated with a thick crust of caked dust. Many found they could not stand upright and sank to the ground before they had emerged. Some faced away and vomited uncontrollably. Others staggered, fell, and needed help to crawl to the buckets of water the rescuers had brought from the ravine.

Among the dead was S. R. Henderson. His body was found 'between our lines and where the Indians had been. Whether he had been killed by soldiers or Indians we couldn't tell.' [10]

Joseph DeCamp, Redwood sawmill operator, who had accompanied Captain Anderson seeking news of his family, was among the critically injured.[11]

Major Joseph R. Brown, former Sioux agent, who had been in the party of worried searchers, had also been wounded, but not critically.

A single wagon stood upright among the shattered ruins of the barricade, its sides scarred, slashed, and pitted by scores of bullets. Two or three rescuers peered inside.

'They seemed perfectly astonished on finding me alive,' said Justina Kreiger. 'The blanket on which I lay wrapped in the wagon was found to have received over two hundred bullet holes during the fight.' [12]

Justina was as resilient after Birch Coulee as she had been fortunate during the battle.

Her second husband's death at Sacred Heart Creek had left the twenty-eight-year-old widow with seven children and step-children, most of them under ten years of age.

She was taken to St. Paul, and there met John Jacob Meyer, a settler whose wife and children had been killed by the Dakotas. 'On the relation of our mutual sufferings we soon became attached to each other,' said Justina. Two months after the battle of Birch Coulee she became Mrs. John Jacob Meyer.

Joseph DeCamp, with all other seriously injured survivors, was taken to Fort Ridgely for hospitalization. There, two days later, he died. At his bedside was the Reverend Joshua Sweet, chaplain of the garrison.

DeCamp's wife, Jannette, and the three young sons had been taken above Yellow Medicine as captives. Here they aroused the sympathy of the mother of Lorenzo Lawrence, a Christian Indian. The mother persuaded her son, at great risk to everyone, to take the DeCamps down-river.

At Fort Ridgely Mrs. DeCamp met the Reverend Joshua Sweet and inquired for her husband.

'I buried him ten days ago,' said the Reverend Mr. Sweet, bursting into tears.

Jannette remained at the fort long enough to give birth to another son. Then she and her four boys went to Mrs. De-Camp's family home in the south, where they stayed during the remainder of the Civil War.

Four years later they returned to Fort Ridgely, Jannette as the wife of the Reverend Joshua Sweet.[13]

Described as 'one of the most desperate Indian encounters ever to occur on the American continent,' [14] the Battle of Birch

Coulee was not an auspicious start for Colonel Henry Hastings Sibley's war of the races. During a whole subsequent generation of warfare with the Plains Tribes, 'Remember Birch Coulee!' was to be a watchword whenever anyone in Indian country was tempted to pick a camp-site which was not in protected ground.[15]

Colonel Sibley decided against taking responsibility for the disaster. In his military reports and in press dispatches he started to refer to the encounter as the 'attack on J. R. Brown's party.'

Captain Hiram Grant, as all military leaders were expected to do, wrote a report on the expedition. 'It was handed back to me,' said Grant, 'and I was cooly informed that I should make my report to Major Joseph R. Brown, who was in command of the expedition. This was the first I had heard of it. We had been gone four days, two of which we had been engaged in deadly fight; no order had been given me by Major Brown, not an intimation that he considered himself in command. To say that I was angry, when told to make my report to him, would only express half what I felt. I then and there destroyed my report.' [16]

Outraged by what seemed to be an attempt to tamper with fact, Captain Grant charged that a meeting had been held immediately after the battle 'at which it was agreed to make it appear Major Brown was in command at Birch Coulee.'

Unlike Hiram Grant, Joseph Brown was not at the time commissioned as a militia officer. He had long been associated with Sibley in American Fur Company activities. He did not outrank Grant, and was called 'Major' only because he had been an Indian agent. He did not start using the title in a military sense until two months later.

'If any blame rests on anyone for selection of camps or in carrying out any details of the expedition, it rests upon me. I had the full charge,' declared Grant.

Efforts to minimize the Birch Coulee calamity by attributing it to unfortunate civilian bungling were no more successful than the event itself had been.

Timothy Sheehan testified that he had heard Sibley order his second in command, Colonel William Crooks, to place Grant in charge of the expedition. Crooks stated he had done so. McPhail's report referred to the men trapped at the coulee as 'Captain Grant's command.' Such participants as Bob Boyd and Ezmon Earle consistently described events in terms of orders issued by Grant. Neither they nor other survivors indicated that Brown had been in command. Any credit to be derived from the Birch Coulee engagement clearly belonged to the willing captain and his reluctant commanding officer.[17]

XX I HAVE DONE THIS MYSELF

Urgent questions, hard to answer, confronted the
Dakotas when they reassembled in the camps above the Yellow Medicine.

What should be the reply to Sibley's letter? Should the
captives be killed, surrendered, or taken away as hostages?
Should the Sioux flee? If so, where should they go? If the
braves killed Little Crow, would the whites think this was
adequate atonement for all that had happened? Would this
action save the lives of hundreds of others?

A series of turbulent councils began when the warriors
came back from Forest City, Hutchinson, and Birch Coulee.
Many factions were present; all demanded to be heard. Complex differences of opinion were expressed. [1]

Present in the councils were partisans of war, advocates of
peace, soldiers' lodge spokesmen, a Christian bloc, a combination of traditionalists and conservatives, Lower Indians, Upper
tribesmen—some clamoring for instantaneous flight, and
others denouncing all talk of departure, one faction urging
immediate surrender of the captives, and another demanding
the prisoners be killed at once.

Composition of the factions was fluid; it followed no static
geographic, or other, pattern. Little Crow, Mazzawamnuna,
and Rdainyanka, son-in-law of Wabasha, were Lower Sioux
who fought any suggestion of peace. Shakopee and Red
Middle Voice, authors of the war, sent warriors to the councils

but did not attend them. Wabasha, Wacouta, and Traveling Hail, also Lower Indians, were articulate exponents of a truce.

Of the Upper Sioux, Red Iron and Standing Buffalo opposed continuation of the conflict on military and economic grounds; the Christian chiefs argued against it for moral reasons; and Strike the Pawnee, son of White Lodge, was an ardent War Party leader.

Threats against Little Crow's life did not actually develop, but the chief had no part in the Birch Coulee triumph. His braves had refused to follow him to the Big Woods, and much of his prestige had vanished. Conservatives and soldiers' lodge members alike blamed him for the plight of the Dakotas. He was despised as a giver of bad advice. He did not seem the logical negotiator of the truce that Sibley appeared willing to consider; but Sibley had addressed his note to Little Crow and would expect an answer to come from him.

No proposition for peace or a truce, but a list of grievances and complaints was the answer to Sibley's letter. The answer came from Little Crow, but was a compromise devised by a council. It was calculated by some to gain sympathy and clemency, intended by others to sound defiant and unremorseful, and designed to fix responsibility on Little Crow. Every faction had a different idea of what the message should contain, and every faction had its way.

'For what reason we have commenced this war I will tell you,' the letter to Sibley said. 'It is on account of Major Galbraith. We made a treaty with the government, and beg for what we get, and can't get that till our children are dying with hunger. It is the traders who have commenced it. Myrick told the Indians they could eat grass or dung. Forbes told the Lower Sioux they were not men. Roberts was working with his friends to defraud us out of our money. If the young braves have pushed the white man, I have done this myself. I have a great many prisoners, women and children.'[2]

Sibley now had 1619 men, more than twice as many as the

Indians could muster, but continued to stay at Fort Ridgely. His failure to advance provided time for numerous Dakota councils and for the exchange of more letters. To the women in captivity the delay was terrifying.

Emissaries from the councils or from the soldiers' lodge circulated through the villages daily or more often, crying the news.

'White women to be killed now very soon; they eat too much. We are going away and they cannot travel; they had better die at once,' the criers would call.[3]

Once, especially, 'there was great alarm, for the Indians said they would kill all the half-breeds and prisoners. When I heard this I dropped as one struck by apoplexy. I could not speak for a while. My teeth chattered and I shivered with fear,'[4] said Mrs. Wakefield.

To the Indians, Sibley's failure to advance was both incredible and amusing. 'The Indians made much sport of the slow movements of Sibley. They said the white people did not care much about their wives and children or they would have hurried on faster.'[5]

Accusations and denunciations filled the councils. Little Crow, often denounced, finally told of the letter his warriors north of the river had not allowed him to send, and explained his position.

The war, he thought, was not going well. No allies were coming to help the Dakotas. He thought the Indians should see what peace terms the whites were willing to offer.

Mankato, Big Eagle, and many others grunted agreement, but a young sub-chief of Mankato's band leaped to his feet. Birch Coulee, he declared, had changed everything. Now the Dakotas could win without any help from anyone.

'Childish talk!' snapped an older chief. 'You know better! Birch Coulee was a glorious victory, but it changed nothing. The whites have miles of soldiers and wagon-guns. There is no way the Dakotas can win. When Little Crow talks about peace terms, he should remember this is not like Black Hawk's war. The whites can win, and they know it. They will not offer a new treaty and pay for our lands a second time. They will not treat Little Crow as they treated Black Hawk. It is time to stop talking like children and start acting like men.' [6]

Rdainyanka arose and faced the council. 'I am for continuing the war,' he said with sad deliberation. 'I have no confidence the whites will stand by any agreement they may make. Ever since we have treated with them their agents and traders have robbed and cheated us. We may regret what has happened, but the matter has gone too far to be remedied. We have got to die. Let us, then, first kill as many whites as possible.' [7]

During the second week of September an answer to Little Crow's note came from Colonel Sibley. 'You have murdered many of our people without any sufficient cause,' read the reply. 'Return me the prisoners under a flag of truce, and I will talk with you then like a man.' [8]

Two answers went back to Sibley. One was signed 'Your truly friend, Little Crow,' and the other, about which Little Crow knew nothing, was signed by Wabasha.

Little Crow's letter said the Lower Sioux held one hundred and fifty-five prisoners near Yellow Medicine, with more at Lac qui Parle. 'I want to know from you as a friend,' requested Little Crow, 'what way I can make peace for my people. In regard to the prisoners, they fare with our children and ourselves just as well as us.' [9]

Wabasha's secret letter, likewise designed to open a channel for peace, implied its author would be a more suitable negotiator than Little Crow.

'You know,' wrote the principal chief, 'Little Crow has been opposed to me in everything our people have had to do with the whites. He has been opposed to everything in the form of civilization and Christianity. He has now got himself into trouble that we know he can never get himself out of, and he is trying to involve those few of us that are still the friends of the Americans.'

Sibley, as a fur trader, had known of Little Crow's attempts to induce his band to take up farming. He knew of no effort on Little Crow's part to involve anyone else in the blame for the massacre. He thought it expedient, however, to send a separate reply to each letter.

'You have not done as I wished in giving up to me the prisoners taken by your people,' he reproached Little Crow. 'You have allowed your young men to commit nine murders since you wrote your first letter. That is not the way for you to make peace.'

The colonel's reply to Wabasha was cautious; between its lines may have been traces of skepticism: 'If you and others who have not been concerned in the murders will gather with all the prisoners on the prairie in full sight of my troops, when a white flag is displayed by you a white flag will be hoisted in my camp, and then you can come forward and place yourself under my protection. I am powerful enough to crush all who attempt to oppose my march, and to punish those who have washed their hands in innocent blood.' [10]

After reading Sibley's letter, Wabasha was not at all sure he had made his position clear. He promptly sent the colonel another note. 'My friend,' he wrote, 'you know that I am not a bad man. I am a kind-hearted man. If you want to make peace with the friendly Indians, we want to hear from you in regard to it. I am trying to do what is right.' [11]

By now it was mid-September. Sibley's sixteen hundred fidgety soldiers already had been obliged to dawdle two weeks at Ridgely for no reason anyone could explain. Their only accomplishment had been burial of the dead before and after the Battle of Birch Coulee.

Sibley's apologists said the long delay was caused by fear that an abrupt move might result in the murder of hundreds of captives. But Little Crow had been the first to call attention to the prisoners. Sibley, writing Ramsey, Pope, and others from the fort, did not express concern for the welfare of the captives; he attributed his delay to the weather, the roads, and a desire for still more supplies.[12]

Such Indians as wanted peace, together with the terrified captives, worried about the delay. As early as September 15 the Christian chiefs wrote Sibley objecting to his slowness. 'If your troops do not reach here till the last of the week,' they warned, 'it may be too late. The lower bands have already held two councils about killing off the captives.'[13]

What to do with the prisoners was as tangled and urgent a problem as any the Dakotas faced. Some of the arguments it provoked nearly ended in violence. Frequently the captives seemed destined to be killed before their rescuers arrived.

A faction led by Little Paul advocated that the captives be surrendered to the whites at once, as a prelude to seeking peace.[14]

Another element demanded the prisoners be slaughtered without delay. As long as the hostages lived, argued this faction, one group or another would try to use them as a wedge for a separate peace.

'Give me the captives,' demanded Little Paul, 'and I will take them to Fort Ridgely.'

'You who favor delivering the prisoners,' sneered Mazza-wamnuna, 'think the whites will spare your lives if you do so. They will not, and you ought to know it.'

'If you do not give up the captives,' thundered Red Iron, 'our soldiers' lodge will take them from you.'

'Disgrace not yourselves by surrender to those who will hang you up like dogs,' pleaded Little Crow, 'but die, if you must, like warriors of the Dakotas. Did we ever do the most trifling thing, and the whites not hang us? I know if they get us in their power they will hang every one of us.'[15]

'Why should the Sissetons and Wahpetons die for the crimes of the Lower bands?' demanded Standing Buffalo.

'If you are not afraid of the whites, fight them on your own land. Make good your boasts and stop your lies!' taunted Little Paul at the final council.

'Kill him! Kill him!' screamed Shakopee's men, the Rice Creekers, and other partisans of war.

'Bluster away!' scoffed Paul. 'I shall not die alone.'

Everyone in the assemblage jumped up, roaring and shouting.

Wabasha, Big Eagle, Standing Buffalo, and a few others prevented bloodshed by bellowing adjournment and pushing their own braves from the council.

As the meeting dissolved, raucous voices broke into song:

Over the earth I come,
Over the earth I come.
A soldier I come;
Over the earth I am a ghost.

It was a Dakota chant signifying reckless defiance. Many did not join in the singing.

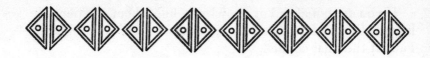

XXI ACCIDENTAL VICTORY

September 18, nearly five weeks after the start of the massacre—Colonel Henry Hastings Sibley, most of the Sixth Minnesota Infantry, parts of the Third, Seventh, and Ninth, thirty-eight Renville Rangers, twenty-eight mounted citizen soldiers, and sixteen citizen artillerists marched from Fort Ridgely toward the Yellow Medicine.[1]

By the customary route, which the army took, it was a little over forty miles from the fort to Upper Agency. Wagons using the route ordinarily made it in one day. George Gleason, taking Dr. Wakefield's wife and children over the road when the massacre started, expected to reach Ridgely in half a day; he would have made it if the Dakotas had not killed him and captured his passengers before they got to Lower Agency. The trip took Colonel Sibley four days.

Because he sent out no advance scouting parties, the colonel did not realize that more than half of the transplanted Lower Sioux encampments were within three or four miles of Wood Lake, a small body of water two miles below the mouth of the Yellow Medicine.

On September 22 Sibley and his sixteen hundred men camped for the night at Wood Lake.[2] When the Indians learned where the army had bedded down they assembled to discuss the possibilities. The prospect appealed to Shakopee, and he even attended the session.

Little Crow and Shakopee suggested a sudden night attack,

complete with shrill war whoops and much shooting from all sides at once.

Messengers were dispatched inviting Upper Indians to participate, and a second meeting was necessary. At this council, Little Crow, Rdainyanka, Mankato, and other Redwood chiefs described the proposed night attack.

'A daylight attack,' sneered one of the Upper Indians, 'would provide greater evidence of bravery than a sneak attack at night.'[3]

This remarkable argument won support when scouts reported Sibley's men had erected breastworks at the Wood Lake camp. An alternative plan, calling for a morning attack, was proposed and adopted. There would be ambush and surprise; it would be fully as exciting as a night attack.

A little more than a mile northwest of the lake a road ran along the Yellow Medicine River. Over it the white troops could be expected to march when they broke camp after breakfast. A large number of warriors would be concealed in the grass along this road.

Near the road as it approached the Minnesota River was a wooded ravine serving as the lake's outlet to the river. A huge force of braves would be concentrated in this ravine.[4] West of the road was a low hill, broad enough to conceal an additional body of warriors on its far side.

Far out on the prairies, to the right and left of the intended battlefield, would be mounted parties, waiting to gallop into the fray on signal.

Colonel Sibley's strung-out troops, surprised by the men concealed in the grass, and overwhelmed by reinforcements closing in from all sides, would be entirely wiped out.

In the early, wet hours, Indian warriors hid themselves according to plan and confidently awaited dawn.

An accident spoiled the plot of the Dakotas and gave Colonel Sibley the only triumph of his expedition.

The accident occurred at seven in the morning, and involved Private De Grove Kimball and a dozen other men of Company G, Third Regiment.

At that hour, while most of the remainder of Sibley's army breakfasted, Private Kimball and his friends took four wagons, intending to go on an unauthorized foraging expedition.[5]

The Third Regiment had been surrendered at Murfreesboro, Tennessee, in the Civil War. Its members considered the surrender an unwarranted and disgraceful act. They had been paroled from a Confederate prison 'not to serve against the Confederacy,' which left them free to fight Indians.[6] Neither their morale nor their discipline was as high as it had been before their imprisonment.

Private Kimball and his comrades did not have a high opinion of the food that Colonel Sibley provided. They had heard of a garden on the Yellow Medicine, filled with potatoes, melons, sweet corn, and other delicacies, abandoned when the inhabitants of the agency fled with John Otherday. The members of Company G thought that a request for four company wagons in which to bring back vegetables probably would be granted, but wanted to be sure of the wagons before the garden was buried in snow. For this reason, they refrained from asking permission and departed while everyone else was busy with breakfast.

By accident the wagons, when they cut across the prairie toward the road along the Yellow Medicine, headed directly for the grass in which some of the Indians lay concealed. This was the circumstance which gave Colonel Sibley his victory.

Two choices confronted the concealed warriors. They could continue to lie in the grass and be noticed while being run over, or they could get out of the way of the wagons and be discovered while doing so.

They chose the latter course, and embellished it by firing at the boys in the wagons. Private De Grove Kimball was shot through the thigh and mortally wounded.

Accidental exposure of the ambuscade brought on the Battle of Wood Lake,[7] but not according to plans made the previous evening.

On the low hill west of the road crouched Little Crow, with three or four other planners, watching the premature start of the conflict.

'Little Crow felt very badly,' said Big Eagle. 'Hundreds of our men did not get into the battle and did not fire a shot. They were too far out.'[8]

As soon as the Indians began to shoot, the boys of Company G jumped from their wagons and returned the fire. They were greatly outnumbered and fell back toward camp. Their comrades of the Third Regiment, seeing the unexpected development, grabbed their muskets. Two hundred of them, led by Major Abraham Welch, poured across the prairie.

Additional Indians, seeing the battle had started, jumped from the grass on both sides of the road.

Major Welch formed his men into line and began to push the Indians toward the Minnesota.

From the ravine emerged additional Indians, intent on getting behind Major Welch's forces and cutting them off.

The Renville Rangers sped out to check the Indians swarming from the ravine.

More Indians appeared. Colonel Sibley sent in five companies of the Seventh Regiment, two companies of the Sixth, and some of the artillerists with a six-pounder and a howitzer.

Awed by the artillery and the show of white strength, the Indians broke and ran. Probably not more than three hundred of the seven hundred and forty warriors in the vicinity got within firing distance of the impromptu battlefield. On the side of the whites most of the fighting was done by troops of the Third Regiment and the Renville Rangers. Less than one-third of Sibley's army fired a shot.

Seven whites, including Private Kimball, were killed or

fatally wounded. Major Welch received a leg wound, and thirty-four others, mostly of the Third Regiment or Renville Rangers, were injured.

Mankato, most daring and perhaps most able of the Lower leaders, was killed by a cannon ball. His warriors carried his body away to a secret burial place. Fifteen other Indians were left dead on the battlefield by fleeing braves. All fifteen were scalped; strenuous efforts were made to blame half-breeds among the Renville Rangers for this. About fifty Indians were wounded. One was taken prisoner.

With Indian fatalities outnumbering those of the whites by more than two to one, the Battle of Wood Lake was, for Colonel Sibley, an unqualified success.

Six days after the battle the colonel, 'for his judicious fight,' was made a brigadier general.[9]

There is no record that the foragers of Company G ever received any special recognition.

When the brief battle ended, all of the Sioux factions recognized that the war on the whites had been lost.

Little Crow, Wabasha, Shakopee, Red Middle Voice, and many other leaders, accompanied by hundreds of braves, went disconsolately upstream when they left the battlefield.

On the way Wabasha and Little Crow discussed their plans for the immediate future. Little Crow said he would leave in the morning, taking any who wished to go with him. Wabasha would remain, he declared, but he asked custody of the captives held by Little Crow. If the white women and children were alive when the soldiers arrived, perhaps the Sioux who remained behind would be allowed to live.

Three days before, after scouts had reported the Army's departure from Ridgely, all captives held near the Yellow Medicine had been moved twenty-five miles up-river to camps opposite the Chippewa's mouth. At the same time prisoners held at Lac qui Parle, ten miles beyond, were brought down. Except for groups of a dozen or twenty, scattered here and there among various bands, most of the captives were now in camps controlled by Little Crow or Wabasha.

During the day some of the captives, aided by half-breeds and by Christian Indians who refused to go to Wood Lake, had moved some of the tepees to a new camp-site.

'While the warriors were gone the women all dug holes to get into,' said a captive, 'expecting that when the Indians returned they would kill all of us.'[10]

By sundown, when the defeated Dakotas reached the camps, they found matters already partly settled. Wabasha moved his band's tepees to the new site, and Little Crow went to his own camp to spend his last night in the upper valley.

During the morning, after he had issued orders for the loading of wagons, Little Crow stepped outside his lodge and gathered his band around him.

'I am ashamed to call myself a Dakota,' he said. 'Seven hundred of our best warriors were whipped yesterday by the whites. Now we had better all run away and scatter out over the plains like buffalo and wolves. To be sure, the whites had wagon-guns and better arms than we, and there were many more of them. But that is no reason why we should not have whipped them, for we are brave Dakotas and whites are cowardly women. I can not account for the disgraceful defeat. It must be the work of traitors in our midst.'[11]

Other camps in addition to Little Crow's were abandoned before noon. Shakopee, Red Middle Voice, Medicine Bottle, and scores of others went north of the river. In Little Crow's immediate party were over one hundred braves. Accompanying Shakopee were even more. Sleepy Eyes, with most of his band, had already fled. So had Hapa, Sacred Rattle, the four Rice Creekers who had spent a Sunday morning murdering settlers at Acton, and many scores of others. Not all who fled were guilty of murder or rape, but many were. Not all of the guilty fled, but most of them did.

Big Eagle, Traveling Hail, Wabasha, Wacouta, the Chris-

tian chiefs, Simon, Little Paul, Akipa, and Cloudman did not
flee. Neither did Chaska, who had been with Hapa when he
killed Gleason, and later was the protector of Mrs. Wakefield
and her children. Red Iron and his men remained to help
guard the captives.

From the newly established camp Wabasha released Joe
Campbell, half-breed captive. He sent Joe to Wood Lake to
inform Sibley that most of the prisoners waited at his village.

Sibley remained at Wood Lake two more days. Altogether,
it took him four days to advance twenty-five miles up-river
over the Lac qui Parle trail, a trip often made in half a day.

'I suppose,' said a captive, 'the troops were fatigued, if they
marched all the way from St. Paul as fast as they did from
Yellow Medicine, taking over fifty hours to travel twenty-five
miles.'[12]

During his second day at Wood Lake Sibley wrote the
guardians of the captives that he feared to proceed because
'if I advanced my troops before you could make your arrange-
ments the war party would murder the prisoners. Now that I
learn from Joe Campbell that most of the captives are in safety
in your camp I shall move on tomorrow.'[13]

'We at last concluded he was afraid,' reported Mrs. Wakefield. 'The Indians began to get uneasy for fear Little Crow
would return and kill us if Sibley did not come soon.'

On the third day Sibley got started, but only made eight
miles that day. He stopped in the afternoon to 'treat the
command to a dress parade,'[14] and in the evening his army
'spent hours intrenching themselves. An army leaving us, a
little handful of persons with only about one hundred men to
protect us! God watched over us, and kept those savages back.
To Him I give all the honor and glory; Sibley I do not even
thank, for he deserved it not,' said Mrs. Wakefield.[15]

Conditions among the captives did not improve notably
after Wabasha and Red Iron took over custody.

Except for the half-breeds, George Spencer was the only

adult male among the prisoners. 'The female captives,' wrote Spencer, 'were, with few exceptions, subjected to the most horrible treatment. In some cases a woman would be taken out into the woods, and her person violated by six, seven, and as many as ten or twelve of these fiends.'

'The night before the troops came,' reported Nancy Faribault, 'twenty or thirty Indians came in with a young white girl of sixteen or seventeen. She was nearly heart-broken, and quite in despair.'[16]

Finally, on September 26, the army reached the camp where the prisoners were held. The men promptly named the place 'Camp Release.'

Sibley, accompanied by his staff and bodyguard, went to the camp and requested a council. Much of the afternoon was spent in speech-making. The colonel expressed determination that all the guilty be caught and punished. Indian leaders delivered orations denying that their own hands were stained with the blood of the whites.

Toward evening Sibley formally demanded custody of all prisoners. Ninety-one whites and one hundred and fifty half-breeds were turned over to him. The released included Jonathan Earle's wife and two daughters, Mrs. Wakefield and her children, Mary Schwandt, Mrs. Adams, Mattie Williams, and more than eighty other whites. The release of additional captives, held in other camps, was promised. Altogether, about three hundred and fifty half-breeds were freed in a day or two.

'The woe written on the faces of the half-starved and nearly naked women and children would have melted the hardest heart,' said an eye-witness.[17]

Wagons were supplied to take some of the released to Fort Ridgely. Orphaned children were sent to the settlements. Women who might usefully testify against their captors remained at Camp Release.

XXII   UTTERLY EXTERMINATE THE SIOUX

During the month his army remained at Camp Release Sibley sought to do two things: first, to seize such Dakotas as were handy, and, second, to 'hang the villains.'[1]

Accomplishing both objectives at the same time proved awkward. As long as the Indians thought that they and their families would be fed and housed if they surrendered as prisoners of war, they waited to be seized. But after the shrewdest, most cautious, or most guilty ones suspected treachery, they took Little Crow's advice to 'scatter over the plains like wolves.'

With comparatively few exceptions, those who had instigated or directed the war or participated in attacks on settlers withdrew three days before Sibley's men arrived. A few did not immediately go far away; they crossed to the north side of the river. Curiosity kept them near enough to be sighted by soldiers approaching to free the captives.

After his arrival Sibley, heeding information supplied by friends among the Indians, promptly became utterly confused regarding the whereabouts of Little Crow, Shakopee, Red Middle Voice, White Lodge, Sleepy Eyes, and hundreds of others he proposed to hang.

Within four days 'intelligence of a reliable character'[2] informed the colonel that Little Crow was one hundred and twenty miles to the north. Three days later the chief and a small band of followers were reported making their way toward the Yankton Sioux, seventy miles west. At nearly the same time Sibley sent a message to Standing Buffalo reproaching him for allowing Little Crow to enter Sisseton territory and to camp on Big Stone Lake, fifty miles to the northwest. Two days later, while the Lake Shetek raiders were taking their captives to the upper Missouri, Sibley heard that White Lodge, accompanied by Sleepy Eyes, and 'one hundred or more fighting men' was on either the Big Sioux River or the James. A week later Little Crow, now said to have only five men with him, again was declared far to the north, 'fleeing to take refuge under the British flag.'

By alternate wheedling, threatening, and deception, less guilty Dakotas lurking in the vicinity were induced to move their families near the captive camp. A second village of the surrendered grew along the Yellow Medicine.

Half-breed messengers, visiting encampments of the reluctant, spread word that those who came in voluntarily would be made prisoners of war, a far kinder fate than starvation.

A week later the colonel sent messengers to tell those who had not come in that 'their only hope of mercy, even to the women and children, will be immediate return and surrender.'³ Those who arrived were assigned to the encampment adjoining Camp Release or to the Yellow Medicine village.

Now the troops got suddenly tough. By order of the commander, soldiers surrounded the nearby camp at night, disarmed the men, and placed them in a log jail previously erected. 'A similar proceeding was ordered at Yellow Medicine and safely accomplished by assembling all the braves within the walls of the agency buildings, under pretense of holding a council.'⁴ It may not have been honorable and may not have yielded many who were actually guilty; but it was certainly safe, and enabled the colonel to report additional prisoners.

Two detachments went upstream, explored the river's upper tributaries, 'scoured the country westward toward the James River,'⁵ surrounded such bands as they found, and brought in a hundred more braves with their wives and children.

Most of the men, whether near Camp Release at the start or brought in later, were 'linked together in pairs, by chains forged to their ankles.' There were not nearly enough manacles to fetter all of them. The colonel was obliged to call for 'what trace-chains and suitable iron rods can be found.'[6]

At the start Camp Release consisted of 'about one hundred and fifty lodges sheltering some twelve hundred souls.' The surrenders and seizures caused the number to swell to about two thousand.

There had been two hundred and fifty adult males to begin with. In three weeks Sibley was able to report, 'I have now about four hundred Indian men in irons and between sixty and seventy under surveillance here and at Yellow Medicine.'[7] Thus, about two hundred men were added by persuasion, threat or seizure.

Feeding two thousand Indians and sixteen hundred soldiers became a difficult problem. Some of the soldiers and prisoners were ordered to harvest corn and potatoes from abandoned fields of Yellow Medicine farmer Indians. Some of the cattle, stolen and otherwise, held by prisoners, had to be slaughtered for food and to save forage.

Two days after reaching Camp Release, Sibley issued an order creating a judicial device 'to try summarily the mixed bloods and Indians engaged in the raids and massacres.'[8] No mention was made in the order of military offenses or participation in battles.

Sibley called his judicial device a 'military commission,' and so did General Pope. Governor Ramsey, writing to President Lincoln, referred to it as a 'military court.' Flandrau called it a 'court-martial' and a 'military tribunal.' Since the Indians were not members of the armed forces, and thus not subject to military law, the proceedings were not actually 'courts-martial.'

Neither military nor civil law provided for precisely the sort of judicial mechanism Sibley created; it could be regarded as an improvisation of the colonel, though by no means as his original invention.

In the furious excitement of the frontier, a civilian court hearing the cases the military tribunal tried might readily have become a lynch court, but the colonel's improvisation did not. It did, however, show a certain disregard for problems of admissible evidence, proof, and jurisdiction.

Isaac V. D. Heard, a St. Paul attorney who had enlisted with Sibley's forces, acted as recorder.[9]

Comprising the commission were five of Sibley's officers. Lieutenant Rollin C. Olin, with help from Attorney Heard, served as trial judge advocate. No regular defense counsel was appointed; this was another irregular aspect of the proceedings.

The Reverend Stephen Riggs, when he emerged in the settlements after the journey from Hazelwood, was asked by Governor Ramsey to accompany Sibley as chaplain and interpreter. At Camp Release Sibley asked him to invite the recently freed women captives 'to make known any acts of cruelty or wrong they had suffered at the hands of Dakota men during their captivity.'[10]

According to Recorder Heard, the Reverend Stephen Riggs was 'in effect, the Grand Jury of the court.' The clergyman's long acquaintance with the Indians, his knowledge of the character and habits of most of them, and his familiarity with their language, eminently qualified him for the position of interrogator. He could 'tell, almost with certainty' who had been implicated.[11]

Consequently, with few exceptions, the prisoners were arraigned on charges resulting from the Reverend Stephen Riggs's interrogation of the women who had been held captive.

First of the suspects to be tried was a mulatto named Godfrey, twenty-seven-year old son of a Canadian Frenchman and a Negro mother. Godfrey had married a squaw of Wabasha's band and had lived in his wife's village for the previous five years. He had 'a very dark complexion, curly hair, lips of medium thickness, eyes slightly crossed, but not enough to disfigure.' For his appearance before the tribunal he wore 'an old plush cap with large ear-flaps on one side of his head.'[12]

Godfrey was charged with murder. There were two specifications. The first alleged 'at or near New Ulm, on or about the nineteenth day of August, he did join in a war party of the Sioux tribe of Indians against the citizens of the United States, and did with his own hand murder seven (more or less) white men, women, and children, peaceable citizens of the United States.'

The second specification charged that 'at various times and places between the nineteenth of August and the twenty-eighth of September he did join and participate in the murders and massacres committed by the Sioux Indians on the Minnesota frontier.'

Three witnesses appeared against the accused. One of them, Mary Woodbury, testified that she saw Godfrey, a few days after the start of the massacre, wearing a breech-cloth and war paint. She heard him whoop and yell, 'apparently as fierce as any of them.' Later she heard an Indian ask him how many he had killed and heard Godfrey say, 'Only seven.'[13]

Mary Schwandt and Mattie Williams, taken captive near New Ulm while fleeing in the wagon of Francis Patoile, Yellow Medicine trader, were the other witnesses. They recalled that Godfrey had been with the Indians taking them captive. He had not been armed, they said, but he 'appeared to be as much in favor of the outrages as any of the Indians,' and had said nothing to the contrary within their hearing.

None of the witnesses accused Godfrey of rape. Nobody had seen him commit any murders. His explanation was that his wife's uncle had told him he would only be safe if he joined the Indians. Another Dakota had told him he would be killed if he did not join in the fighting. He denied having killed anyone and said he had boasted of murders to keep the good will of the others.

'His voice,' reported Heard, 'was one of the softest I have ever heard. He had such an honest look and spoke with such a truthful tone the commission was inclined to believe there was a possibility of his sincerity.'

Neither Godfrey's guilt nor innocence had been clearly established, the commissioners felt. They found the defendant guilty of murder and sentenced him to be hung, but recommended the penalty be commuted to ten years' imprisonment.

After Godfrey's case came trials of half-breeds, including some who had deserted from the Renville Rangers before the first attack on Ridgely. Among those found guilty and sentenced to die were Baptiste Campbell, brother of Little Crow's captive secretary, and Hypolite Auge, relative of Corporal James Auge, Birch Coulee interpreter.

Chaska and his mother had protected Mrs. Wakefield and her children during nearly six weeks of captivity. Unlike his cousin Hapa, Chaska had decided not to flee. When Sibley and the Reverend Stephen Riggs first reached Camp Release, they asked Mrs. Wakefield to point out the Indian who had saved her. They shook hands with Chaska and for a while 'made quite a hero of him.'[14] But when the Indian camp was surrounded, Chaska was put in irons along with most of the others.

At his trial Mrs. Wakefield was called as a witness. 'I told them all I could say would be in his favor,' she reported. 'They thought it very strange I could speak in favor of an Indian.'

Chaska had been present when Hapa killed George Gleason, but took no part in the murder. Now Hapa had fled. The tribunal found Chaska guilty of being present at the murder, and sentenced him to hang.

Of all those tried by the military commission, 'the most repulsive-looking prisoner,' said Heard, 'was Cut Nose. He was foremost in many of the massacres. The first days of the outbreak he devoted his attention particularly to the Beaver Creek settlement.'

Even before the soldiers had arrived Cut Nose proclaimed belief in the futility of flight and announced that he expected to be executed. He was one of the few defendants whose guilt was proved beyond doubt.

Most of the charges against the others were no more specific than those against Godfrey. 'After a few instances, the specifications became stereotyped.'[15] The accused were charged with 'participation in the murders, outrages, and robberies' and 'particularly in the battles at the Fort, New Ulm, Birch Coulee, and Wood Lake.'

In a large proportion of the trials the proceedings consisted of an arraignment and 'a confession by the accused that he had been in one or more of the battles. Believing they would be considered prisoners of war, the Indians had no hesitation in confessing to presence in the battles.'

'The trials,' said Heard, 'were elaborately conducted until the commission became acquainted with the details of different outrages and battles. Then, the only point being the connection of the prisoners with them, five minutes would dispose of a case. As many as forty were sometimes tried in a day.'

'In a few weeks,' reported the Reverend Stephen Riggs, 'instead of taking individuals for trial, the plan was adopted to subject all the grown men, with a few exceptions, to an investigation, trusting the innocent could make their innocency appear. This was not possible in the case of the majority, as conviction was based on admission of being present at the battles.'

'The battles were not ordinary battles,' Recorder Heard explained for the benefit of anyone who might question death sentences for military participation. 'They were directed against villages defended by civilians, hastily and indifferently armed.' And besides, 'the code of the Indians, which takes life for life, justified it.' New Ulm was a village, critics conceded, but Fort Ridgely, Birch Coulee, and Wood Lake were not. Most of those sentenced to die, asserted the Reverend Stephen Riggs, 'were condemned on general principles, without any specific charges proved.' The convictions 'were only justified by the consideration they would be reviewed by a more disinterested authority, and were demanded by the people.'

At the start of the trials Sibley intended to hang immediately anyone found guilty.

'They will be forthwith executed,' he wrote Pope. 'Perhaps it will be a stretch of my authority. If so, necessity must be my justification.'[16]

General Pope did not object. 'It is my purpose utterly to exterminate the Sioux. They are to be treated as maniacs or wild beasts,' he instructed the colonel.[17]

But the responsibility, because of the large number of prisoners taken, was greater than either Sibley or Pope had contemplated. On September 28 only sixteen were to be tried, but by October 21 four hundred were in irons. On October 7 Sibley had twenty prisoners 'under sentence of death by hanging,' but by the 21st there were more than one hundred.

Before mid-October Sibley wanted to 'send all below' instead of doing the executing at Camp Release, and General Pope had asked Washington whether he needed 'further authority to execute Indians condemned by military commission.'[18]

With the end of October approaching, Sibley became concerned about the location of his army and concentration camps, and his shortage of food for humans and forage for horses and cattle. If roads to the settlements became impassable thirty-six hundred soldiers, condemned prisoners and Indian women and children, together with hundreds of head of livestock, might be stranded without food for the winter. He decided to suspend the military tribunal for a few days, moving his camp to Lower Agency.

One trouble was that nearly three hundred prisoners remained to be tried. Just the same, when October 23rd came court was adjourned and everyone moved to the Lower area. Here, in the kitchen of Trader La Bathe's partly wrecked house, the trials were resumed.

'The avenging nemesis had brought the guilty to an appropriate spot,' observed Heard, 'for it was here the mad saturnalia began.'

Now the trials proceeded at an accelerated pace. Between October 25 and November 5 two hundred and seventy-two cases were disposed of. In a little over a month, the military commission had tried three hundred and ninety-two prisoners and had sentenced three hundred and six of them to be hung.

Sibley sent the names of the convicted to General Pope. The general had received no clarification of his authority from Washington. To President Abraham Lincoln he telegraphed the names of the condemned, and to Governor Ramsey he announced, 'the Sioux prisoners will be executed unless the President forbids it, which I am sure he will not do.'[19]

Pope's telegram cost more than four hundred dollars. The *New York Times* was moved to suggest that the cost be deducted from General Pope's salary. On November 10 came an acknowledgment from President Lincoln.

'Your dispatch giving the names of Indians condemned to death is received. Please forward as soon as possible the full and complete record of the convictions; if the record does not fully indicate the more guilty and influential of the culprits, please have a careful statement made on these points and forward to me. Send by mail.'[20]

General Pope's reaction was an indignant snort. He reached for a sheet of paper to compose a protest.

'The only distinction between the culprits is as to which of them murdered most people or violated most young girls. ... It is certain the criminals condemned ought to be executed without exception.'[21]

He promised, however, to comply with the President's wishes immediately.

When Lincoln received the trial records he could not help observing that they were far from full and complete. To George Whiting and Francis Ruggles he assigned the task of trying to distinguish between those guilty of crimes and those guilty only of participation in battles.[22]

Grave crimes no doubt had been committed on the border, but few genuine criminals seemed to have been caught. Lincoln did not propose to give the Confederates reason to declare to the world that he had agreed to the execution of three hundred prisoners of war.

THE COURT-HOUSE OF THE MILITARY COMMISSION

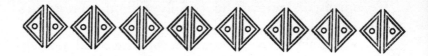

XXIII FEARFUL COLLISION

It had been late summer when Sibley's troops reached Camp Release. A month later, when the soldiers herded their two thousand charges downstream, winter had nearly come.

Autumn had glided past, getting little attention. It had stripped leaves from trees and bushes. It had turned prairie grass brown and brittle.

Now the country looked desolate. Summer's growth had died; the color of autumn was gone; decay had begun, but snow had not arrived to hide the damage.

Each night was cold. Every morning the ice in the water buckets was a little firmer than it had been the morning before. More and more firewood needed to be cut, and more blankets from the supply wagons passed to the tents.

Late each afternoon many pairs of Indians, hobbled together, clanked to the river. They squatted on its banks, wordless and glum, heads bent, blankets sweeping downward from shoulders to cross over updrawn knees.

A smell of burning prairie hovered everywhere. After dark, redness glowed dully from burning dry marshes across the river. Sometimes during the day swirls of icy wind, heavy with ashes and soot, swept from the northwest where the prairie was smoldering. Occasionally it came in gusts strong enough to uproot trees; often it leveled tents. Always, said one of the soldiers, it made white men look as though they had been 'suddenly resurrected from dirty graves.'[1]

Flights of brant sped across the sky. Larger wild geese

passed higher, not always seen, but their honking always heard. Cranes and ducks wheeled overhead, challenging soldiers to shoot.

Some days were clear and bright, but more were cloudy and bleak. Often the sun hid until noon; some days it never appeared.

Word of departure was cheering news to the soldiers, two months away from the settlements. The Indians left with sadness, knowing few would ever come back to the valley.

An auxiliary camp filled with wives and children of the condemned stood along Redwood River near the road. When the prisoners passed near it the women 'began to weep and set up a dismal wail.'[2]

During the ten-day pause at Lower Agency, hundreds crossed to explore the area north of the river. Near Sacred Heart Creek they saw the blackened ruins of the Krieger cabin; inside lay the charred remains of the seven children who had died in its flames.

Herds of cattle, in two months grown wilder than buffalo, bellowed in terror and thundered away from the soldiers. A pack of rabid dogs, snarling and unpredictable, circled near the invaders, running their lives out.

Fire had swept the prairie, skipping occasional sloughs but scorching thousands of acres of hay land. In the black stubble sprawled reeking corpses of settlers, often in family groups, killed while fleeing or trapped by flames the attackers had set. To the four score buried by Hiram Grant's men before the Birch Coulee battle, were added other scores. One group from Lower Agency in one day found and buried twenty-five more.

From Yellow Medicine and the Redwood camp, mostly afoot, came Indians and half-breeds held to be innocent. Nine out of ten were women or children. Guards were assigned to escort them to Fort Snelling. There were seventeen hundred; they made a scraggly procession four miles long.

At Henderson hundreds of citizens with clubs, knives, guns,

and stones assailed the column. 'Before the guards could drive them back, they maltreated many. One infant, snatched from its mother, was so injured it died a few hours later. The body was quietly laid away in the crotch of a tree.'[3]

On the bottom land near Fort Snelling a flat tract, outlined by a high board fence, had been designated as the winter camp-site. Behind the fence two hundred and fifty tepees were pitched; here the occupants lived on army rations.

Throughout the winter one alarming rumor after another swept the camp. There were predictions of slavery, of mass execution, of banishment to remote islands, and of similar fates. Only the missionaries held out hope for the future. Bishop Henry Whipple, Father Augustin Ravoux, Dr. Thomas Williamson's son, John, the Reverend Samuel Hinman, and a dozen less regular visitors, baptized hundreds of converts. Wabasha, one of the few major chiefs sent to the Fort Snelling camp, became an Episcopalian. Simon and Little Paul, also in the winter camp, had been elders at the Hazelwood Congregational mission and remained members of that denomination.

Two days after the exodus from Lower Agency of those deemed innocent, the cavalcade of the condemned resumed its journey. It was destined for a stockade named Camp Lincoln, on the banks of the Minnesota southwest of Mankato, near the now-extinct town of South Bend.

New Ulm was on the route. Here the procession crawled slowly through streets lined by scores of hooting women. Some had aprons filled with rocks. Others carried pots full of scalding water. The rest were armed with pitchforks, scissors, hoes, knives, and bricks.

'The Dutch she-devils were as fierce as tigresses,' complained Sibley in a letter to his wife.

Fifteen prisoners were injured; one sustained a broken jaw. Some of the escorts also were hurt.

By the time the condemned neared the South Bend stockade, President Lincoln began to feel two kinds of pressure.

One kind came from the Far West and the other from the East.

'I hope,' wrote Governor Ramsey, 'execution of every Sioux Indian condemned by the military court will be at once ordered. It would be wrong upon principle and policy to refuse this. Private revenge would on all this border take the place of official judgment.'[4]

'It is to be noted,' General Pope reminded the President, 'that the horrible outrages were not committed by wild Indians, whose excuse might be ignorance or barbarism, but by Indians who have been paid annuities for years, and who committed these crimes upon people among whom they had lived, at whose homes they had slept, and at whose tables they had been fed.'[5]

On the other hand, Lincoln 'was inundated with appeals for mercy from friends of the Indian who had never seen one, from people opposed to the death penalty, and from those who regarded the convicts as prisoners of war.'[6]

Most eloquent of the appeals came from the frontier. Bishop Whipple, calling on Lincoln in person, talked 'about the rascality of this Indian business until,' said the President, 'I felt it down to my boots.'

Indian Commissioner William P. Dole thought the 'indiscriminate punishment of men who have laid down their arms and surrendered themselves as prisoners' would be 'a stain upon our national character and a source of future regret.'

From the Far West came dire threats and ominous warnings.

Henry Hastings Sibley foresaw 'a fearful collision' between his army and the residents of the border if the condemned were not hung promptly. 'Thousands of men in all parts of the state' were about to besiege the South Bend stockade. 'Should the president pardon the condemned, there will be a determined effort to get them in possession, which may cost the lives of thousands of our citizens.'[7]

General Pope called the President's attention to the hundreds of unconvicted in the Snelling winter camp, and thought it would be 'nearly impossible to prevent the indiscriminate massacre of all—old men, women, and children' if all the condemned were not executed forthwith.[8]

There was a collision, but it was not very fearful. During the evening of December 4, after a few rounds of drinks, patrons of Mankato House became convinced they should march to South Bend. As they trudged toward the stockade they enlisted recruits from other taverns. By the time the marchers reached South Bend, shortly before midnight, there were, not thousands, but more than one hundred and fifty.

They 'assaulted the guard,' reported Sibley, 'with the avowed intention of murdering the condemned prisoners.'[9] The guards 'surrounded the assailants and took them prisoners, but subsequently released them.' The assailants agreed to return quietly to Mankato House or to other, nearer taverns.

Thousands from all parts of the state did not converge on South Bend. Residents of the frontier were far from indifferent, but knew the stockade contained few genuine rapists and murderers.[10]

On December 5 a resolution of the United States Senate asked President Lincoln for such information as he possessed regarding the massacre and the trials conducted by Sibley's commission.

By now George Whiting and Francis Ruggles had analyzed the trial evidence and prepared an abstract of their findings.

Lincoln reported to the Senate that, contrary to his expectations, the abstract showed only two inmates of the South Bend stockade had been proved guilty of violating women.[11] Evidence proved that only forty were connected with 'wanton murder of unarmed citizens.' This meant that more than two hundred and sixty were guilty, at most, of participation in battles.

Hundreds of wanton murders and violations of women had occurred. Clearly, most of the rapists and killers had not waited to be tried, but had scattered over the plains.

XXIV   MORE A GROWL THAN A CHEER

Hammer blows sounded across the road and rang through the stockade. On the river's bank a busy swarm of soldiers built an enormous square scaffold.

Wide platforms composed the scaffold's four sides. Above each side were beams supported by sturdy upright posts. Each beam was notched for ten ropes.

Peering between logs of their enclosure, the prisoners watched the construction.

Some of the watchers recalled Little Crow's words about 'those who will hang you up like dogs,' and thought they had been fools to surrender.

In a day or two the sight from the peepholes lost its novelty and few in the stockade watched. The hammering continued.

A letter arrived from the White House. Inside the stockade the Dakotas heard about it from the soldiers and wondered what it said.

It was the Reverend Stephen Riggs's task to inform the prisoners of its contents. With head bowed, he entered the enclosure in which the warriors squatted on the ground or leaned against the walls.

'I have known you for many years,' began the clergyman, looking slowly around the room. 'I have pointed you to the cross and prayerfully endeavored to convince you allegiance to God and the Great Father at Washington was your duty. With a broken heart I have witnessed your cruelty to inoffensive men, women, and children; cruelty to your best friends. You have stained your hands in innocent blood, and now the law holds you to strict accountability. It pains me to inform you that your Great Father in Washington says you must die for your cruelty and murders, and I am directed to inform you that some of you will be hanged by the neck until you are dead.'[1]

At this point Stephen Riggs unfolded two long sheets of paper.

'Here,' he said, 'is a letter to General Sibley from President Abraham Lincoln. I will read it to you.' He began:

'Ordered that of the Indians and half-breeds sentenced to be hanged by the Military Commission lately sitting in Minnesota, you cause to be executed the following named, to wit: Te-he-hdo-ne-che, Number Two by the record; Tazoo, Number Four by the record; Wy-a-teh-to-wah, Number Five by the record. . . .'[2]

Riggs read on, carefully intoning each name and record number. In all, there were thirty-nine names.

'The other condemned prisoners,' continued the missionary, reaching the end of the final page, 'you will hold subject to further orders, taking care that they neither escape nor are subjected to any unlawful violence.'

There was a stoical silence when the clergyman finished reading. One or two Indians knocked ashes from their pipes. The sound was loud in the quiet enclosure. One or two others filled pipes from small cloth bags, but this made no sound whatever. If any of those whose names had not been read sighed in momentary relief, their sighs could not be heard. The hammering across the road had ceased, and no noise came from that direction.

The Reverend Stephen Riggs folded the letter carefully, and again looked slowly around the room. 'May God have mercy on your souls,' he said quietly. A guard stepped quickly behind him to suggest that those whose names had been read be separated from those not listed.

To Joseph R. Brown, 'who better than any other man knew

all these condemned men, and he did not recognize all perfectly, was mainly committed the work of selecting those who were named to be executed.'[3]

What made identification difficult, as Stephen Riggs explained it, was the circumstance that 'among the condemned were several persons of the same name. In the findings of the commission they were all numbered, and the order for the executions was given in accordance with these numbers. But no one could remember which number attached to which person.'[4]

There was, for instance, a Chaska, a Chaskadon, a Chaskay, and a Chaskastay.

'The Indian named Chaskadon, that the president ordered to be hanged, killed a pregnant woman and cut out her child, and they hung Chaska, who was only convicted of being present when Mr. Gleason was killed,' complained Mrs. Wakefield, who had been protected, with her children, by Chaska and his mother during captivity.[5]

Few questioned the guilt of some of the thirty-nine picked by George Whiting and Francis Ruggles, listed in the President's letter.

There was Tazoo, convicted of rape on the testimony of Mattie Williams; Mazabomdoo, found guilty of killing an elderly woman and two children; Hapan, confessed member of the party killing Francis Patoile and taking his passengers captive; and Wyatehtawa, who admitted firing at a white man at the same time another warrior did, but maintained he did not know whose shot had been fatal.

Nobody quite believed Cut Nose guilty of the twenty-seven killings the bitter fatalist boasted, but nobody doubted he was guilty of enough to deserve hanging.

Tehehdonecha and Dowanea had been comrades of Cut Nose on forays north of the river. One of the captives accused the former of rape, and another witness had seen the latter commit murder.

Then there was Wakpadoota, who admitted having shot a white man; Hinhanshoonkoyagmane, accused by Alexander Hunter's widow of having killed her husband; and Napashue, father of an Indian girl deserted by a trader after she had borne him two children. Napashue may not have killed the nineteen he claimed, but evidence supported part of his boast.

Regarding others of the doomed, evidence was less conclusive. Some claimed to be political scapegoats. Some said they were prisoners of war.

Wahehna protested he had not killed anyone; nobody testified to seeing him do so. If he had believed himself guilty of murder, muttered Wahehna, he would have fled with Little Crow; his only crime was soldiers' lodge membership.

White Dog declared he was a victim of misunderstanding, and not even properly a prisoner of war. He had stood across the river, shouting at Interpreter Quinn, the day Captain Marsh's men walked into ambush. He insisted that his shouts were intended as a warning, but survivors of the ferry ambuscade thought differently. No evidence of White Dog's participation in any non-military event was introduced.

Crimes against settlers or captives were not charged in the case of Rdainyanka, son-in-law of Wabasha. Witnesses identified him, however, as a scornful critic of the Peace Party.[6]

'You have deceived me,' he wrote his father-in-law while waiting to die. 'You told me if we gave ourselves up to the whites all would be well. I have not killed or injured any white person, and yet today I am set apart for execution and must die in a few days, while men who are guilty will remain in prison. When my children are grown up let them know their father died without having the blood of a white man to answer for to the Great Spirit. My wife and children are dear to me. Let them not grieve for me. Let them remember the brave should be prepared to meet death. I will do as becomes a Dakota.'[7]

Not all who had been active in the war's leadership were hung. Most prominent among those recognized as unmistakable prisoners of war was Big Eagle, sentenced to imprisonment.[8]

Most of the war's instigators, and most of the perpetrators of civilian massacres, were not on the list of those to be hung for the reason that they had not waited to surrender.

Missing were Red Middle Voice and most of his Rice Creekers, including Brown Wing, Killing Ghost, Runs Against When Crawling, and Breaking Up, the four who had argued about eggs at Acton.

Absent were Shakopee, Little Crow, White Lodge, Medicine Bottle, White Spider, Sleepy Eyes, and dozens of other chiefs and head soldiers.

Few or none of the participants in raids on Lake Shetek, Big Stone Lake, or Leavenworth, and only a handful of those taking part in the Sacred Heart Creek or Beaver Creek massacres, were present.

Not on the list were Sacred Rattle, who dashed out the Adams infant's brains; Hapa, murderer of George Gleason; Mazzawamnuna, head soldier of Shakopee's band; Pawn, betrayer of the Shetek settlers; Walker Among Sacred Stones, leader of the night raid on Forest City; Plenty of Hail, killer of James Lynd, first Lower Agency casualty; or many hundreds of others.

Probably less than one in twenty, and certainly not more than one-tenth, of the rapists and murderers that Sibley had been sent to capture were on the list.

It was Tuesday afternoon when the Reverend Stephen Riggs read the President's letter with its list of the doomed. The execution was to take place Friday.

Those who were to die were moved to a stone structure. There they broke into a rhythmic 'Hi-yi-yi' chant, a mourning Dakota wail of death. Their keepers had heard nothing quite like it before. Lest the chant be a war song, presaging an effort to break from the stockade, the guards called for reinforcements and chained the condemned to the floor.

Wednesday was Christmas Eve. Most of the doomed had friends or relatives among the Indians held elsewhere in the stockade. These were brought to the stone enclosure for farewell visits.

Many had families in the winter camp at Fort Snelling, but wives and children were not brought to Mankato for leave-taking.

Knives, rings, personal trinkets, money, and articles of clothing were bestowed on visitors, or given to be sent to absent relatives as parting momentos. A few who had trinkets or rings but no relatives gave souvenirs to the missionaries or to newspapermen from Mankato and St. Paul who had been admitted to the enclosure.

Thursday was Christmas, the final day before the scheduled hanging.

Three clergymen, the Reverend Stephen Riggs. Father Ravoux, and Dr. Williamson, were in the stockade. They spent the day in the enclosure, hearing confessions and talking to the warriors. More than three-fourths of them asked Father Ravoux for baptism.

'This,' explained the Reverend Stephen Riggs, 'was because one of the Campbells, a half-breed and a Roman Catholic, was of the number.'[9]

Friday morning was much like any other morning, but now there were more people than usual outside the stockade, and the demeanor of the guards was subtly less brusque.

From the road in front of the stockade came the clatter of passing feet, the sound of voices, and occasional bursts of laughter.

As soon as the prisoners had eaten, guards placed a cap of white muslin on the head of each. The muslin was rolled back loosely to leave the wearer's face uncovered.[10]

Each condemned man's hands were then crossed in front of him and his wrists bound together tightly. After this had been done the iron manacles were removed.

Shortly after nine o'clock Father Ravoux entered the enclosure and began to say a final prayer. Most of the prisoners lay on the floor. Some turned their heads to the priest, some wriggled nearer, and many mumbled responses.

The provost marshal entered the enclosure to announce that the time to mount the scaffold had come.

Now the muslin caps were pulled down over each face. Although the prisoners objected, there was nothing they could do but tug uselessly at the cords holding their wrists together.

They were ordered to form a line.

All had stood while the cloth was being pulled down, but now nobody could see well enough to take his place in line. By shoving and leading, the guards formed all in a compact row behind the marshal. There were thirty-eight prisoners in the line instead of the thirty-nine the president had listed. Tatemima had been respited.[11]

More than fourteen hundred soldiers formed solid ranks around the scaffold when the masked prisoners were led forth.

Hundreds upon hundreds of spectators crowded the roofs and windows of nearby buildings, a sandbar below the bank, and the river's opposite side.

In the stockade prisoners not being hung crowded to crevices and watched with stolid interest. They demonstrated neither anger nor sorrow. They merely observed, attentive and silent.

The provost marshal climbed the steps leading to the drop. Behind him, guided and pushed by guards, crowded the thirty-eight.

On the platforms forming the outer sides of the great scaffold, guards guided the Indians to positions beneath dangling ropes and adjusted nooses over their heads.

Facing inward, the Dakotas again broke into the mournful

wail which had frightened their keepers on Tuesday night.[12]

This time the 'Hi-yi-yi' was punctuated by occasional screams, and accompanied by swaying and stomping. The gallows platform, built to hold forty reasonably passive men, rocked sharply from side to side until the provost marshal's shouts ended the swaying.

Still protesting about the muslin covering their faces, the Indians shouted their own names and names of others. They swung their bound arms from side to side, and a few succeeded in grasping hands of neighbors.

The provost marshal and the guards scampered off the scaffold.

Three slow, rolling beats boomed from a drum. On the final beat a young man with a deeply lined face stepped forward, holding a long knife in one hand. He was William J. Duley,[13] formerly of Lake Shetek, father of two massacre victims, and killer of Lean Bear during the attack on the slough near Shetek. Now, standing before the scaffold, he glanced uncertainly from side to side.

The provost marshal motioned sharply.

Duley stepped forward and quickly cut a taut rope under the near side of the scaffold. The platforms fell, and thirty-eight bodies dangled in the air, legs kicking, arms flailing.

Soon after the platforms crashed, the rope holding one of the bodies broke and a figure tumbled to the ground. It was the body of Rdainyanka. His neck had been broken before his body fell; there was no flailing when he was hung up again.

As the platforms fell there was a brief, subdued roar from the soldiers and watching citizens. It was more a growl than a cheer.

One by one the bodies were cut down and examined by physicians. Then they were placed in army wagons and hauled to a sloping part of the river bank.

Here, among the willows, a grave twelve feet wide and three times as long had been dug. In it the bodies were placed in two rows, heads to the outside, and covered with blankets. It was a shallow grave, only four feet deep, and was speedily filled with sand and earth.

Late that night a group of doctors from Mankato, St. Peter, and Le Sueur dug the bodies out and took them away, explaining that the high water in the spring would open the grave in any event.

Dr. William Mayo drew the body of Cut Nose. The skeleton of the terror of Beaver Creek was cleaned and articulated. A few years later, when the doctor's two young sons showed an interest in medicine, their first knowledge of osteology came from the skeleton of Cut Nose.[14]

After the execution the platforms surrounding the big scaffold were raised and tied back into place. As they peered from their enclosure, the surviving prisoners wondered when another letter with an additional list of names would arrive.

Snow fell on the scaffold and winter winds switched the dangling ropes from side to side. Then one day soldiers swarmed over the scaffold again. This time they whacked it asunder. The watchers in the stockade heard the screeching of boards being pulled apart, and knew that no additional list had arrived.

INTERIOR OF INDIAN JAIL

XXV NIMBLE ADVERSARY

To Little Crow the Wood Lake fiasco was a grievous disappointment, but no reason for despair. Now that everyone needed to make a final choice, traitors and cowards would purge themselves from the ranks of the Sioux; the remaining Dakotas would be better off without the timid and disloyal.

Another stand against the soldiers could not be attempted at present. The Lower bands needed to vacate the valley. They could do so easily enough without trespassing on land guarded by Standing Buffalo.

Once the Dakotas got beyond reach of the soldiers, important additional matters needed attention. For one thing, powerful support might be recruited from Sioux in the west. For another, a serious appeal could be made for help from the British.[1]

Crossing the river, Little Crow and his followers went sixty miles north, jogged westward forty miles, and emerged in the valley of the Red River of the North. Not once had they set foot on Sisseton land.

Leading north into Canada, the Red River passed within fifty miles of Devils Lake. The lake, also known as Mini Wakan, was five hundred miles northwest of St. Paul, near the northeast corner of Dakota Territory, and not far from British America. It was huge, shallow, and surrounded by scores of smaller lakes.

For generations the region had been a summer hunting base for Dakotas, Chippewas, Assiniboines, Arikaras, Minnetarees, or whatever tribe reached it first in the spring. Now it could serve as winter headquarters. It offered game, fish, and wood in abundance. It was here that Little Crow and his followers went.

In every respect the location was ideal. From the lake, envoys could reach Mandans, eastern Tetons, and Yanktons, all possible allies, without trespassing on Chippewa territory. From it Little Crow could go to St. Joseph and Fort Garry for talks with the British.

Emissaries went first to some of the western tribes. Some encountered scorn and hostility, but most were received with respectful attention.

White Spider was jeered by Mandans and driven from camp. Some Yankton villages welcomed Little Crow's messengers, but others were coldly disdainful. Little Crow's war, though, had created great interest and excitement, even among those who considered it foolish. In the end, most bands approached by the messengers voted to journey to Devils Lake, not to join Little Crow, but to see and hear him.

During the winter thirty thousand Indians,[2] with warriors at times numbering six thousand, poured from the southwest and west. Arriving were Yanktons and Yanktonais. Tetons came from as far west as the Black Hills and from as far south as the North Platte. Included were a few Ogalallas, Hunkpapas, Mineconjous, and others from farther west. Bands of Sissetons and Wahpetons, fearing undeserved reprisals if they remained on reservation land, wandered into the region from the southeast. Such Medewakantons as Shakopee, Red Middle Voice, Medicine Bottle, and hundreds of others had followed when Little Crow came.

Most arrivals were full of curiosity. They yearned for detailed accounts of the summer's exploits. But they were determined to do nothing detrimental to their own bands.

Little Crow's exhortations were stirring. His denunciations of the whites were impressive. **His predictions of what would** happen if the Indians failed to drive back the invaders were alarming.

Whites, proclaimed Little Crow, were swindlers, liars, and cowards, but they were numerous. Driving them out and keeping them away was no job for the Lower bands alone. It was a job for all the Sioux, and maybe also Cheyennes, Pawnees, and even Chippewas. United action was the only way the Plains country could be saved for the Indians.

The chief's famed eloquence won attention and sympathy, but did not achieve unity. Few of the grievances that Little Crow recited applied, thus far, to any but the annuity bands.

When spring came, the thousands of warriors at Devils Lake remained tribesmen with separate interests, sometimes conflicting. They had not been welded into a unified force under a single command. Little Crow had no more army than he had had the previous fall.

It was now that the chief decided to visit St. Joseph and Fort Garry. Any concession gained from the British might strengthen his prestige at the lake and help him achieve the unity he needed.

He made two trips, visiting Fort Garry, near Winnipeg, and St. Joseph, international trading post forty miles west of Pembina.[3] Sixty braves accompanied him to attract attention with war dances. The chief wore a long black broadcloth coat with a velvet collar, fit attire for calling on officials. Vividly colored silk shawls were wrapped around his head and middle.

At every appearance Little Crow made a speech. He reminded the British of Sioux help in the War of 1812. He requested ammunition, 'only for hunting.' He asked for a grant of land in western Canada where he and his followers could settle. He said the Dakotas had surrendered all their white captives, but complained that the Americans held hundreds of Sioux in prison; he implored authorities to intercede with the United States for release of the prisoners.

The authorities shook their heads. They knew of no treaty

obligations resulting from Sioux help fifty years before. Killing unarmed settlers was cowardly and shameful; it had won no friends for the Sioux in British America. Granting of ammunition or land was unthinkable; in any case, such grants were beyond the power of authorities in frontier forts or trading posts. Canada was no place for Sioux to settle; Chippewas would kill them. The authorities in the east and in London were being carefully neutral during the Civil War; they would never interfere to ask that prisoners be freed.

Wowinapa, sixteen-year-old son of Little Crow, went along on the second trip. It was June when the party returned to the lake. On the journey back to camp Little Crow, for the first time, acknowledged failure of his efforts.[4]

No allies had been recruited from the west. No ammunition or land had been gained from the British. There was no chance for success in the chief's fight with the United States. Flight was the only possibility, and for flight Little Crow's family needed horses. He would make a final foray to the settlements, get horses, and take his wives and children to some remote place west of the Missouri or in western Canada. When his family was safe he would return to see about continuing the war.

In the settlements, scouts reported, great plans were afoot for exterminating the Sioux. General Pope had made his appeals for men heard above the Civil War tumult. He was assembling eight thousand troops to capture Little Crow. Four thousand were gathering on the upper Minnesota, at the mouth of the Redwood, under Brigadier General Sibley's command. The other four thousand, led by General Alfred Sully, were on the Missouri in the northwest corner of Iowa.[5]

Pope's strategy was apparent. One force would come up the Red River to a point east of Devils Lake. The other would approach along the Missouri until they were west of the lake. Then the two armies, with Little Crow between them, would swing together, capturing or killing the Sioux. The answer was as obvious as the strategy; by the time the armies were in position there would be no Sioux at Devils Lake.

As soon as word of Pope's preparations reached them, some of the Indians began to depart.

Red Middle Voice, who had as much to fear from the soldiers as anyone, started for Canada. A stray band of Chippewas encountered his party. Red Middle Voice and his entire family were slaughtered.[6]

Shakopee, Medicine Bottle, most of the Rice Creekers, and more than eight hundred others, succeeded in crossing the border south of Fort Garry. Some formed an encampment of sixty lodges on the Assiniboine River twenty-five miles from the fort. Others scattered to Manitoba and other parts of Canada's Far West.

Despite the eight thousand troops Pope had amassed west of the border, peace and security did not return to the Minnesota frontier.

Raiders from bands overlooked in the area scoured by Sibley's forces the previous autumn and small detachments from Dakota Territory continued to make forays. Thirty more settlers were killed during the spring.

South of New Ulm the family of Swenson Roland was attacked and a twelve-year-old son shot to death. In the same area Ole Palmer, Gabriel Elingson, and other Norwegian immigrants were killed. Henry Basche was murdered within two miles of New Ulm.

North of the river Gilbert Parker, fishing on Long Lake, was butchered and scalped.

In late June the family of Amos Dustin started across the prairie forty-five miles west of St. Paul. In their wagon were six, including three young children and Dustin's widowed mother. In the over-due wagon, when searchers found it, were the lifeless, mutilated bodies of Dustin, his four-year-old son.

and his mother. In a meadow near the road lay Dustin's wife, mortally wounded.[7]

James McGannon, homesteader seventy miles west of Minneapolis, was murdered July 1. A gray coat was stripped from McGannon's body, and his horse was taken.

'While Sibley's army is moving, with ponderous steps and slow, to crush the Sioux under the heel of strategy,' raged the St. Paul *Press*, 'his nimble adversary is crawling through his legs and running all around him.'

Six miles northwest of Hutchinson, near the western edge of the Big Woods, lived a settler named Nathan Lamson. Late on the afternoon of July 3, three days after James McGannon had been killed, Lamson observed that it was time to round up the horses for the night. He asked his oldest son, Chauncey, to help him. A clearing in the woods, less than a mile from Lamson's shack, was a favorite grazing place of the horses. Carrying guns, Nathan and Chauncey headed for it, the father in the lead. As they neared the clearing Nathan held out his hand. Father and son came to a stop.[8]

Just the day before, in Hutchinson, Lamson had heard details of the finding of Amos Dustin's wagon. He was glad both he and Chauncey were armed.

In the clearing were clumps of bushes and a few slender poplars, but no large trees. On the near side, stripping berries and eating them, were two figures. Enough late afternoon light filtered into the clearing so that there was no question that both berry pickers were Indians.

The Lamsons dropped to the ground and crept slowly ahead, keeping a clump of bushes between themselves and the pickers.

At the edge of the clump was a slim poplar. Nathan steadied his gun against it, aimed at the nearest Indian, and fired.

The Indian yelled loudly and leaped into the air. Two guns lay nearby in the grass. The wounded Indian stumbled backward, clutched one of the guns, turned it toward Lamson, fired, and reached for the other weapon. His companion, a younger Indian, grabbed the empty gun and reloaded it.

Nathan and Chauncey continued to crouch behind the bushes. As far as either knew, there might be more Indians in the clearing. If so, having heard the two shots, they would be gliding nearer. Nathan glanced quickly around. The clump behind which he and Chauncey lay afforded concealment from only one side.

He decided to try for the trees.

As he broke from the bushes, both Indians fired. Buckshot struck Nathan's left shoulder, knocking him down. Chauncey saw the impact on the side of his father's jacket. Nathan fell several yards short of the trees, and did not stir.

As the two Indians fired, Chauncey shot at the one his father had wounded. The ball from Chauncey's gun grazed the stock of one of the weapons and ricocheted into the older Indian's shoulder. The wounded man fell, rasped a few words to his companion, and lay motionless.

Chauncey looked toward the spot where Nathan lay. He concluded his father was dead, slid out of the clearing, and reached the trail. Then he ran to Hutchinson. He reached the settlement at ten that night and returned to the berry patch with a party of soldiers and citizens.

Nathan was not in the clearing. His wound had only stunned him. He soon crawled into the woods and, avoiding the trail, had dragged himself almost home by the time the rescuers reached the patch.

The only occupant of the clearing was the older Indian. He was dead. A gray coat, the one stripped from James McGannon's body three days before, had been folded and placed under his head. His hands were crossed over his body.

Early next day, the Fourth of July, the dead Indian was taken to Hutchinson. There the body was viewed by scores of citizens.

The dead man appeared to have been of medium height.

His hair was partly gray. He had a double set of teeth. His left arm was withered and the other one appeared to have been partly crippled. It looked as though the bones, probably broken by a bullet, had not been properly set.

'Many persons recognized the body as that of an Indian well known in the place,' but nobody could identify it.

In the evening the scalp was removed, and the corpse tossed into a pit generally full of rotting beef entrails. A report of the killing was sent to St. Paul.

A week later dogs dragged what remained of the corpse from the pit. Someone pried the head off and left it 'lying on the prairie for several days, the brains oozing out in the broiling sun.'[9]

Citizens who had viewed the body continued to talk about it. Some thought they had detected a resemblance to Little Crow. Others contended Little Crow's complexion was darker. Anyway, eight thousand troops were approaching Devils Lake, and what would the chief, with only one companion, have been doing four hundred miles southeast of the lake?

Perhaps, though, the deformed arms were a clue worth checking; it was known that the chief's wrists had been damaged years before in a tribal shooting. Presently the wrist-bones and skull were retrieved from the entrail pit.

With the scalp, they were shipped to St. Paul. Medical inspection supported the theory that the bones had been shattered and improperly set. This, however, did not prove the body was that of Little Crow.

Twenty-six days after the berry patch shooting came conclusive identification. A party of half-breed hunters picked up, near Devils Lake, 'a young man half-starved and nearly naked.' He was, he declared, Wowinapa, son of Little Crow.[10]

He told of having been in the clearing when his father was shot. It was he who had folded the gray coat and placed it under his father's head, and he who had crossed the fallen chief's hands over his body.

'A short time before father was killed,' explained Wowinapa, 'an Indian named Hiuka, who married the daughter of my father's second wife, came to him. He had a gray-colored coat he had taken from a man he had killed. He gave the coat to father, telling him he might need it when it rained. Hiuka said he had a horse now, and was going back to the Indian country.'

Little Crow and Wowinapa had been on the same foray, for horses, when disaster overtook them in the berry patch.

In the Indian country, with the summer of 1863 half gone, General Pope's campaign to exterminate the Sioux had run into trouble.[11] Most of General Sully's four thousand troops did not get within one hundred and sixty miles of their destination. Sully's supplies were to go up the Missouri in barges. Snags, sandbars, and muddy shallows caught the barges and held them.

General Sibley's four thousand men carted supplies overland in two hundred and twenty-five wagons. By the end of July, having moved at an average rate of fifteen miles a day, they were within forty miles of Devils Lake's south end.

Scouts reported the separate armies' progress each day. By the time Sibley's forces were a hundred miles distant, four thousand warriors and most of the Indian women and children had moved west of the Missouri.

In a delaying action designed to give stragglers time to reach the new encampment, two thousand braves engaged Sibley's forces in inconsequential skirmishes at Big Mound and Stony Lake, near present-day Bismark, North Dakota.

That was the end of the 1863 campaign. General Sibley sent a messenger to inform General Sully that the Devils Lake area had been cleared of the enemy. Then he turned his troops to the southeast and marched them to St. Paul. General Sully's army skirmished at White Stone Hills, burned what the General estimated was 'four hundred thousand to five hundred thousand pounds of dried buffalo meat,'[12] made captives of one hundred and twenty-four Indian women and children and thirty-two warriors. On September 5 they headed for the settlements.

Red Middle Voice had been killed by Chippewas. Little Crow had been shot by Chauncey Lamson, assisted by his father. Mankato had been killed by an artillerist at Wood Lake. Cut Nose, willing to die, had been hung at South Bend.

Only Shakopee, of the massacre's major instigators, remained alive.

Participants who were not self-exiled in British America crossed the Missouri and scattered over the plains. Some joined one band, some another. After a few more months they were dispersed too widely ever to be overtaken and identified, and widely enough to sow seeds of rebellion among a hundred western bands.

Promised a reward by the Americans, British subjects at Fort Garry seized Shakopee and Medicine Bottle the following winter and turned them over to authorities at Pembina.[13] It was May, 1864, when the captives reached Fort Snelling; November before Sibley appointed a special military commission to try them; and November, 1865, before they were hung. The charges on which they were tried were not considered very substantial; the evidence on which they were convicted was thought inconclusive by many.

'We do not think serious injustice will be done by the execution,' brooded the St. Paul *Pioneer* the day before the hanging, 'but it would be more creditable if some tangible evidence of guilt had been obtained.'

Shakopee and his companion died on a wooded hillside near the Minnesota's mouth.[14] According to legend, the first steam locomotive to reach the area hooted mournfully below the hill at the moment they ascended the gallows. Shakopee, said the myth,[15] waved an arm toward the train and exclaimed: 'As the white man comes in the Indian goes out!'

XXVI   THE CAPITOL WAS DRAPED IN BLACK

Nobody knew how many residents of the frontier were chopped or shot to death during one week of August, 1862. Nobody ever will.

Thousands of newcomers were in the ravaged land. After the devastation, land offices could say how many claims had been filed in each locality, but they could not say how many families had occupied the land or how many members each family contained.[1]

Even an accurate count immediately before the killings would not have helped; thousands fled, some never to come back and some going to different localities when they did. Other thousands, not present before the carnage, first came when the population returned. No before-and-after comparisons meant much.

Tallies of casualties could not be kept during the killings. Settlers who paused in flight to bury murdered neighbors might themselves be slain before they reported the burials.

A count of graves could not determine the number of casualties. Except by disinterment, it could not be known how many bodies each mound covered. Some graves were not found, and never would be. Some victims were not buried; wind and rain erased the remains of some who perished in flames of lonely cabins. Those who died in swamps, thickets, or deep prairie grass would never be known.

Six months later Jane Grey Swisshelm, pioneer editor and lecturer, said that fifteen hundred lives had been lost.[2]

Senator Morton Wilkinson informed President Lincoln that 'nearly or quite one thousand' had been murdered.

President Lincoln placed the number at 'not less than eight hundred.'[3] His estimate seemed, and continues to seem, as realistic as any, and more so than some.

Agent Thomas Galbraith made an area-by-area tally and reached a total of six hundred forty-four civilians and ninety-three soldiers, or a grand total of seven hundred thirty-seven. 'More there may be,' said Galbraith, 'and I think there are.'

Fifty years after the massacre an effort to list all civilian and military casualties produced four hundred and forty-seven names,[4] but by then those whose graves had been plowed under or whose ashes had blown away had been long forgotten.

'It is our impression,' asserted the St. Peter *Tribune* six weeks after the killings, 'that nearer two thousand than one thousand have been massacred. Doubtless hundreds that have been slain and left upon the surface will never be found, as decomposition is nearly complete, and the prairie fires now ravaging the whole upper country will consume what may yet remain.'

When this estimate was published, burial parties continued to inter as many as forty-seven bodies a day, and searchers were still finding survivors hiding in forests and swamps.

Explanations of the outbreak's causes varied as widely as estimates of casualties. Everyone voiced an opinion regarding the disaster's origin; most of the opinions differed.

Agent Galbraith attributed the revolt to 'ingrained and fixed hostility of the barbarian to reform, change, and civilization.' Specifically, he was inclined to think 'encroachments of Christianity upon the habits and customs of the Sioux' was a cause.

The Reverend Stephen Riggs blamed the Democrats. When Republicans took over Indian affairs, they paid annuities partly in goods; the Democrats had paid entirely in cash. This

gave the Democrats 'a grand opportunity to work on the
hopes and fears of the Indians, and they seem to have carried
it a little too far.' [5]

Martha Riggs opined the massacre had occurred because
whites had taught Dakotas to swear and drink liquor, and
'violated the rights of womanhood among them.'

'The federal government, through maladministration of
the Indian department,' was at fault, in the belief of Attorney
Isaac Heard.

'The whites always acted as if they were better than the
Indians,' complained Big Eagle, 'but the Dakotas thought
there were no better men on earth than they were.' [6]

'The war was in full force in the South,' explained Charles
Flandrau. 'Thousands of men were being sent out of the state.
This led to the belief the whites were in desperate trouble and
caused the Indians to think it was a good time to recover their
country, redress all their grievances, and re-establish themselves as lords of the land.' [7]

These causes, combined with fraudulent treaties, insolent
traders, swindling fur companies, and dishonest agents, certainly helped make the rebellion. But grievances alone would
not have produced so violent a blood-letting. Without grievances the uprising could not have occurred; with nothing but
grievances, it could not have happened either. The other
essential was leadership.

Shakopee, Red Middle Voice, and the Rice Creek soldiers'
lodge could provide the kind of leadership needed for slaughter of unarmed settlers, and did so. But they could not author-
ize and lead a general war, and they knew it. Sanction and
respectability had to come from a leader with prestige and
authority; Little Crow supplied it.

To his contemporaries, both red and white, Little Crow's
leadership of the conflict, considering the kind of war it turned
out to be, seemed entirely out of character. For years there-

after survivors would debate, explain, and try to comprehend his position.

How could a pants-wearing, church-going farmer, planning a new brick house, have led a vicious and deadly assault on his pants-wearing, church-going neighbors?

Had taunts and jibes over his new wagon, his trousers, or his support of the 1858 treaty stung him beyond endurance?

Had loss of the speakership caused Little Crow to decide that adjustment to the whites' way of life made, after all, 'very little good sense'?

Had the mob's roar at the pre-dawn council caused Little Crow to fear for his life?

Had rage, when Red Middle Voice ridiculed him as being afraid of the whites, unbalanced Little Crow's judgment for a critical moment?

Had the mob won his acquiescence by trickery?

One or another of Little Crow's acquaintances offered each of these explanations. Alone, each seemed an oversimplification. Together, they rendered almost believable the endorsement wrung from the chief.

In the broadest and truest sense, though, the war did not start at Acton or Lower Agency, and was not launched by the pre-dawn council.

Instead, it began three centuries before Little Crow's day. It commenced when the first Europeans poked exploratory canoes into North America's inland waters, exclaiming over the beauty, fertility, and emptiness of the land.

The trickle of migration in the wake of the canoes had become a tidal wave. It had engulfed tribe after tribe in the eastern part of the land, extinguishing some and causing others to fall westward. Now it was washing the eastern edge of the Great Plains, whose possessors and guardians were the Sioux, Cheyennes, Pawnees, and others.

When Little Crow was killed his body was tossed into an

offal pit. Later his brains oozed out in the broiling sun. When Henry Hastings Sibley died he was buried with ceremony, and the capitol of his state was draped in black.[8]

This was not because Sibley was a better or abler man than Little Crow. It was because Little Crow existed at the end of one era, and Sibley was the fore-runner of the next. Almost anything Little Crow did was doomed to fail. Almost anything Sibley undertook, with the exception of fighting Indians, was bound to be successful.

As sometimes happens in wars, all the winners of the 1862 war were not immediately wholly victorious.

In the score of counties entirely depopulated and in the half dozen partly abandoned, no settlers returned for a year and a half. 'All the property of the settlers, including their growing and garnered crops, was totally lost, and many of their houses, outbuildings, and fences were burned or destroyed.'[9]

When settlement was resumed it was slow. Few who returned could afford promptly to buy implements, seed, cattle, horses, or to rebuild what had been destroyed. Many were without families. Their wives and children might be 'scattered in distant places subsisting on the generosity of friends, or charity.'

Many who came back did not remain. The Duleys returned to Lake Shetek, 'but found someone had jumped their claim so they did not stay.'[10] They moved to Beeson, Alabama.

Other survivors or participants scattered elsewhere.

Jonathan Earle, his taste for the frontier lost, took his family back to New York. His son, Ezmon, became a physician at Rochester.

Mary Schwandt married William Schmidt, a St. Paul businessman. Her brother, August, who had watched the attackers rip open his sister, Caroline, grew up to become a hardware dealer in Portland, Oregon.

Agent Galbraith moved to Montana Territory and was made a district judge.

Joseph and Valencia Reynolds, keepers of the public house on Yellow Medicine road, became keepers of a hotel at St. Peter.

After withdrawing from the state supreme court, Charles Flandrau moved to Nevada, lived there two years, returned, moved to St. Paul, and there developed a successful law practice.

Another who moved to St. Paul was Henry Hastings Sibley. He became president of the St. Paul Gas Company, the City Bank, the state historical society, and the state university's board of regents. He helped organize the city's Chamber of Commerce, served as chairman of the Committee on Relief of Grasshopper Sufferers, and was a director of the First National Bank and the Sioux City Railroad.[11] He died at the age of eighty, and the state went into mourning the day he was buried.

Lieutenant Tom Gere went south with the Fifth Minnesota Infantry. He participated in the capture of Vicksburg. At the close of 1864, in the Battle of Nashville, he 'captured a battle flag on the enemy's works, and in other respects showed the most daring gallantry.'[12]

Although a negligible number of guilty Dakotas surrendered for punishment and few died in the fighting, effects of the conflict on most of the others left no doubt as to who were the losers.

John Otherday, given a farm near Henderson to reward him for leading Yellow Medicine whites to safety, was one of the few Dakotas better off after the conflict than before.

The reprieved prisoners at South Bend were removed to a camp at East Davenport, Iowa, when river navigation reopened. After three years they were released to rejoin their tribesmen.[13]

Occupants of the Fort Snelling winter camp were moved in the spring to a tract of barren, unproductive land on Crow Creek, Dakota Territory.

'The very memory of Crow Creek became horrible,' wrote a missionary who accompanied them. 'They still hush their voices at mention of the name.' [14]

Three years later they were allowed to move to more arable land in the valleys of the Big Sioux and Niobrara.

Wabasha and Wacouta, after accompanying the other exiles to Crow Creek, spent their remaining years on the Niobrara reservation in northeastern Nebraska.

Of the Sioux who took an active part in the war's leadership, Big Eagle was one of the few to return to Minnesota. He adopted the name 'Jerome' and lived for forty years on a farm near Granite Falls, not far from the site of the former Upper Agency.[15]

Wowinapa, son of Little Crow, was tried by one of General Sibley's military commissions, found guilty of helping his father try to steal horses near Hutchinson, and sentenced to be hung. The army's Judge Advocate General disapproved of the proceedings. Wowinapa was sent to East Davenport. On release from prison camp he changed his name to Thomas Wakeman. He became an active church member and a deacon.

Some who fled without having been implicated in the massacre, notably Wahpetons and Sissetons, returned after a few years to the eastern part of Dakota Territory. They had not found hunting grounds comparable to their own, had 'lived so miserably, and undergone such privations, that they returned in despair to put themselves under the protection of the government.' [16] But they could not quite return to their former reservation. During their absence a string of six forts had been established in the Upper Missouri area to serve as a rampart against the Sioux. Most of the returnees stopped at the line of forts, or west of it.[17] Descendants of many now live on Sisseton Reservation in northeastern South Dakota.[18]

Those who were deeply implicated stayed far away. Thirty years after the massacre at least two of the Rice Creekers who had been at Acton still lived in Manitoba. Plenty of Hail, confessed slayer of James Lynd, was a resident of Canada in the early years of the present century.

More of the thoroughly guilty lost themselves and their identities among western bands of the Sioux, where their experience and talents were welcome. Joining remote bands, they spent the winter and then the summer of 1863, reciting grievances, boasting of exploits, spreading word that they had found whites to be cowardly incompetents, and joining Teton raids on wagon trains.

In the following year, 1864, came an act of white savagery matching the Minnesota performance of the Sioux. In November a regiment directed by Colonel J. M. Chivington, a vengeful, fanatical ex-abolitionist, attacked two Cheyenne villages on Sand Creek, Colorado. Three hundred Indians, most of them unarmed squaws and children, were murdered. Scores of bodies were mutilated; more than one hundred were scalped. The Sand Creek camp-site had been authorized by the governor of Colorado, and the Cheyennes had supposed they were under military protection. The raid was as brutal and unprovoked as any deed of the Rice Creekers.

All surviving Cheyennes became allies of the Sioux; the Sioux war became the War of the Plains Indians.[19]

At Platte Bridge the following summer Cheyennes wiped out a wagon train, its military escort, and a detachment of Kansas cavalry. In Wyoming Territory a year later Sioux and Cheyennes collaborated to exterminate Captain Fetterman's eighty-one officers and men.[20] The next summer, also in Wyoming, thirty wood-haulers from Fort Phil Kearny, armed with rapid-fire repeating rifles, fought off two hundred Sioux in the Wagon Box Fight.

Extermination of General George Custer with two hundred and eight troops on Montana's Little Big Horn in 1876 was a joint operation of Cheyennes and such Sioux as the Brules, Ogalallas, Hunkpapas, and Minneconjous. Among many [21] reported to have killed Custer were Spotted Calf, a Minnesota Sioux and two sons of Inkpaduta, also of the Lower bands.

The closing act of the struggle for the Great Plains did not take place until mid-winter, 1890. It was an event that Red Middle Voice might have admired. Three thousand soldiers butchered two hundred Minneconjous and Hunkpapas, again mostly unarmed squaws and papooses, at Wounded Knee Creek in western South Dakota as they approached Pine Ridge reservation for sanctuary.

Three days later a detachment of soldiers gathered frost-stiffened corpses from a two-mile area over which the terrified victims had tried to flee, tossed the bodies into a long trench, and threw frozen earth over them.[22]

Victory for the invaders had ended, after twenty-eight years of the nation's most ignominious war.

BIBLIOGRAPHICAL NOTES

Some who survived events related in this narrative, or participated in them, told what they had experienced, done, or seen. A few of their accounts were in writing. Others were told to investigating commissions. Many related to single happenings or to a series of connected events. Because of the nature of the outbreak nobody saw more than a fraction of what occurred. Two accounts, written within two years of the uprising contained first-hand testimony of various witnesses regarding numerous events, and were held together by descriptions of what was then known of the whole affair. These accounts, and major sources of more fragmentary accounts, are as follows:

Bryant, Charles A. and Murch, Abel B. *A History of the Great Massacre by the Sioux Indians.* Cincinnati. Rickey & Carroll. 1864.

Heard, Isaac V. D. *History of the Sioux War.* New York. Harper & Bros. 1863.

Riggs, Stephen R. *Mary and I; Forty Years with the Sioux.* Boston. Congregational S.S. and Pub. Society. 1887. (Written earlier and first published as a book in 1880.)

Wakefield, Mrs. Sarah F. *Six Weeks in the Sioux Tepees.* Shakopee, Minn. Argus. 1864.

Flandrau, Charles E. *The History of Minnesota.* St. Paul. E. W. Porter. 1900. (Some of the most vivid of Flandrau's recollections appeared earlier in 'Minnesota in the Civil and Indian Wars,' 'Encyclopedia of Biography of Minnesota,' and elsewhere.)

Collections of the Minnesota Historical Society. St. Paul. Pioneer Press Co. Various years and writers.

Minnesota in the Civil and Indian Wars. St. Paul. Pioneer Press Co. In two volumes. 1890 and 1893. Various writers.

Here, sometimes filled with anguish, pride, doubt, self-righteous-
ness, or anger, and often told with prejudice, are the stories of
captives, military men, citizen soldiers, missionaries, and the Sioux.

Because of the frequency with which these sources are named
in the chapter notes, they are designated as *Bryant, Heard, Riggs,
Wakefield, Flandrau, Collections,* and *M.C.I.W.* The sixth volume
of the *Collections,* published in 1894, contains an unusual number
of narratives relating to the outbreak. The second volume of
M.C.I.W. holds most of the military reports and correspondence
concerning the uprising. Thus, unless otherwise noted, *Collections*
refers to Volume 6 and *M.C.I.W.* to the second volume of this set.

In addition to these publications, a number of others were
accounts closely related to the outbreak. Some consist of important eye-witness accounts confined to a single phase or event.
Some add supplemental detail without contributing information
not already established. Some were not written until many years
had elapsed. Some contain first-hand accounts but in the main are
second-hand reports. This does not necessarily detract from their
interest and value, because some contain carefully recorded information not reported elsewhere. They include:

Boyd, R. K. *The Battle of Birch Coulee.* Eau Claire, Wisc. 1925.

Buck, Daniel. *Indian Outbreak.* Mankato, Minn. 1904.

Connolly, A. P. *Minnesota Massacre.* Chicago. 1896.

Earle, E. W. *Reminiscences of the Sioux Massacre.* Fairfax, Minn.
Undated.

Folwell, William Watts. *A History of Minnesota.* St. Paul. 1924. (In
four volumes. Vol 2 is most pertinent.)

Gilman, S. C. *The Conquest of the Sioux.* Indianapolis. 1900.

Holcombe, Return I. and others. *Minnesota in Three Centuries.*
Mankato, Minn. 1908. (In four volumes. Vol. 3 is most pertinent.)

Hughes, Thomas. *Indian Chiefs of Southern Minnesota.* Mankato,
Minn. 1927. *Old Traverse des Sioux.* St. Peter, Minn. 1929.

McConkey, Harriet E. *Dakota War Whoop.* St. Paul. 1864.

Neill, E. D. *History of the Minnesota Valley.* 1882.

Pettijohn, Jonas. *Autobiography*. Clay Center, Kan. 1890.

Robinson, Doane. *A History of the Dakota or Sioux Indians*. Aberdeen, S. D. 1904.

Roddis, Louis H. *The Indian Wars of Minnesota*. Cedar Rapids, Ia. 1956.

Satterlee, M. P. *A Detailed Account of the Massacre in 1862*. Minneapolis. 1923.

Swisshelm, Jane Grey. *Crusader and Feminist*. St. Paul. 1934.

Tarble, Helen. *The Story of My Capture and Escape*. St. Paul. 1904.

Related to earlier or later events, to the setting in which the outbreak took place, or to the immediately subsequent War of the Plains Indians, are such publications as:

Adams, James Truslow, editor. *Atlas of American History*. New York. 1943.

Black Hawk. *An Autobiography*. Edited by Donald Jackson. Urbana, Ill. 1955.

Burt, Struthers. *Powder River*. New York. 1938.

Clapsattle, Helen. *The Doctors Mayo*. Minneapolis. 1941.

De Trobriand, Philippe. *Army Life in Dakota*. Chicago. 1941.

De Voto, Bernard. *The Course of Empire*. Boston. 1952.

Eastman, Charles A. *Indian Boyhood*. New York. 1902.

Fremont, John Charles. *Memoirs of My Life*. Chicago. 1887.

Grinnell, George Bird. *The Fighting Cheyennes*. New York. 1915.

Havighurst, Walter. *Upper Mississippi*. New York. 1937.

Hyde, George E. *A Sioux Chronicle*. Norman, Okla. 1956.

Kingsbury, George W. *History of Dakota Territory*. Chicago. 1915.

Mayer, F. B. *With Pen and Pencil on the Frontier in 1851*. St. Paul. 1932.

Parker, Nathan H. *The Minnesota Handbook*. Boston. 1857.

Rollins, Philip Ashton, editor. *Robert Stuart's Narratives*. New York. 1935.

Sharp, Mrs. Abigail Gardner. *History of the Spirit Lake Massacre.* Des Moines. 1895.

Shea, John G. *Early Voyages Up and Down the Mississippi.* 1861.

Sibley, Henry Hastings. *Iron Face.* Chicago. 1950.

Spindler, Will H. *Tragedy Strikes at Wounded Knee.* Gordon, Neb. 1955.

Stewart, Edgar I. *Custer's Luck.* Norman, Okla. 1955.

Sullivan, Maurice S. *Jedediah Smith.* New York. 1936.

Vestal, Stanley. *New Sources of Indian History.* Norman. 1934. *Sitting Bull, Champion of the Sioux.* Boston. 1932.

Wellman, Paul I. *Death on Horseback.* New York. 1947.

Many of these publications are mentioned again in the chapter notes. The bibliographical listings do not contain the names of all publications cited. Newspapers, magazines, Army, Indian Bureau, or Congressional publications, for example, are not included in any of the lists, but are generally fully identified in the notes.

CHAPTER NOTES

CHAPTER I—*YOU ARE AFRAID OF THE WHITE MAN*

1. Events at Acton were described in *Heard* and *Bryant*, and by Big Eagle in *Collections*. Big Eagle reported the happenings and discussions as they were told him 'by all four of the young men who did the killing.' Both Heard and Bryant related the Cox incident, Bryant in greater detail.

2. The 1851 Treaty prohibited the sale of liquor in the ceded territory. In practice the prohibition applied to Indians but not to whites.

3. Holcombe, in *Minnesota in Three Centuries*, Vol. 3, condensed Mrs. Howard Baker's testimony as it was recorded by Judge Abner Smith of Forest City. Judge Smith later wrote a history of Meeker County in which he included an account of the inquest.

4. *Bryant*. The site of the massacre's start, about seven miles southwest of the present town of Litchfield, is marked by Acton State Monument.

5. Holcombe, *Minnesota in Three Centuries*, Vol. 3, quoting an interview with Big Eagle.

6. Earle, *Reminiscences of the Sioux Indian Massacre*.

CHAPTER II—*PLANT A GOOD DEAL OF GROUND*

1. *Minnesota in Three Centuries.* Vols. 3 and 4. The territory's representatives exaggerated the white population by about 50,000 in their claim of population growth.

2. The names 'Dakota' and 'Sioux' were used interchangeably by Sioux bands living east of the Missouri. Both names appeared in early treaties, and both were used by the Indians themselves. Big Eagle, in his account in *Collections*, used both, and so did the Reverend Stephen R. Riggs when he wrote *Dakota Grammar and Dictionary* and *Forty Years with the Sioux*. The Ogalallas, Hunkpapas, and other bands west of the Missouri used their tribal names much of the time, but were known collectively as the Teton Sioux. They rarely used the name 'Dakota.' In present-day usage the eastern bands still call themselves both 'Sioux' and 'Dakota,' while the western bands continue to use the collective term 'Teton Sioux.' The notion that the name 'Sioux' is resented because it was derived from a word meaning 'enemy' may account

for such comparatively recent nomenclature as 'Teton Dakotas,' applied to the western bands. 'Teton Dakota' is not an incorrect designation, and is used by some present-day Indians, but the term 'Teton Sioux' was more widely used in the past.

3. In early dealings with explorers, traders, and other non-Indians, the eastern bands were more peaceful than those west of the Missouri. According to Maurice S. Sullivan's *Jedediah Smith*, Sioux suspicion of Americans originated in 1811 when a member of the overland party of Astorians, to test the accuracy of his aim, shot and killed a Sioux warrior standing on the opposite bank of a stream.

4. Five dollars an acre for farm land not near markets was considered a fair average price at the time. 'Public land' was being sold to pre-emptors at $1.25 an acre, and sometimes was resold without improvements for $5.00 or more. The price of land near settlements in the more populous eastern part of the state varied from $5.00 to $30.00 an acre, according to Parker's *Minnesota Handbook, 1857*.

5. Provisions of the 1851 and 1858 treaties are discussed at some length in William Watts Folwell's *History of Minnesota*, Vol. 2 and Neill's *History of the Minnesota Valley*. Hughes's *Old Traverse des Sioux* describes one of the two 1851 treaty councils. The other council that year was at Mendota, down-river near the Mississippi. Traverse des Sioux, a short distance downstream from St. Peter, Minnesota, was the site of one of the valley's earliest trading posts, but did not survive as a town.

6. Translation of pertinent parts of Le Sueur's journal may be found in John G. Shea's *Early Voyages Up and Down the Mississippi*.

7. *Wakefield*. Mrs. Wakefield's criticisms of traders, agents, and rescue operations led to accusations that she had been unduly friendly with the Indians during captivity. She wrote *Six Weeks in the Sioux Tepees* in 1864 to defend her reputation, and in it described reservation life as well as conditions behind the Sioux lines during the outbreak. Unlike imagined 'captivity yarns' (Ann Coleson's *Narrative of Her Captivity among the Sioux*, also published in 1864, is an example), the Wakefield account was a factual report.

8. Indian agents were barred by law from having an interest in the Indian trade. Joseph R. Brown, agent at the time of the payment, could not file a direct claim, but the record, said Folwell's *History of Minnesota*, showed an allowance of $21,597 for 'the Browns.' Hughes, in *Old Traverse des Sioux*, described the traders' claims in detail, using figures on claims and allowances derived from the report of a subsequent investigation of Ramsey's handling of the funds.

9. Half-breeds often were products of the seduction of Indian women by traders or their employees, although some were the offspring of legitimate marriages. With notable exceptions, such as Nancy and David Faribault, they tended to be misfits, not wholly acceptable either to whites or Indians.

10 'Major' was a courtesy title assumed by all Indian agents and, in this connection, had no military significance.

11. Folwell's *History of Minnesota* quotes an acquaintance of Galbraith as saying that Galbraith was 'a hard drinker . . . really unfit to hold official position. Half of the time he was out of his head.'

CHAPTER III—*THE GREATEST AMONG THE CHIEFS*

1. 'Medewakanton' is a compromise spelling of this tribe's name. Hughes wrote it Mdewahkonton, Riggs had it as Mdaywakantonwan, Heard made it M'dewakanton, Bryant spelled it Medawakanton, and Big Eagle, in talking to Holcombe, pronounced it Midawa-Xanton. Although the name no longer is used extensively, it continues to appear in reports of the Bureau of Indian Affairs, where it is variously spelled Mdewakanton and Medawakanton. The spellings of such other tribal names as Wahpeton and Wahpekute were subject to similar variation. Even 'Sioux' had numerous spellings. In his notes for *The Discovery of the Oregon Trail*, Philip Ashton Rollins listed twenty variations, ranging from 'Sue' to 'Sceouex.'

2. Although the name 'Santee' was seldom used before the outbreak, it originated much earlier. At one time the eastern bands lived on Knife Lake in the Mille Lacs region of Minnesota and were called Isanyati, or 'Dwellers on Knife.' That, said *Riggs*, is where 'Santee' came from. After the outbreak the name replaced 'Medewakanton,' especially, and became the name of a reservation in northeastern Nebraska. The Wahpekute village at Lower Agency was led by a chief named Hushasha. It was located down-river from the agency a little beyond the Medewakanton encampments. Because of distance, it is possible few Wahpekutes arrived in time for the early attack on the agency. They were present for the battle at the ferry, however, and one of their warriors was killed in that engagement. Hushasha's band was not a large one, and the Wahpekute's main claim to distinction is that the outlaw Inkpaduta was a native son. Inkpaduta was absent at the time of the outbreak, but he or his sons, or both, participated in many activities of both the eastern and Teton Sioux between the Spirit Lake Massacre of 1857 and the Battle of the Little Big Horn in 1876.

3. Little Crow's Indian name was interpreted as meaning 'His Scarlet People,' 'His People Are Red,' 'His Red Nation,' and 'The Sacred Pigeon-Hawk That Comes Walking.' It was written 'Taoyatechata,' 'To-wai-o-ta-doo-ta,' 'Chetan wakon mani,' and in other ways. The French called the chief 'Petit Corbeau.'

4. *Minnesota in Three Centuries*, based on recollections of members of the former Kaposia band.

5. *Flandrau*: 'I can truthfully say one of the happiest and most harmonious families I ever knew was that of Little Crow.' Polygamy was common among the Dakotas.

6. The Sioux and Chippewas were inveterate enemies. Warfare between them was recorded over a period of at least three hundred years.

7. *Minnesota in Three Centuries.*

8. James W. Lynd in *Collections*, Vol. 2. Lynd, a clerk at Myrick's store, was the first reservation casualty at the outbreak's start.

9. *Flandrau.*

10. Frank B. Mayer, *With Pen and Pencil on the Frontier in 1851.*

11. T. W. Wood. The portrait was reproduced in *Minnesota in Three Centuries*, Vol. 3, and *Collections*, Vol. 12. It shows one feather clearly, and suggests the possibility of one, or even two, others.

12. Wowinapa, Little Crow's son, recited twenty-two children the chief had fathered. More than half of them had died.

13. Helen Carrothers, whose narrative appeared in *Bryant*, described Little Crow's house.

14. Many settlers in the vicinity of New Ulm and in the Beaver and Sacred Heart Creek localities across the river in Renville County were German immigrants. Those who had begun to farm former reservation land north of the river were especially despised. The blanket Indians promptly applied the name 'Dutchman' to all farmers, Indian and white.

15. Thomas Hughes, *Indian Chiefs of Southern Minnesota.*

16. Big Eagle, *Collections*. The outcome of the speakership race, in Big Eagle's opinion, strongly influenced Little Crow's subsequent conduct.

17. Ho-choke-pe-doota is the way the name was written by Holcombe, *Minnesota in Three Centuries.*

18. Early accounts said the Rice Creek encampment was north of the river on land no longer part of the reservation, but narratives of captives clearly established its location on the river's south side. Rice Creek was a tiny stream entering the Minnesota a short distance above present-day North Redwood.

19. *Bryant, Heard, Riggs,* and *Wakefield* discussed conditions and events among the bands in the upper part of the reservation.

20. By custom, July 1 had come to be the date by which payment was expected, although no treaty provision stipulated this date. In 1862 Congress, preoccupied with Civil War financing, did not appropriate funds for the annuity payments until July 5. Then the Treasury, concerned over its gold supply, brooded until August 8 over the possibility of making the payment in greenbacks before finally sending gold.

21. Bishop Henry B. Whipple of the Episcopal church declared March 6, 1862, in a letter to President Lincoln, it was a 'tradition on the border that an Indian agent can retire upon an ample fortune in four years.' After the outbreak, in a letter quoted by *Heard*, he called the 'Indian system' an 'organized system of robbery.'

22. By treaty stipulation annuity funds were to be paid 'to the chiefs in such manner as they shall request,' but the agents, in reality, generally handled distribution of the money. This enabled those who had secret financial interests in the Indian trade to hold back whatever they chose, 'Cheating the creatures very much.' (*Wakefield*).

23. *Bryant, Heard,* and Galbraith's report in *M.C.I.W.* discussed formation of the Rice Creek soldiers' lodge. In *Iron Face* Sibley described the traditional organization and functions of soldiers' lodges. *Riggs* wrote of the Lower Agency lodge, 'if the outbreak did not have its inception in this soldiers' lodge, it found there a prepared and powerful ally.'

24. *M.C.I.W.* and *Bryant.*

25. In *New Sources of Indian History,* Stanley Vestal informatively described the powers of chiefs.

26. *Minnesota in Three Centuries.*

27. Folwell, *History of Minnesota.* Also, *Minnesota in Three Centuries.*

CHAPTER IV—*LITTLE CROW WILL LEAD THEM ALL*

1. Big Eagle, in *Collections,* told of the meeting in Shakopee's village and the subsequent council at Little Crow's house.

2. Holcombe, *Minnesota in Three Centuries.*

3. Big Eagle, *Collections.*

4. In 1857 Inkpaduta of the Wahpekute band led a group of renegades in an attack on a settlement at Lake Okoboji in Iowa, almost on the Minnesota border. Inkpaduta's bandits killed more than thirty settlers and carried four white women into captivity. The Wahpekutes subsequently said they had outlawed Inkpaduta prior to the raid. The attack, today called the Spirit Lake Massacre, was not punished. (See *History of the Spirit Lake Massacre,* Abigail Gardner Sharp.) When it became unsafe for Inkpaduta to appear at his home village he drifted westward and was identified with later activities of the Teton Sioux, according to Vestal's *Sitting Bull,* Stewart's *Custer's Luck,* and others.

5. Agent Galbraith had formed a unit of Civil War recruits at Yellow Medicine Agency earlier in the month, and was leading the unit to Fort Snelling at the time of the outbreak. The recruits, said Galbraith's *Annual Report,* included mixed bloods, traders' clerks, government employees, reservation visitors, and 'persons from the opposite side of the river,' an area which, a short distance below the agency, was beginning to be known as Renville County. Galbraith's unit chose 'Renville Rangers' as its name. Called back before they reached Fort Snelling, the Rangers helped defend Fort Ridgely and were prominent in the action at Wood Lake. Joseph Renville, Sr., a half-breed trader at Lac qui Parle, was a leading figure in the early history of the upper valley. His post, protected by a stockade, was sometimes called 'Fort Renville.' He was an enthusiast for education, and helped Riggs compile his *Dakota Grammar and Dictionary,* although Riggs declared that 'It was never certainly known whether Mr. Renville could read his French Bible or not.' Joseph's wife, said Hughes in *Indian Chiefs of Southern Minnesota,* was an aunt of Little Crow.

6. *Heard* enumerated tribes the Dakotas thought might be allies. Also *Flandrau.*

7. Hughes' *Indian Chiefs of Southern Minnesota* contained much information regarding this important council. Big Eagle, in *Collections,* discussed the council, but not in detail. *Heard* also described the event.

8. Hughes, based on information supplied by a son of Little Crow who attended the council.

9. When the Dakota chiefs were escorted to Washington in connection with the 1858 Treaty they were shown an impressive array of troops and guns.

10. *Collections,* Big Eagle's account.

11. Two years after the council at Little Crow's house more than three hundred peaceful Cheyennes, of whom over two-thirds were women and children, were butchered in Colorado by Col. J. M. Chivington's cavalry. This event transformed the Cheyennes into eager allies of the Teton Sioux, already excited by the outbreak and by a steady stream of eastern Sioux who had been joining them. By 1865 the War of the Plains Indians had spread to the Rocky Mountains. Presently it involved nearly all of the Cheyennes, some of the Arapahoes, and all bands of the Teton Sioux. Development of the war was described by George Bird Grinnell in *The Fighting Cheyennes,* Paul I. Wellman in *Death on Horseback,* and Stanley Vestal in *Sitting Bull, Champion of the Sioux.*

CHAPTER V—*LET MYRICK EAT GRASS*

1. *Heard* and *Bryant* were among those to relate the outbreak's events at Lower Agency.

2. *Wakefield.* Also *Collections.*

3. *Bryant,* quoting Spencer.

4. In *Collections* Big Eagle disagreed and claimed he saved Spencer's life.

5. Folwell, *History of Minnesota,* Vol. 2.

6. *Heard* quoted the Reverend Samuel Hinman's account of the Humphrey family's fate. In *Collections,* Vol. 15, almost fifty years later, John Ames Humphrey described his family's attempted flight.

7. Mrs. Joseph DeCamp's narrative, *Collections.*

8. Few authentic heroes have had their names as ill-remembered. Heard said the ferry operator's name was 'Old Mauley.' Holcombe wrote it 'Miller.' Folwell recorded it as 'Millier.' The Renville County section of E. D. Neill's *History of the Minnesota Valley* listed 'Martel, the ferryman.' Mrs. DeCamp thought the name was 'Manley.' The ferryman's first name was variously recalled as 'Hubert' and 'Jacob.'

9. *Collections.*

10. *Bryant,* Mrs. Valencia Reynolds' statement.

11. Mary Schwandt's most vivid narrative appeared in *Bryant.* Thirty years

later she wrote a less graphic account for *Collections.*

12. *Heard* reported Patoile's name as 'Patville.'

13. *Collections,* Mrs. DeCamp's account.

14. *Wakefield.*

15. *Wakefield* supplied details of the trip with the children and Gleason.

16. *Bryant* contained a brief account of the killing. Quotations, however, are from *Wakefield.*

CHAPTER VI—*THE FUN OF KILLING THE WHITES*

1. One Indian, a member of the Wahpekute band, died at Redwood Ferry on the outbreak's first day, but he was killed by a soldier rather than a settler. Both *Bryant* and *Heard* described the manner in which the massacre spread after the agency was attacked.

2. *Minnesota in Three Centuries,* Vol. 3.

3. Nearly fifty casualties among farm families in the New Ulm vicinity on the first day of the uprising were estimated by Folwell in *History of Minnesota.*

4. *Collections.* 'The Story of Nancy McClure' is Mrs. Faribault's narrative.

5. *Collections.*

6. Early accounts spelled the name 'Eune.' Folwell, acquainted with one of the younger members of the family in later years, wrote it 'Juni.'

7. 'Narrative of Jonathan W. Earle,' in *Bryant.*

8. *Reminiscences of the Sioux Indian Massacre,* by Ezmon W. Earle, also related these events.

9. Mrs. Carrothers's first account, a comparatively brief narrative, appeared in *Bryant.* Later, as Mrs. Helen Tarble, she wrote *The Story of My Capture and Escape,* a more detailed account. The Bryant narrative did not mention Medicine Man or his feud with the Hendersons, but both accounts referred to Mrs. Carrothers's knowledge of the Dakota language. Her discussions with the Indians were reported in *The Story of My Capture and Escape.*

10. The flight of David Carrothers and Henderson was described in both accounts. The quotation is from the longer narrative.

11. Mrs. Carrothers did not witness the murder of Mrs. Henderson and her children. In *Bryant* she stated: 'We saw a fire where Mrs. Henderson had been last seen, and supposed they had burned her and her little children. This turned out to be true, as I afterward learned.'

12. *Bryant,* Jonathan Earle's account.

13. *Heard.*

14. Ibid.

15. Samuel Brown, fifteen-year-old son, related the adventures of the Browns and Charley Blair to *Heard.*

16. *Heard* quoted Little Crow's speech.

17. The speeches of John Otherday and Little Paul, recited by half-breeds who attended the councils at which they were made, were quoted by *Heard.*

18. The Minnesota town of Shakopee was not named for the chief who helped launch the outbreak. It had been founded a decade earlier near a site long occupied by the young chief's ancestors. Mankato, located where the Minnesota River makes a great bend toward the northeast, similarly was not named for the outbreak's Chief Mankato. The town and the chief, said Hughes's *Indian Chiefs of Southern Minnesota,* were both named for a bank of colored clay in the Blue Earth River, which joins the Minnesota at the latter's great bend.

19. The killing of numerous undefended women and children could not be denied, nor could evidence of mutilation and some instances of torture. Mutilation after death was in the Sioux tradition but torture before death was not. Decapitation of victims had become almost a hallmark of Sioux killings in parts of the Great Lakes region, just as torture of enemies was part of the death ritual among a number of northeastern tribes. Without question some of the outbreak's atrocity stories were false and others were greatly exaggerated. Probably the torture accounts contained more inflation than the mutilation reports. Some mutilation may have been intended to horrify and terrorize the whites, speeding their departure, and some of the torture evidence may have had the same purpose. (For an account of torture practices of northeastern tribes see *Saint among the Hurons,* Francis X. Talbot, S. J.)

CHAPTER VII—*GOD IS THE REFUGE OF HIS SAINTS*

1. The present Granite Falls, Minn., located five miles upstream from the former Upper Agency area, is the Yellow Medicine region's largest town. Downstream from the Upper Agency site, four miles south of the Minnesota River, is Wood Lake State Monument. Thirteen miles northwest of Granite Falls is a state wayside that marks the site of Camp Release. The area between Wood Lake and Camp Release was occupied at the time of the outbreak by the Upper Agency and the Hazelwood and Pajutazee missions of the Reverend Stephen Riggs and Dr. Williamson. No parks or waysides call attention to their sites. State Road No. 67, along the river's south side after it leaves Granite Falls, goes through much of the former mission and agency area.

2. *Bryant.*

3. Before John Otherday's conversion to Christianity he was a 'peculiarly abandoned and fierce savage,' said a contemporary report quoted by Folwell's *History of Minnesota.*

4. *Riggs.*

5. *Bryant.*

6. Ibid.

7. Estimate in *Bryant,* based on information supplied by Patoile.

8. *Riggs.*

9. Stephen Riggs's autobiography contained much the most vivid account of the escape of the missionaries and teachers. Its descriptions of the flight, while not published for years, appear to have been written soon after the outbreak.

10. *Riggs.*

11. Ibid.

12. Ibid.

13. *Bryant.*

14. *In Sioux Claims Commission* testimony, Agent Galbraith listed seventeen wholly and sixteen partly depopulated counties.

CHAPTER VIII—*RIDGELY WAS IN NO SENSE A FORT*

1. *Flandrau.*

2. *M.C.I.W.,* Vol. 1; letter from Marsh to Sheehan.

3. *Heard.*

4. Lieutenant T. P. Gere's account of events at Redwood Ferry in *M.C.I.W.* is the most complete report of this action, more detailed than the account of Sergeant John Bishop, who was present at the event.

5. Exactly what White Dog shouted across the river was long disputed. *Heard* said White Dog advised the soldiers to cross. Gere's account in *M.C.I.W.* said White Dog shouted 'Come across!' Big Eagle, in *Collections,* declared he had been told by Indians that 'White Dog did not tell Mr. Quinn to come over, but told him to go back.' In *History of Minnesota* Folwell quoted White Dog as having said 'first he called to them to come over, but when he saw the ambush he beckoned Captain Marsh to stay back.'

6. In talking to the Reverend Stephen Riggs, White Dog was said to have denied giving the Indians a signal to fire. *Riggs* did not refer to the denial.

7. *M.C.I.W.,* Vol. 1.

8. Big Eagle, *Collections.*

9. In *Collections,* Mrs. DeCamp described Wabasha as looking 'as if just out of one of Catlin's pictures.'

10. Mary Schwandt, *Collections.*

CHAPTER IX—*TWO HEAVY BOXES*

1. *Heard.* Also, *Minnesota in Three Centuries.*

2. Lt. Tom Gere's account of events at Fort Ridgely was embodied in Gen. L. F. Hubbard's narrative, both volumes, *M.C.I.W.*

3. Gere, *M.C.I.W.*

4. Ibid.

5. *M.C.I.W.*

6. Gere thought 'about 600 Sioux warriors are now approaching the fort and will undoubtedly attack us.'

7. Gere, *M.C.I.W.*

8. *Heard,* quoting Samuel Brown.

9. Holcombe, *Minnesota in Three Centuries,* Vol. 3, estimated 120 warriors remained with Little Crow after the dissension and placed the fort's strength at seventy-five men, presumably including the troops approaching from the northeast.

10. *Minnesota in Three Centuries.*

11. Gere, *M.C.I.W.*

CHAPTER X—*SURELY HELP IS ON THE WAY*

1. Alice Felt Tyler, 'William Pfaender and the Founding of New Ulm,' *Minnesota History,* March, 1949.

2. Folwell, *History of Minnesota.*

3. *M.C.I.W.* and *Heard.* The latter said there were about twenty in the chief's party.

4. Holcombe, *Minnesota in Three Centuries.*

5. Early accounts declared Jones found his artillery jammed with rags. This was supposed to have been the work of a few half-breeds among the Renville Rangers who subsequently deserted. Folwell, in *History of Minnesota,* called this report 'farcical.'

6. Gere, *M.C.I.W.*

7. *Bryant* said 'the glad shout of rain! rain! thank God! thank God!' echoed through the 'beleaguered garrison' as the first drops began to fall.

8. *M.C.I.W.*

9. *Minnesota in Three Centuries.*

10. Ernestina Broberg's statement, *Bryant.*

11. *Bryant.*

12. Anton Manderfeld's narrative, *Bryant.*

13. *Bryant.* Theodore C. Blegen's *Building Minnesota* had a condensed version of the Guri Endreson narrative.

CHAPTER XI—*EVERYONE'S FRIEND*

1. Until a dike was built across one of the northern parts of Lake Shetek, a tributary of the eastward-flowing Cottonwood originated in the lake. Now the lake's outlet is at its southern end. A stream leaving Shetek near the town of Currie flows southward into the Des Moines.

2. Charlie Hatch's diary provided the basis for a description of Lake Shetek events in *Conservation Volunteer*, May-June, 1953.

3. The villages of Lean Bear and White Lodge were nearly forty miles distant from the cabins east of Lake Shetek. It seems improbable more than two score Indians from them had invaded the neighborhood.

4. Lavina Eastlick's narrative, *Bryant*.

5. Alomina Hurd's narrative was also in *Bryant*. Mrs. Hurd was not among the settlers trapped in the slough. Her account was concerned mainly with her own experiences and those of her children.

6. The slough is now drained and has been converted into farm land. Since 1862 it has been known locally as 'Slaughter Slough.' It is a short distance east of Lake Shetek State Park, northeast of Slayton, Minn.

7. Mrs. Eastlick's narrative, *Bryant*, provided much information regarding events in Slaughter Slough.

8. Without discussing the merits of Ireland's claim, Folwell's *History of Minnesota* said Thomas Ireland declared he had shot Lean Bear.

9. Recalled Lavina Eastlick: 'He lay with his right hand on his face. I kissed him two or three times. I felt his face and hands. They were cold. . . . I knew it was the last time I should ever see him.'

10. Alomina Hurd's narrative, *Bryant*.

11. 'When I came in sight of the children,' Mrs. Eastlick remembered, 'I could hardly wait for the horse to get to them. Merton stood by the side of the road, with Johnny sleeping in his arms. O, how I wanted to press him to my bosom! He had carried his little brother a distance of fifty miles!'

12. Arthur Mitty, now farming some of the land in the one-time slough and on the prairie above it, described the graves in an interview with the author.

13. Duley, generally credited with the shooting of Lean Bear, was invited to participate in the December executions at Mankato.

14. Mrs. Eva Roberts, *Murry County Historical Society*.

CHAPTER XII—*THAT GUN WAS TERRIBLE*

1. *M.C.I.W.* Also *Bryant*.

2. Big Eagle, *Collections*.

3. *Wakefield*.

4. The number of Indians participating at Fort Ridgely and in other actions was based by early writers on the estimates of half-breeds and Indians, and by Folwell on testimony in the *Sisseton-Wahpeton Claims Case.*

5. Gere, *M.C.I.W.*

6. *Heard.* Also *Minnesota in Three Centuries.*

7. Gere, *M.C.I.W.*

8. *M.C.I.W.*

9. Holcombe, *Minnesota in Three Centuries.*

CHAPTER XIII—*A VERY FINE SPECTACLE*

1. South Bend, like Traverse des Sioux, did not survive as a town. It was gradually absorbed by its larger neighbor, Mankato.

2. From the rosters of citizen soldiers, *M.C.I.W.*

3. *Bryant.*

4. Helen Clapesattle, *The Doctors Mayo.*

5. *Flandrau.* Descriptions by Flandrau of some of the New Ulm events appeared in *Bryant* and *M.C.I.W.*

6. *M.C.I.W.*

7. *Bryant,* quoting Flandrau.

8. *Flandrau.*

9. Ibid.

10. *M.C.I.W.*

11. Folwell, *History of Minnesota.*

12. *Flandrau.*

CHAPTER XIV—*WITH UTMOST PROMPTITUDE*

1. *M.C.I.W.*

2. J. Fletcher Williams, 'Henry Hastings Sibley. A Memoir,' *Collections.*

3. John Charles Fremont, in *Memoires of My Life,* described Sibley's Mendota home as having 'much the character of a hunting lodge.' There were 'many dogs around about. Two large wolfhounds, Lion and Tiger, had the run of the house.' Tiger presently displayed 'a temper of such ferocity, even against his master, as eventually cost him his life.' Lion, on the other hand, was 'companionable and affectionate,' but on Sibley's marriage 'so far resented the loss of his first place that he left the house, swam across the river, and ended his days at the fort.'

4. Major Lawrence Taliaferro's autobiography, *Collections*. Taylor, later President of the United States, commanded Fort Crawford, Prairie du Chien, Wisc., at the time of the remark.

5. J. Fletcher Williams' memoir, *Collections*.

6. *Minnesota in Three Centuries*.

7. Henry Hastings Sibley is sometimes confused with Henry Hopkins Sibley. The latter was a Southern-born graduate of the U.S. Military Academy, who fought Seminole and Navajo Indians, invented the Sibley field tent, and in 1862 was a brigadier-general in the Confederate Army.

8. *M.C.I.W.*

9. Sibley to Flandrau, *M.C.I.W.*

10. *Bryant.*

11. Folwell, *History of Minnesota*.

12. Sibley, in *Iron Face*, acknowledged having met Frazer at St. Peter. He did not credit Frazer as the source of his information regarding the situation among the Sioux, but described him as bringing messages 'through to St. Peter to the commander of the forces.' No such messages became part of the military record, possibly because they may have been delivered orally rather than in written form.

13. Correspondence in *Governor's Archives*, St. Paul, quoted by Folwell.

14. *M.C.I.W.*

15. Sibley to Ramsey, *M.C.I.W.*

16. Folwell, *History of Minnesota*, cited the criticisms, editorial comments, and letters to the governor. Defenders of Sibley's performance contended he was handicapped by raw recruits, an inexperienced staff, deserting cavalry, inadequate weapons, and insufficient supplies.

CHAPTER XV—*NO CALAMITY RECEIVED LESS ATTENTION*

1. C. F. Holland, *Morgan and His Raiders*.

2. Jane Grey Swisshelm, *Crusader and Feminist*.

3. *Bryant.*

4. *Chicago Tribune*, Aug. 23, 1862.

5. Fletcher, not fully identified in the dispatch, may have been Major J. E. Fletcher, long-time agent among the Winnebagoes, who knew the Dakota language.

6. Folwell, *History of Minnesota*.

7. Secretary Smith's *Report to Congress*. On Oct. 9, 1862, the *New York Tribune* opined that the 'Dakota Sioux have doubtless been tampered with by Secessionists,' expressing a view widely held by Northern papers.

8. *M.C.I.W.*, *Bryant*, and *Flandrau* all mentioned the parolees. The condition of their release by the Confederates, explained Flandrau, was 'of not fighting against the Confederacy during the continuance of the war.'

9. *M.C.I.W.*

CHAPTER XVI–*KILL, IF INDIAN*

1. *M.C.I.W.* Also *Bryant*, quoting Oscar Malmros, the state adjutant general. Malmros' account named Captains Grant and Anderson as being in charge.

2. Ezmon W. Earle, *Reminiscences of the Sioux Indian Massacre*.

3. Grant, *M.C.I.W.*

4. 'The Narrative of Justina Kreiger,' *Bryant*. Subsequent writers followed Bryant's spelling of the name, but descendants of Justina's second husband, living in Renville County after the outbreak, spelled the name 'Krieger.'

5. *Bryant*.

6. Ibid. The conversation is from Justina's narrative.

7. Ibid.

8. Ibid.

9. Ibid.

10. Robert K. Boyd, *The Battle of Birch Coulee*. Boyd was a member of one of several burial units functioning separately. His estimate of the number of bodies buried during the day is higher than the number reported in other accounts. No total count appears to have been kept.

CHAPTER XVII–*THE CAPTORS WERE ANNOYED*

1. *Minnesota in Three Centuries*. Chiefs of villages in the vicinity of Lake Traverse were not altogether successful in restraining their young men. Stables and herds at Fort Abercrombie, a post forty miles north of Lake Traverse, on the west side of the Red River, were raided three times in late August and early September. While later reports indicated about 100 Sissetons participated, contemporary accounts and estimates of the number of Indians involved tended to exaggerate the importance of the Fort Abercrombie activities.

2. Across the river from the present town of Montevideo, Minn.

3. *Wakefield*.

4. *Collections*, 'Mrs. DeCamp Sweet's Captivity.'

5. Holcombe, *Minnesota in Three Centuries*: 'When Little Crow and his army came up above the Yellow Medicine, Red Iron put his warriors into line and threatened to fire upon the hostiles if they tried to come upon his land.'

6. *Minnesota in Three Centuries.*

7. *Heard,* based on interview with Joseph Campbell.

8. *Heard.*

9. Holcombe, *Minnesota in Three Centuries,* derived in part from information supplied by Campbell.

10. Folwell, *History of Minnesota.*

11. *Heard.*

12. Ibid.

CHAPTER XVIII — *MY MOTHER'S PEOPLE*

1. Big Eagle's story, *Collections.*

2. Grant, *M.C.I.W.*

3. James J. Egan's statement, *M.C.I.W*

4. Robert K. Boyd, *The Battle of Birch Coulee.*

5. Big Eagle, *Collections.*

6. Ezmon W. Earle, *Reminiscences of the Sioux Indian Massacre.*

7. Robert K. Boyd, *The Battle of Birch Coulee.*

8. Justina Krieger's narrative, *Bryant.*

9. Robert K. Boyd, *The Battle of Birch Coulee.*

10. Ibid.

11. Big Eagle, *Collections*: 'We had an easy time of it.'

12. Robert K. Boyd, *The Battle of Birch Coulee.*

13. Ibid. Also Grant, *M.C.I.W.*

CHAPTER XIX — *REMEMBER BIRCH COULEE!*

1. *Riggs.*

2. McPhail to Sibley, *M.C.I.W.*

3. McPhail, *M.C.I.W.*

4. *M.C.I.W.*

5. Big Eagle, *Collections.*

6. Grant, *M.C.I.W.*

7. Folwell, *History of Minnesota*, quoting Dr. J. W. Daniels.

8. Folwell, *History of Minnesota*.

9. Robert K. Boyd, *The Battle of Birch Coulee*.

10. Ezmon W. Earle, *Reminiscences of the Sioux Indian Massacre*.

11. A. P. Connolly, *Minnesota Massacre*.

12. Justina Krieger's narrative, *Bryant*.

13. *Collections*.

14. Malmros, *M.C.I.W.*

15. Robert K. Boyd, *The Battle of Birch Coulee*.

16. Grant, *M.C.I.W.*

17. Harriet E. McConkey, *Dakota War Whoop*. The 1864 revised edition of this account contained a report of the Birch Coulee activities addressed to Sibley and signed 'Joseph R. Brown, Maj. Gen., 3rd Division Minnesota Volunteers, Mil. Com. Detachment.' If Brown had been entitled to sign reports 'Maj. Gen.,' he would, of course, have outranked Colonel Sibley. The 'Maj. Gen.' seemingly had the purpose of making it appear Brown outranked Captain Grant. In reality, Brown was a civilian at the time of Birch Coulee, with no military title of any kind. The attempt to pretend Brown was in command at Birch Coulee failed; *M.C.I.W.* published Grant's report, and earlier or subsequent accounts of participants uniformly named Grant as the officer in charge.

CHAPTER XX–*I HAVE DONE THIS MYSELF*

1. *Heard* quoted speeches by Little Crow, Mazzawamnuna, Strike the Pawnee, Paul Mazakutamane (Little Paul), Rdainyanka, Wakinyantociye, Standing Buffalo, and many others, reported to him by half-breeds who had attended the councils.

2. *Heard*.

3. *Wakefield*.

4. Ibid.

5. Ibid.

6. Black Hawk's war had taken place during the youth of leaders of the 1862 outbreak. Its effects on the Sauk and Fox tribes had been observed with much interest by the Sioux. The peace settlement ending hostilities was clearly more advantageous than the terms of a treaty three decades earlier. Black Hawk served a brief prison term, after which he was taken on what was called a 'triumphal tour' of eastern cities.

7. *Heard*.

8. Ibid.

9. Ibid. The quotations from correspondence, like those from speeches, are excerpts.

10. Ibid.

11. *Minnesota in Three Centuries.*

12. *M.C.I.W.*

13. *Heard.*

14. Mrs. Wakefield described Little Paul as 'continually hanging around, wanting me to go with him as his wife.'

15. *Heard.*

CHAPTER XXI—*ACCIDENTAL VICTORY*

1. *M.C.I.W.*

2. *Heard.* The encampment actually was on Lone Tree Lake, a smaller body of water in the vicinity, but the name of the larger lake became firmly identified with events in the locality.

3. *Minnesota in Three Centuries.*

4. Big Eagle, *Collections.*

5. E. T. Champlin's account, *M.C.I.W.*

6. *Minnesota in Three Centuries.*

7. *M.C.I.W.* Sibley called the encounter a 'battle.' Pope referred to it as a 'skirmish.'

8. Big Eagle, *Collections.*

9. *M.C.I.W.*

10. Folwell, *History of Minnesota,* quoting Nancy Faribault.

11. Hughes, *Indian Chiefs of Southern Minnesota.* Samuel Brown, half-breed who had been with Wahpeton relatives during much of the outbreak, heard Little Crow's departing speech and repeated it to Hughes.

12. *Wakefield.*

13. *M.C.I.W.*

14. Folwell, *History of Minnesota.*

15. *Wakefield.*

16. *Collections.*

17. *Heard.*

CHAPTER XXII—*UTTERLY EXTERMINATE THE SIOUX*

1. Sibley to Pope, *M.C.I.W.*

2. *M.C.I.W.*

3. Ibid.

4. *Heard.*

5. Folwell, *History of Minnesota.*

6. *M.C.I.W.*

7. Ibid.

8. Ibid.

9. *Heard* said, 'The writer acted as recorder.' Subsequent accounts sometimes have referred to him as the judge advocate.

10. *Riggs.*

11. *Heard.*

12. Ibid.

13. Ibid.

14. *Wakefield.*

15. Folwell, *History of Minnesota.*

16. Sibley to Pope and Sibley to Flandrau, *M.C.I.W.*

17. Pope to Sibley, *M.C.I.W.*

18. Pope to Halleck, *M.C.I.W.*

19. Pope to Ramsey, *M.C.I.W.*

20. Lincoln to Pope, *M.C.I.W.*

21. Pope to Lincoln, *M.C.I.W.*

22. Folwell, *History of Minnesota.*

CHAPTER XXIII—*FEARFUL COLLISION*

1. *Heard.*

2. Ibid.

3. Folwell, *History of Minnesota.*

4. Ramsey to Lincoln, *M.C.I.W.*

5. Pope to Lincoln, *M.C.I.W.*

6. Folwell, *History of Minnesota*.

7. Sibley to Elliott, *M.C.I.W.*

8. Pope to Lincoln, *M.C.I.W.*

9. Sibley to Elliott, *M.C.I.W.*

10. Only mild interest elsewhere in the nation in the fate of the sentenced Indians is reflected in contemporary newspaper accounts. *The New York Daily Tribune,* December 13, 1862, reported the President had 'received appeals by telegraph for their execution from some parties, and in their behalf from others.'

11. *Executive Documents,* 1862.

CHAPTER XXIV—*MORE A GROWL THAN A CHEER*

1. *Heard* and *Bryant* quoted the instructions Riggs received from Colonel Stephen Miller, who was in charge of the execution.

2. Doane Robinson, *History of the Dakota or Sioux Indians,* reproduced the two-page letter. The original was in Lincoln's handwriting.

3. *Riggs.* This statement has caused confusion. Since the selection had already been made, the Reverend Stephen Riggs may have meant Brown was responsible for 'identification' rather than selection.

4. *Riggs.*

5. *Wakefield.*

6. *Heard.*

7. Ibid.

8. Big Eagle, *Collections.* Big Eagle served three years in prison, protesting that a prisoner of war who had surrendered in good faith should be held only briefly.

9. *Riggs.*

10. An account in the *St. Paul Pioneer,* Dec. 28, 1862, provided details for many contemporary reports of the mass execution.

11. *Riggs* said Round Wind (Tatemima) was 'reprieved by an order from the president.' *Flandrau* declared 'the pardoned Indian was hanged and one of the others liberated by mistake.' Doane Robinson said the respited man was Henry Milord. Folwell's *History of Minnesota* reported the record of suspension of sentence had not been found.

12. *St. Paul Pioneer,* quoted by *Bryant.*

13. *Heard.*

14. Clapesattle, *The Doctors Mayo.*

CHAPTER XXV—*NIMBLE ADVERSARY*

1. Before Little Crow left the Yellow Medicine area, said *Heard,* he had written the British at Pembina: 'Our fathers have told us that when the English fought the Americans the Sioux helped them, and captured a cannon, which they gave to them, and which was called the "Little Dakota." Do you recollect this? We have helped you when you were in trouble. . . . Now we are in difficulty, and want that cannon and your assistance.'

2. A letter from Governor Alexander Dallas, written in early 1864 to Thomas Fraser, Hudson's Bay House, London, told of his having been in communication with 'the chiefs of the Sioux on the Missouri, where they have one camp of 5,000 lodges, in addition to straggling bands.' The customary population of this many lodges would have been about 35,000. Many bands other than eastern Sioux would need to have been present for the number to be nearly this large.

3. *Heard.*

4. Little Crow described his plans to his son, Wowinapa, whose statement appeared in *Heard* and *Bryant.*

5. *M.C.I.W.*

6. Hughes, *Indian Chiefs of Southern Minnesota.*

7. Folwell, *History of Minnesota.*

8. *Heard.* An account of the event, related much later by James Lamson, a brother of Chauncey, appeared in *Collections,* Vol. 15.

9. *Heard.*

10. Ibid.

11. *M.C.I.W.*

12. Kingsbury, *History of Dakota Territory.*

13. The kidnappings were in violation of international law, a fact promptly recognized by newspapers on both sides of the border, and brought out in the trials of Shakopee and Medicine Bottle. Robin W. Winks, in *North Dakota History* (July, 1957), attributed capture of the two chiefs to American citizens.

14. The knoll, known as Pilot Knob, was formerly an Indian burial ground and is the present site of Acacia Park Cemetery.

15. Four railroads operated in the vicinity at the time.

CHAPTER XXVI—*THE CAPITOL WAS DRAPED IN BLACK*

1. *Bryant.*

2. Swisshelm, *Crusader and Feminist.*

3. Folwell, *History of Minnesota,* quoting Lincoln's message of December 1, 1862.

4. Satterlee, *Victims of the Indian Massacre.*

5. *Riggs.*

6. *Collections.*

7. *Flandrau.*

8. *Collections.*

9. *Bryant,* quoting the annual report of Col. Clark W. Thompson, listed eighteen counties, with a population of 40,000, from which 30,000 inhabitants had fled.

10. Mrs. Eva Roberts, *Murray County Historical Society.*

11. *Collections.*

12. *M.C.I.W.*

13. *Flandrau:* 'The only proper course was to have exiled them to some remote place, such as the Dry Tortugas.'

14. *Riggs.*

15. Hughes, *Indian Chiefs of Southern Minnesota.*

16. Philippe de Trobriand, *Army Life in Dakota.*

17. Forts Wadsworth, Bufort, Totten, Ransom, and Stevenson were built within five years of the outbreak. Berthold, previously built as a trading post, was garrisoned in 1865.

18. *House Report No. 2503, Second Session, 82nd Congress,* showed a combined population of 4,914 on the Santee Sioux Niobrara reservation in northeastern Nebraska and the Sisseton-Wahpeton reservation near the eastern borders of North and South Dakota. The Niobrara reservation is the home of the main present-day concentration of Medewakanton and Wahpekute descendants. Smaller groups live at Pipestone, Morton, Granite Falls, and elsewhere in Minnesota, and in several South Dakota localities. Hundreds of Wahpeton and Sisseton descendants are on the Fort Totten reservation in North Dakota. The number of descendants of outbreak participants living among the Teton Sioux or in Canada is not known, and there is no record to show how many have renounced reservation life to join the general population.

19. Grinnell, *The Fighting Cheyennes.*

20. Some Arapahoes, to whom the Cheyennes had also 'offered the war pipe,' were believed to have been participants.

21. Custer's death was also attributed to Sitting Bull, Rain in the Face, White Bull, Two Moons, Medicine Bear, Harshay Horse, Hawk, Flat Hip, Brave Bear, and others. In addition, the general was said to have committed suicide.

22. Spindler, *Tragedy Strikes at Wounded Knee.*

INDEX

Oehler, Charles M
      The great Sioux uprising. New York, Oxford Univer-
sity Press, 1959.

272 p. illus. 22 cm.

Includes bibliography.

1. Dakota Indians—Wars, 1862–1865.   I. Title.

E83.86.O33   973.7   59–5183 †